AF540596

Electronic Governance

S. Pankaj

A.P.H. Publishing Corporation
Ansari Road, Darya Ganj
New Delhi - 110 002

Published by
S.B. Nangia
A.P.H. Publishing Corporation
4435–36/7, Ansari Road, Darya Ganj,
New Delhi-110002
Phone: 011–23274050
e-mail: aphbooks@gmail.com

2026

Rs. 2995/-

Typeset by
Ideal Publishing Solutions
C-90, J.D. Cambridge School,
West Vinod Nagar, Delhi-110092

Printed at
RD DIGITAL PRINTERS
Ansari road , Daryaganj, Delhi-110002

Dedication

I am thankful to my entire family for providing me support and motivation to compile this book. My parents Sh. R.D. Sharma, My Mother Smt. Indra Sharma, my uncle Sh. M.P. Sharma, my aunt Smt. Sharda Sharma and my wife Pratibha have provided me support for compiling this book.

Preface

There is a lot of discussion and interest generated globally on the concepts of e-Governance and e-Government. Though both these terms are used interchangeably, 'e-Government' refers to the larger process of using IT for improving both the internal operations of the Govt. as well as its external interface in several forms, while the term 'e-Government' relates mostly to improving the Govt. interface with the citizens and the business.

Traditionally, the interaction between a citizen or business and a government agency took place in a government office. With emerging information and communication technologies it is possible to locate service centers closer to the clients. Such centers may consist of an unattended kiosk in the government agency, a service kiosk located close to the client, or the use of a personal computer in the home or office.

The Internet has proven to be a powerful tool for reinventing governments. It encourages transformation from the traditional bureaucratic paradigm, which emphasizes standardization, departmentalization, and operational cost-efficiency, to the "e-government" paradigm, which emphasizes coordinated network building, external collaboration and customer services.

All over the world governments are attempting to manage e-technology in a different way. Governments are capitalizing on e-technology to improve people's lives. Generally governments are aiming to make e-technology the servant of society in order to improve the quality of neighbourhoods, to make economies stronger and to bring people closer together. E-governance fosters the partnerships and collaborations of those who have a stake in enriching the processes. This includes all levels of government (county, municipal, state, regional, tribal and federal), the private sector, the academic community and foundations

E-governance is the evolutionary binding of government structures and functions with Internet technologies to serve citizens, virtual constituents and the public good. Governments of today are feeling the need to reinvent the very process of governance. There are various challenges faced by the governments in proper implementation of the e-government infrastructure major among them are issues like cultural differences, digital divide and low level of ICT infrastructure. This particular text aims at providing a birds eye view of the process of e-governance.

The book envisages the national perspective on the subject dealing with major issues in a comprehensive manner. The major issues covered are core governance technology and ICT, e-governance initiatives in Indian states and legal issues. It also presents a national comparative mapping on the subject. The book also explores the various models and developments through case studies. The case studies are helps us in understanding the growth that India has witnessed due to the process of e-governance.

—S. Pankaj

Contents

1

E-Governance

Traditionally, the interaction between a citizen or business and a government agency took place in a government office. With emerging information and communication technologies it is possible to locate service centers closer to the clients. Such centers may consist of an unattended kiosk in the government agency, a service kiosk located close to the client, or the use of a personal computer in the home or office.

The Internet has proven to be a powerful tool for reinventing governments. It encourages transformation from the traditional bureaucratic paradigm, which emphasizes standardization, departmentalization and operational cost-efficiency, to the "e-government" paradigm, which emphasizes coordinated network building, external collaboration and customer services.

All over the world governments are attempting to manage e-technology in a different way. Governments are capitalizing on e-technology to improve people's lives. Generally governments are aiming to make e-technology the servant of society in order to improve the quality of neighbourhoods, to make economies stronger and to bring people closer together.

E-governance is also defined as the transformation of (governance) processes (resulting from) the continual and exponential introduction into society of more advanced digital technologies.

E-governance focuses on how these new technologies can be used to strengthen the public's voice as a force to reshape the democratic processes, and refocus the management, structure, and oversight of government to better serve the public interest.

E-governance fosters the partnerships and collaborations of those who have a stake in enriching the processes. This includes all levels of government (county, municipal, state, regional, tribal and federal), the private sector, the academic community and foundations.

E-governance is the evolutionary binding of government structures and functions with Internet technologies to serve citizens, virtual constituents and the public good. I do not agree with the many writers who contend that government is in the midst of a technological revolution.

Rather, the re-engineering and deployment of governance processes *via* advanced Internet technologies is an evolutionary process of structural and functional adaptation. Traditional government functions are binding, in a genetic sense, to Internet driven, electronic governance delivery systems. It is the breakneck speed at which e-governance deployments are taking place that generates the illusion of revolution.

Electronic government (e-government), the ability for government to provide access to services and information twenty-four hours a day, seven days a week, is an emerging force today. In the aftermath of a successful Y2K rollover, government is turning attention and resources to providing information and services on-line, exploring digital democracy, and using technology for economic development. As a result, government service will be revolutionized as we progress into the Digital Age.

E-Government also refers to the use by government agencies of information technologies (such as Wide Area Networks, the Internet, and mobile computing) that have the ability to transform relations with citizens, businesses and other arms of government.

These technologies can serve a variety of different ends: better delivery of government services to citizens, improved interactions with business and industry, citizen empowerment through access to information, or more efficient government management.

The resulting benefits can be less corruption, increased transparency, greater convenience, revenue growth, and/or cost reductions.

In this new age, good government is accessible government. Good government correlates to immediate access to pertinent information. Good government is faster, cheaper and more efficient.

E-Government can provide many opportunities to improve the quality service to the citizen. Citizens can get service or information in minutes or hours.

It is estimated that in the US more than 60 percent of all Internet users interact with government websites.

The e-government vision of the US President aims at reforming government. It emphasizes that "government needs to reform its operations—how it goes about its business and how it treats the people it serves". The vision is guided by three principles:

— Citizen-centered, not bureaucracy-centered;

— Results-oriented; and

— Market-based, actively promoting innovation.

It is estimated that when E-Government initiatives would be deployed effectively, conducting business with the government will be easier, privacy will be protected and security provided. Citizens and businesses can visit one point-of-service online or by telephone that will reflects the concept government at doorsteps.

The US federal department focuses on four citizen-centered groups, each providing opportunities to transform delivery of services.

— *Individuals / Citizens:* Government-to-Citizens (G2C); Which aims at making at an infrastructure which is easy to find, easy to use, one-stop points-of-service that make it easy for citizens to access high-quality government services.

— *Businesses:* Government-to-Business (G2B); This infrastructure will aim at reducing government's burden on businesses by eliminating redundant collection of data and better leveraging E-business technologies for communication.

— *Intergovernmental:* Government-to-Government (G2G); Make it easier for states and localities to meet reporting requirements and participate as full partners with the federal government in citizen services, while enabling better performance measurement, especially for grants. Other levels of government will see significant administrative savings and will be able to improve programme delivery because more accurate data is available in a timely fashion.

— *Intra-governmental:* Internal Efficiency and Effectiveness (IEE); Make better use of modern technology to reduce costs and improve quality of federal government agency administration, by using industry best practices in areas such as supply-chain management, financial management and knowledge management.

A policy document of New Zealand states that the E-government infrastructure will provide:

— **Better services** — more convenient and reliable, with lower compliance costs, higher quality and value;
— **Cost effectiveness and efficiency**—cheaper, better information and services for customers and better value for taxpayers;
— **Improved reputation**—building an image of New Zealand as a modern nation, an attractive location for people and business;
— *Greater participation by people in government*—making it easier for those who wish to contribute; and
— *Leadership*—supporting the knowledge society through public sector innovation.

Uncertainty is probably greater in e-technology than in many other policy areas. The opportunities and problems of technology are not yet entirely known. More importantly, the human dimension cannot be predicted so it is not known exactly how e-technology can benefit a common man life.

Strategy

Once e-government is defined, local government can move into the next stage, development of an e-government strategy. This strategy is fundamental to navigating through the exploding e-government market place, re-engineering processes and procedures to support e-government, and implementing e-government initiatives.

Government is quickly realizing that this strategy must be enterprise-wide to most effectively and efficiently serve the digital society.

This strategy should include:

The organization's definition of e-government that includes key areas to be addressed and identification of all customers;

- — A vision that is easily understood and succinctly expresses the organization's concept of and plans for e-government;
- — Specific goals and objectives that can be monitored and measured;
- — Identification of policies necessary to support e-government;
- — A methodology for determining organizational readiness;
- — A process for identifying and prioritizing e-government initiatives;
- — A business model to sustain e-government initiatives.

Issues for E-Governance

Governments all over the world are trying to utilize IT for various purposes. The initial motivation usually comes from the need to improve efficiency of processes in the government. This may be concurred or followed by the second step comprising re-engineering of the processes.

E-government applications bring governments into more than efficient and effective government in delivery of services and internal administration and communication. E-government brings countries, and, concomitantly, its citizens, into the international stream.

This brings cultural change both within the government itself and in the overall society. Increased links, by government and the citizen alike, to international web sites, news groups, chat rooms, email communications, building of international networks through the use of email and the powerful wireless technologies, all contribute to an emerging linked world that operates continuously.

We must admit the great potential of new technologies for enhancing democracy without supposing either that this is yet happening or that it will necessarily happen without a lot of sustained effort.

There are very considerable opportunities, but so too are there risks. Those can most effectively be minimized if we first open our eyes to both the benefits and the potential costs of the change in the culture of democracy that the new technologies are bringing about and are likely to continue to bring about.

Gartner, an international consultancy firm, has formulated a four-phase e-governance model. This can serve as a reference for governments to position where a project fits in the overall evolution of an e-governance strategy.

According to Gartner, e-governance will mature according to the following four phases *viz.*, Information, Interaction, Transaction and Transformation.

E-government is itself a process, or a means to an end, rather than an end in and of itself. E-government is still in the earliest stages of development and promises to evolve with advances in technology and increased acceptance and trust in electronic communications. Initial forays into e-government initiatives have focused mostly on providing enhanced access to information and basic services

Although the full transformative effects of e-government remain largely unrealized at this time, the rapid growth in interest and resources dedicated to e-government initiatives may contribute to swifter changes.

A set of motivation may come from the need to provide various social services to citizens for improving the quality of life of the citizens. A parallel set of motivation may be to strengthen the democratic foundations of governance (opinion polls, voting etc.).

These social services and democratic enablements correspond to the new activities that become economically viable due to the altered cost structure due to use of information technology.

Government grows up exponentially once e-governance is introduced. This is because the ease of transactions introduced by e-governance would encourage citizens and businesses to have more transactions with the government. In order to manage this enormous amount of data such that system performance does not get degraded, and such that the system is scalable, there is a need to automate the record management functions.

Although there exists solutions for document archival system based on network-centric groupware (Berchtold et al. 1999; Crespo and Garcia-Molina 1998) but they do not address the issue of archival based on policies of multiple. While initiatives have been emanating from various directions, they are often at cross-purposes and so repetitive and wasteful.

Many governments are struggling with massive internal reengineering in relation to technology to improve efficiencies and deliver government services electronically to citizens. Thus e-governance would require setting up of LANs/ Intranets/ Extranets, along with data warehousing, administrative process revamp, and training and capacity enhancement in government organizations.

Economic benefits accruing to governments from technology integration have historically been viewed in terms of cost savings and return on investment from specific projects. Effective use of technology is therefore key to successful deployment of electronic governance.

Accordingly critical issues need to be clearly delineated and solutions worked out. Whatever may be the middleware chosen, the system should be highly reliable, must have capability for future expansion, must be able to be managed with ease, must have high performance but above all should have very good security in transactions. In order to achieve this an EAI system, like e-Governance, must have some built-in services which will not only make the applications to have smooth interactions but also make the users feel that the entire operation is user friendly.

Vendors of a typical middleware like IUNA, BEA, Netweave, etc. provides these services. We must understand that e-government is about transformation and technology is a tool. E-government is about transformation that helps citizens and businesses find new opportunities in the world's knowledge economy. It holds great potential.

Yet, if e-government is not part of a larger programme for reform—reforming how government works, manages information, manages internal functions, serves citizens and businesses—then it may not produce all the benefits expected from the time and money invested. Use e-government to rethink the role of government. Use it as a tool to further economic development and good governance.

The infrastructure needs and issues of e-governance cannot be generalized. The e-governance infrastructure varies according to the governance objectives and needs of the society. The architecture options are decentralized architecture, hybrid architecture and centralized architecture.

Social Issues

Social issues play an important role in the success and failure of the e-governanace efforts. As we have seen earlier that societies unlike individuals behave in a separate manner and thus it is extremely necessary to determine the dynamics of the social changes which happen on a constant basis. E-governance is not just a technology-oriented effort rather it aims at creating the concept of social change.

This change can be at the level of the administration, politics, social, economical or individuals. The society is a dynamic body. Civil society as a concept can be difficult to understand, but although there are a number of conflicting definitions there is widespread agreement that during the past few decades, civil society receded and political/commercial society advanced in terms of their impact on people's lifestyles.

Civil society is based on voluntary participation, whereas the state is based on coercion. It can be argued that political society in pseudo-democracies has a leg in each camp, consisting as it does of competing self-serving organized gangs intent on gaining control of state apparatus. Government is institutiona-lized coercion. and must be so since we have governments in order, essentially, to protect civil society from internal and external predators.

Some define civil society to include only non profit organizations, others define it to include only self-organizing communities of common interest, others apply the descriptor to all forms of non governmental cooperation including big business, while yet others define it to exclude all forms of institutionalized human activity.

Sorting the range of different definitions in use isn't helped by the fact that what once distinguished government from the market was coercive force, present in the one and absent in the other.

However, capital has steadily become more concentrated in fewer hands, and governments have relied more and more on big business to finance election campaigns. Therefore quite apart from governments' innate propensity to drift towards crony capitalism, the above differentiating line has faded almost to non-existence.

Here we wont do dissection of the society rather we will just view it as a dynamic body which lies at the center of growth.

The basic objective of the e-governance exercise is to create a transparency among the various stakeholders of the society namely the government administration, business and common masses. But most of the societies are fearful of the transparency due to the possible pilferages that might occur due to this factor of transparency.

Various stakeholders have their own personal motives, which can act as barrier in successful implementation of an e- governance structure in place. This gets more critical in the under developed nations where typically the administration and the politics tend to thrive on the red tapism, bottlenecks and corruption. With an e-governance structure in place they become vulnerable to the checks and balances. Often it is observed that the powerful strata of the society tend to adopt a non-cooperative approach towards the entire issue. The social awareness is thus an extremely important component to determine the success of the e-governance endeavour.

Andhra Pradesh one of the pioneers in the e-governance practices follows a clearly defined system of architecture. The government's architecture is comprised of a series of interrelated components. The twelve components of the architecture, in concert, provide the basis for the state to take advantage of adaptive systems in support of its business.

The twelve architecture components are:

— Application
— Information
— Groupware
— Component ware
— Data
— Applications Middle ware
— Integration
— Network
— Platform
— Security and Directory Services
— Systems Management

Here we must state that e-governance is not just a technical issue rather it's a social issue. The worthiness of the initiative lies in its usage, and as a first point to be noted is the need to use local languages in the IT implementation process.

However, in a broader context it is essential that a clear strategy to have access to local level databases maintained in regional languages as well as to use appropriate interfaces to aggregate such data. Here, a focused effort would have to be made in improving the technologies for transliteration.

Similarly, an effort would have to be undertaken for perfecting the OCR technology for local languages. This is critical, as an effective OCR technology is required to convert the data that is scanned and stored in local languages into meaningful and workable databases.

This could also help in substantially simplifying the efforts at content generation and data warehousing. Government data is huge and complex. There exists a large inventory and repository of appropriate technological platforms with which to perform public functions in a cost and time effective manner.

However, common platform availability is an issue in this. A major portion of the government data is in the form of what we categorize as legacy data. Integration of the legacy data into the e-governance initiative is not only time consuming but also expensive. Software is not the only issue those posses a challenge to the e-governance initiatives

Only Computerization of government work will lead to automation of existing manual work. There is a real danger of investments being made in hardware, application software and even in training and still the issue of prompt and regular service, updating of data not being effectively addressed.

The e-governance initiative has to address the technological problems objectively by identifying functional areas in every government organization to initiate the process of computerization and choosing appropriate hardware platform and software applications for cost effective delivery of public services.

Simply drafting a law or issuing an order from political leaders, as with all reforms, cannot achieve e-government. It requires changing how officials think and act, how they view their jobs, how they share information between departments.

We should create different level and model of computer applications for Ministry, Department, Directorate and Offices in urban and rural areas that could be suitably customized as per location and work specific requirements.

The issue of Management of change, which have to be made quite rapid at times, is the other major issue to be addressed while implementing IT for good governance. Changes in the decision making procedures, processes, delegation of power etc. would lead to mandatory organizational and Institutional changes effecting both peoples and methods at all the bridges of delivery chain.

For this, acceptance of changed processes would have to be properly understood, accepted, adopted and improved to enable full advantage of the Information technology being adopted for e-governance.

The e-governance initiatives are likely to induce a great degree of change in how governments are functioning today. Change management is a subject matter that is currently sweeping public and private sector organizations. It is not new but has been evolving as a discipline over the past decade.

Change management is addressing the changes being faced by modern public administrators, both internally and externally. In the past three decades governments have had to contend and deal with, many societal evolutions that have significantly altered the way public administrators function in their jobs.

Globalisation, free trade, the increased movements of people and goods, internationally, on a scale never before known, new attitudes of a citizenry that is expecting more from governments, changing social attitudes and new technologies, especially information and communication technologies, have all contributed to the challenges now facing politicians, executives and managers alike.

Change management, in the context of e-government, is all about how members of the public service make the transition from the traditional approaches to management, pre-Information and Communication Technologies (ICTs) era, to new means of administering in new and evolving environments. The latter principle is one of the many ways in which change management is different for the public sector.

Although e-government encompasses a wide range of activities and actors, three distinct sectors can be identified. These include government-to-government (G2G), government-to-business (G2B), and government-to-citizen (G2C). Some observers also identify a fourth sector, government-to-employee (G2E).

Government-to-Government (G2G) : In many respects, the G2G sector represents the backbone of e-government. Some observers suggest that governments at all levels must enhance and update their own internal systems and procedures before electronic transactions with citizens and businesses can be successful. G2G e-government involves sharing data and conducting electronic exchanges between governmental actors. This involves both intra-and inter-agency exchanges at the national level, as well as exchanges between the national, provincial and local levels. G2G applications constitute the maximum chunk of the e-governance functions.

Government-to-Business (G2B) : Government-to-Business (G2B) initiatives receive a significant amount of attention, in part because of the high enthusiasm of the business sector and the potential for reducing costs through improved procurement practices and increased competition. The G2B sector includes both the sale of surplus government goods to the public, as well as the procurement of goods and services. Although not all are directly dependent on the use of information technology, several different procurement methods are used in relation to the G2B sector. Tendering, auctions and information and administrative management tools form the core of this sector.

Government-to-Citizen (G2C) : The third e-government sector is Government-to-Citizen (G2C). G2C initiatives are designed to facilitate citizen interaction with government, which is what some observers perceive to be the primary goal of e-government. These initiatives attempt to make transactions, such as renewing licenses and certifications, paying taxes, and applying for benefits, less time consuming and easier to carry out. G2C initiatives also often strive to enhance access to public information through the use of dissemination tools, such as Web sites and/or kiosks. Another feature of many G2C initiatives is the effort to attenuate the agency-centric, and at times, process-laden nature of some government functions.

The basic aim of any e-governance initiative is aimed at good governance and government citizen interface is thus the most critical aspect of the entire exercise. Digitization of all public domain information like official gazette notifications, acts, rules, regulations, circulars, policies and programme documents are some of the important portions of this exercise.

The ministry of innovation and technology of Italy is implementing e governance through a model, which is composed of six key elements:

— *Service provision* : A set of high-quality services delivered with innovative methods to user-customers (citizens and businesses). In order to focus development efforts, a number of priority services for users have been identified for inclusion in digitalisation initiatives. These services will be provided through a unified access point even when they involve more than one government department. In other words, the complexity of the public administration will not be apparent to users.

— *Digital identification:* Techniques for user identification and secure signatures adopting the Electronic ID Card, the National Services Card and digital signatures.

— *Access channels* : A multiplicity of innovative channels for accessing services: the Internet, call centres, cell phones, third-party networks, etc.

— *Service provision agencies* : Efficient and low-cost back office operations for service providers.

— *Interoperability and cooperation* : Establishment of standards for interfaces between departments that permit efficient and transparent communication with the outside world.

— *Communication infrastructure* : A communication infrastructure that links all government departments.

Models and Issues for Effective E-governance

E-government is a much more massive transformation than electronic service delivery. E-government is multi-faceted: it deals with information technology as a tool of government, as an object of government's attention, and as a major factor in shaping the social and economic environment in which government acts. Looked at this way, e-government can and does implicate all aspects of public service.

E-governance is no more and no less than governance in an electronic environment. It is both governance *of* that environment and governance *within* that environment, using electronic tools. This is a very broad definition, reflecting the far-reaching implications of information and communication technologies.

Closely related to e-governance is "e-government". For our purposes the terms are interlocking, though not interchangeable. E-government, in my view, defines a terrain — the public sector — as well as the institutions, people and processes that operate within that terrain. E-governance is about how that terrain operates, and how it gains and maintains legitimacy.

In designing e-participation tools, we are looking for the technology to support informed, collective decision-making. However, in doing so, we cannot use an e-commerce model. While a lot of the work done to develop e-commerce technology can support e-government, there is an important difference; there people except a level of trust and equity in dealing with government.

In the area of e-consultation, we typically seek participation in formulating policy on specific topic, although there is also the traditional form of consultation where the draft policy has been developed, but requires scrutiny.

E-Governance seem to have greater marginal benefits in countries with moderate development indices, and where alternate channels of communications are weak and governance processes are largely democratic to the extent that they are Information- Driven. Example in Brazil, India, Malaysia, Estonia etc.

In such cases, e-governance strengthens the two-way communication channel-enabling the civil society to get more acquainted with decisions (as well as decision-makers) which affect their quality of lives and providing them avenues to express/ make an informed choice. The latter is usually provided through conventional Governance processes.

Information age governing presents an entirely new set of challenges for decision-makers, public sector professionals and citizens. The technological advances driving e-government are fundamentally altering how individuals and businesses interact with government. This transformation has public sector professionals considering questions like :

— How will e-government affect the performance of public organizations?
— What are the structural effects of e-government and information technology on the public organization?
— What skills do public employees need in order to maximize their performance in an information age?
— What new leadership skills will be needed in the e-governing age?
— Will e-government instill individuals in public sector organizations with a greater degree of autonomy, enabling them to re-think conventional administrative practices?

The changes in technology that have enabled many e-government initiatives, the opportunities and pitfalls posed by new legislations, the increased focus on security and corporate governance, and a continuing and increasing awareness of the need to control costs, all need to be balanced against the requirement to maximise the value to be extracted from existing and proposed new systems.

E-governance has a nice sound to it but we must remember that the e-word doesn't mean an instant change from old systems to this new electronic world. This is an ongoing exercise whereby systems need to be evaluated, new architectures designed, processes modelled, infrastructure built and staff trained. There are also the issues of accessibility, usability, security and transparency. However, security may conflict with access and transparency with ease of use.

Therefore, we need to balance the need for straightforward access to the system with necessary security issues, and we also have to balance easy and flexible navigation with the need for transparency and the need to provide sufficient information to assist individuals to be informed.

During this building phase, one of the challenges will be to adhere to governance requirements knowing that information may reside in a combination of legacy and new systems. Adherence to e-governance translates directly to availability of and access to all requisite information, regardless of where that information may sit within the various departments.

Further to this, e-governance means ensuring that as new methods of conducting business are adopted, so the back-end processes must be implemented to secure and protect that information for the period required by legislation.

Access to information being the core will become a focus area, not only to be compliant, but also to service an increasingly computer-literate customer base. As government, business and private individuals become more computer-literate and -enabled, so the need for client self-service increases.

An interesting challenge is to balance the demands of a few very literate, very demanding customers, with a majority who will still take some time to move to the electronic world. This may mean duplicate systems, with information stored in different forms —paper reports and invoices for many, electronic bill presentment and payment for some.

As we are all aware the paperless office is still a long way off, and e-government doesn't mean totally paperless. The public will only be prepared to interact with departments electronically if they see real benefit in doing so and the service is easily accessible. Trust is needed so that people are comfortable with providing personal information on-line.

There is a need to be a significant mindset change among employees and customers, the majority of whom are still very comfortable working the old way. Implementing new systems is 10% about technology—the rest is ensuring that the people who will use the technology are adequately trained and comfortable with moving to the new ways.

There are many stories about technology implementations, which failed purely because the people were resistant to change. Technology change requires organisational change—new processes require buy-in from staff and other stakeholders. We've all seen and heard about the technology, and we know it exists—now we need to extract the real benefits it promises.

E-governance, requires a fundamental change in how the government operates by constantly reinventing itself by delivering its obligations to the citizens with greater accountability and a responsive sensitivity. Therefore, the quality of e-governance shall eventually depend on the intent of the government and the set of men behind the computers. For an effective and efficient e-governance model, IT deployment has to be backed by flat structures, a healthy work ethos, transparent systems and simple procedures.

The word balance seems to crop up often when looking into the immediate future. One of the delicate juggling acts facing us over the next few years will be to satisfy political agendas and social needs, at the same time as moving into a more technological world. In many instances, technology implementations lead to more efficient processes, more automation and possibly the need for fewer staff.

Government's responsibility to its political partners and constituency must by default have implications for the well-being of society at large, and the continuing employment of people in the country. Some trade-offs will need to be made, and the process needs to be carefully managed to ensure that introduction of technology doesn't lead to reduced employment rates.

There are many challenges associated with the e-governance process. Technology challenges are the most significant of them. Achieving the benefits of e-Governance may not be easy and goes far beyond mere computerization of government processes.

Its successful implementation not only poses technical challenges but also requires a fundamental change in the manner in which the government operates today. In fact, the challenges the Governments are likely to face would be, how to cope with re-engineering the government processes and functions and related issues of new responsibilities for civil servants, businesses and citizens.

The old model was one of information technology (IT) automating the internal workings of government by processing data. The new model is one of information and communication technologies (ICTs) supporting and transforming the external workings of governance by processing and communicating data. e-Governance should be seen to encompass all ICTs, but the key innovation is computer networks — from intranets to the Internet — creating a wealth of new digital connections:

— Connections within government — permitting 'joined-up thinking'.

— Connections between government and NGOs/ citizens—strengthening accountability.
— Connections between government and business/ citizens — transforming service delivery.
— Connections within and between NGOs — supporting learning and concerted action.
— Connections within and between communities — building social and economic development.
— E-government must be a shared vision Encourage stakeholders— government and non-government—to participate in defining the vision. If the public and private sectors are consulted only after e-government plans have been developed and implementation has begun, e-government programmes risk being underused or even irrelevant.

A shared vision ensures that key constituents and communities will "buy into" and support e-government programmes from beginning to end. A shared vision of e-government means a shared stake in the outcome. Involving key stakeholders— citizen groups, associations, businesses, government officials, NGOs, unions and other civil society groups—does not mean that all decisions on e-government must await broad public or across-government consensus.

E-government requires a champion and political leadership. However, defining the vision and selecting priority areas need input from stakeholders, and not only a few elite experts or officials

In many countries, including developing countries, citizens distrust their governments, especially where there has been a history of dictatorship, political instability or large-scale corruption. To ensure that the public and stakeholders will be partners in the e-government effort, it is important to try to build trust in government. Lack of trust by the public can lead to the failure of or serious delay in e-government initiatives.

The mechanisms for receiving input from various stakeholders will vary, but making an effort to include non-government stakeholders in building the vision for e-government will pay off.

Governments must give serious consideration about who should help define the e-government vision and how to secure their input. In some places, governments can organize public meetings or conduct polls of citizens (and businesses or officials). In others, citizens and the private sector are included in committees that develop an e-government plan in an open, collaborative way.

The vision should be citizen-centered. Ultimately, e-government must be about meeting the needs of citizens and improving quality of life. Borrowing a lesson from the private sector, e-government must be customer-driven and service oriented. This means that a vision of e-government implies providing greater access to information as well as better, more equal services and procedures for the public and businesses.

Even when e-government projects seek to improve internal government processes, the end goal should be making government serve citizens better. And this means recognizing the diverse roles that citizens have as parents, taxpayers, constituents, employers, employees, students, investors and lobbyists.

Communication of the vision is another important aspect of the e-government process. Once the vision for e-government is established, it is crucial that leaders from government and non-government sectors communicate the vision and key objectives across government and to the public.

Establish a communications strategy to ensure that people understand the vision the changes that will occur and the tangible benefits for them from e-government. To communicate the e-government vision to the broadest possible audience, it is best to use the media most likely to reach target audiences.

For the public and businesses, this might mean town meetings, newspapers, TV/radio broadcasts or through Web sites. For civil servants, discussing the vision in speeches, department meetings or trainings might be effective.

The communication strategy will depend upon the circumstances of each society and the nature of the e-government application.

To the extent that increased transparency, accountability and predictability (of rules and procedures) are made priorities, e-government may offer a weapon against corruption.

E-government, however, does not guarantee the end of corruption. Officials who master technology-empowered processes can find new opportunities for rent seeking. Under such circumstances, e-government may simply cause an intergenerational shift in corruption toward younger, more tech-literate officials.

One especially sensitive issue, right from the start, is whether fighting corruption should be part of the e-government vision. Each society must answer that question for itself.

For countries where corruption is a serious concern, as in many developing countries, this question should be considered when the e-government vision and priorities are discussed. If the answer is "yes", it will be important to decide what forms of corruption the e-government programme will address and how it will be accomplished.

Publicize e-government's anti-corruption goals or not? If fighting corruption is included in the vision, the next key question is when to announce the anticorruption goal to the public. If fighting corruption is publicly announced as a major part of the e-government agenda, it could help build coalitions and public pressure for anti-corruption results.

However, publicity too early in the e-government process runs the risk of causing fear and resistance from corrupt officials, who are likely to exert negative pressure even upon their uncorrupt colleagues.

Another option is to not publicize the anti-corruption goals of an e-government programme but rather "sell" e-government (especially within the government) as a programme to accomplish other goals such as improving government services, increasing attractiveness of the country for investment, reducing costs to the public/business or improving the competitiveness of the local private sector.

Given the sensitivity of these issues, involvement of non-government stakeholders in the discussion is important.

For example Mexico's federal government established Compranet for government procurement as part of its efforts to curb corruption by automating procurement procedures. By facilitating a process of bidding and reverse bidding online, it seeks to make government purchasing more efficient and transparent. The system allows the public to see what services and products the government is spending its resources on and what companies are providing them with these services. There are more than 6,000 public sector tenders logged daily, and more than 20,000 service-providing firms are regular users. Other countries in the region are looking to imitate Mexico's successful Compranet.

Thus it for an effective e-governance process it is extremely necessary that we take care of all the issues mentioned above.

Related Concepts

Electronic Democracy (E-Democracy)

Over the last century we have witnessed a revolution in communications that has moved much of the public discourse and agenda setting from the individual and community level to the mass level. As communication technologies and their use by people continue to evolve there are indications that this trend is now reversing with some notable globalization exceptions. With computer-meditated communications, people are reclaiming their communications power from mass institutions.

Just as individuals are using the Internet for their own personal interests, so to are traditional political, government, media and other organizations. Most existing organizations will determine how to use the Internet and electronic communications to represent and further their own interests.

If most of the interests in society "get online", does that mean that democracy will be improved? Will this by default improve citizen participation, public discourse and public problem solving? In my general opinion, the answer is no, but it doesn't have to be.

Democracy has evolved from many cultures to the point where it is somewhat different to its small community origins.

In the process, many of its earlier features have become difficult to sustain due to the large size and complexity of communities today.

Electronic Democracy using the Internet information technology medium has the potential to change the democratic process to something more like its original form.

The Internet has the ability to enhance interactive communication and the exchange of information while coping with the constraints of scale, distance and time. This ability can facilitate the transfer of some power from the government back to the people.

The creation and the spread of the Internet and other computer networks have sparked a debate about "electronic democracy" in the United States. Not only media pundits, but also scholars of political science ask if it is possible to foster democratic development with the help of communication technology (for example, Bertelsen 1992; Calabrese/Borchert 1996; Friedland 1996; Ogden 1994).

Research on the relationship between computer networks and democracy has turned up ample evidence that concepts of electronic democracy contribute both to democratic theory and our understanding of the working of a democratic political system in the information age.

According to Steven Clift , E-democracy represents the use of information and communication technologies and strategies by democratic actors (governments, elected officials, the media, political organizations, citizen/voters) within political and governance processes of local communities, nations and on the international stage.

To many, e-democracy suggests greater and more active citizen participation enabled by the Internet, mobile communications, and other technologies in today's representative democracy as well as through more participatory or direct forms of citizen involvement in addressing public challenges.

Broadly, Electronic Democracy (E-Democracy) refers to the processes and structures that encompass all forms of electronic communication between Government and the Citizen.

The term has become the one most often used by those dealing with implications of computer technology for the political process (Dutton 1992; London 1994; Van de Donk' Tops 1995). To some extent, "digital democracy" (as used by Fineman 1995), would be a more precise term.

Other synonyms for the concept are also possible: "Cyberdemocracy" (Ogden 1994, Poster 1995), "Virtual democracy", or "Information Age democracy" (Snider 1994). However, it is now the term "electronic" which has become to imply the application of "interactive technology" itself, as London (1994) has pointed out.

"An Electronic Democracy" is any democratic political system in which computers and computer networks are used to carry out crucial functions of the democratic process—such as information and communication, interest articulation and aggregation, and decision-making (both deliberation and voting).

In a narrower perspective, E-Democracy refers principally to the processes and structures that encompass all forms of electronic communication between the electorate and the elected.

As is typical of Electronic Governance, in order to enable all citizens and diverse communities of practice, expertise, interest, inter-dependence and conviction to plug in, it is essential to have basic access, to the requisite technology, which is affordable, in addition to having a literate population able to use the technology.

A landmark day in evolution of E-democracy was in September 1995 when Sweden proposed that a G7 GOL project should be started on issues related to the provision of online services to the public in support of the democratic process.

The proposed online support for democracy was more precisely seen to concern the area of dialogue between the citizens and government. Another project area would be how to tailor and provide technology and human resources when citizens meet the public authorities in one-stop shops (neighbourhood offices, citizens offices, etc.).

A concern that should be stressed is that IT support for democracy should be tailored so as to reach and be attractive to all citizens, and not just a few.

With technology advances shaping every aspect of our individual and collective future life, it is only a matter of time before our democracy opens itself upto the power of advanced communication and other technological advancement. How will these new technologies influence elections, initiative campaigns, access to government information, access to government service, etc. are certain issues to be seen.

E-Republic

The concept of an E-Republic is derived from elements of self-determination, cosmopolitanism, technological idealism and civil society. An E-Republic maintains that a group of people who share a claim to a common heritage (ethnicity, language, culture, traditions or religion) and shared value systems (common beliefs, common laws, shared economic space, community of interest, universal ethics) have the right and the responsibility through self-determination to form an affiliation.

It recognizes that the prime determinant of personal identity is not necessarily ethnicity, nationality or geography and that in the future other forms of identity will become paramount.

People who freely choose to affiliate themselves with others are entitled to establish a governance structure with common citizenship and a political, social and economic structure that is independent of or co-dependent of geographical location or existing nation-state. It is quite probable that some nation-states will evolve or extend into global E-Republics.

E-Business

It is conceivable, on the basis of the above, that the benefits of E-Government will continue to depend on the realization of technical advances in Electronic Business (E-Business) in the broadest sense. Electronic Business (E-Business) refers to a broader definition of Electronic Commerce (E-Commerce), not just buying and selling but also servicing customers and collaborating with business partners, and conducting electronic transactions within an organizational entity.

According to Lou Gerstner, IBM's CEO: "E-Business is all about time cycle, speed, globalization, enhanced productivity, reaching new customers and sharing knowledge across institutions for competitive advantage". Perceived as E-Business, Electronic Government will comprise the following categories:

- Government-to-Government (G2G) exchange of information and commodities;
- Citizen/Consumer to Government (C2G) exchange of information and commodities;
- Government to Business/Private (G2B) exchange of information and commodities;
- Business/Private to Government (B2G) sale of goods and services; and
- Intra-Government E-Business.

The Stages of E-government Development

Stage 1 : Emerging web presence

A country has a formal but limited web presence through a single or a few independent government websites that generally serve as public information sources. The site(s) provide users with static information on the government and or its ministries, agencies, elected officials etc. contact information like addresses, phone numbers, office hours, calendars, etc. are posted. Special features like frequently asked questions may be found.

Stage 2 : Enhanced web presence

A country's web presence expands as users can access dynamic and specialized information that is regularly updated through an increasing number of official websites. An official national government website or homepage may serve as an entry point linking users to other branches, ministries, departments and sub-national government sites. Official government publications, legislation, newsletters and other useful documents can be downloaded or ordered online. Search features, e-mail and areas for posting comments are accessible.

Stage 3 : Interactive web presence

A country's presence on the internet expands dramatically with an increase in the number of official websites providing access to a broad range of government institutions and the services they provide. A national government website frequently acts as a portal directly linking users with ministries, departments and agencies. Formal interactions between citizens and service providers take place on a more sophisticated level allowing users to directly access information based on their specific interests or needs. Users can search specialized databases; download forms and applications or submit them online; make appointments with officials; participate in online town-hall meetings. Secure sites and user passwords begin to emerge.

Stage 4 : Transactional web presence

Users will have the ability to conduct complete and secure transactions online like obtaining visas, passports, birth and death records, licenses, permits or specialized government services. A single national government website will allow the user to customize a secure one-stop-shop portal that will enable direct access to most government services. Such portals will allow direct access to services based on a users specific need or priorities rather than by the functions of a department or agency. Sites will ultimately be secure making it possible for citizens to safely file and pay taxes online, pay parking fines, automobile registration fees, utility bills. Digital signatures will be recognized.

Stage 5 : Seamless or fully integrated web presence

Country provides all services and links through a one-stop-shop portal. By clicking on the national government's official site, users will have the ability to instantly access any service made available in a & quantified package. Ministerial/departmental/agency lines of demarcation are blurred in cyber-space. Governments will cluster services along common needs through one universal portal. All transactional services offered by government will be available online.

UNPAN Global Survey of E-Government

Role of ICT in E-Governance

Governance can be defined as the process through which institutions, businesses and citizen groups articulate their interests, exercise their rights and obligations and mediate their differences.

Information and communication technologies (ICTs) can help to sustain this process in three ways: (i) they can support tasks that involve complex decision making, communication and decision implementation, (ii) they can automate tedious tasks done by humans, and (iii) they can support new tasks and processes that did not exist before. When ICTs are properly aligned with governance goals, they can help to create gains in both efficiency and effectiveness.

The basis of Governance is strongly rooted in the power of strategic information and knowledge :

— Information and Knowledge / forms the basis of decision-making and action.
— Informed and judicious decision-making depends on the quality and timeliness of information.
— Circumscription of information and knowledge to a selected few enables its manipulation for exploitative purposes.

Citizens the world are demanding that governments be more open in their interaction with the civil society. Access to information and knowledge about the political process, about services and about choices available, is a characteristic requirement in all good governance systems.

But the prime question remains as to what is it that citizens really want from e-government? Is there more to e-government than e-commerce translated to the public sector? Do the standard engineering metrics — faster, better, cheaper —capture the potential of the Internet and World Wide Web to connect citizens to one another and to their government?

What do we know about the ways that citizens search for information on very large, government websites? How do they pose questions on all those search engines and do they receive the answers they're seeking?

The aspirations and the demands of the e-governance applications should meet with the objectives of it. OECD Public Management Service commissioned a report in 1998 to explore how the new information and communications technologies (ITCs) and the emerging "information society" (IS) are changing the way governments handle information in the policy making process, and to discuss some of the issues these changes raise for the conduct of democratic government. In its report Impact of the Emerging Information Society on the Policy Development Process and Democratic Quality, it found out that, the new information and communications technologies (ICTs) have many strengths:

— Speed (compression of time and distance);
— Informality;
— Relative ease of access;
— Targetability;
— Relative low cost.

As a result of these changes, more information is available more readily. These changes are affecting the major players in the policy process in many different ways:

— The media are better informed, more questioning and better able to play a role in government accountability in the emerging Information Society (IS).
— Interest groups are also better informed, better linked through networks, and, in most of the countries visited, better able to bring pressure to bear, especially on the middle level of bureaucracy; access to the top is still, however, limited.
— Lobbyists who do not use the new technologies to rally support around their clients' interests could lose some power as their principals get direct access to information they used to pay lobbyists to obtain; lobbyists will, however, continue to sell their prime asset: access to decision-makers.
— Political parties have become more electoral than policy machines as they have adapted to the emerging IS and adopted many of the new technologies to raise money, organise workers, get out their messages and neutralise the opposition.
— Legislatures are increasingly squeezed between the general public and the executive; the new technologies make plebiscitary democracy more feasible and this possibility is putting pressures on representative democracy.
— Relations with the general public have not, and are unlikely to, change much; they will be able to communicate faster, but not necessarily to greater effect with policy-makers.
— The bureaucracy appears to be increasing its influence as it has the resources to enhance its synthesising and advising role.
— The study concludes that the ICTs have not improved the links to decision-makers or the democratic quality of policy and governance.

"The IS and the new technologies have done little to enhance democratic values such as the frequency and quality of participation in or the transparence of policymaking and governance. Nor have they improved government credibility.

The growth of a confrontational media has done little to advance these values. On the other hand, in a positive vein, the purposeful use of the ICTs has the potential to advance some of the other important touchstones of democracy —accountability, political equality, freedom of speech and association and the treatment and role of minorities — especially if they become simpler to use and more widely distributed."

The report argued that the ICTs have altered the environment for policymaking, often in negative ways, and driven a number of important developments which are affecting the ability of governments to govern and their willingness to embrace the new technologies:

— "The policy-making process has become more complex.
— It is increasingly difficult for governments to set and maintain their agenda; once decisions are taken it is more and more difficult to make them stick; it is more difficult for governments to get their way on issues;
— This has resulted in an enormous stress on "marketing" policy decisions, facilitated by the new technologies with their ease in segmenting markets and speeding delivery of tailored messages. Increasingly vast amounts of time and resources are spent on communications planning and implementing communications strategies.
— There is a tendency for governments to move into the infotainment business. This is accentuated by the need of governments to be seen to be doing something; the media often drive governments to develop "symbolic" or short-term solutions to symptoms rather than root causes with the result that major issues are left untouched."

The democratising potential of the ICTs must be accompanied by other important changes:

— "The advent of a new technically literate generation to positions of power (since the spread of new technology requires leadership from committed users at the top);
— Improved technologies for interactivity, synthesis and feedback;

— Higher priority and greater political will on the part of decision-makers to better link the public to the decision-making process in a substantive way; decision-makers must contain their propensity towards secretiveness and their instinct to "ration democracy"; and last but not least;

— Greater desire on the part of the public to participate actively in the policy process."

A more informed citizenry is in a better position to exercise its rights, play its roles, carry out its responsibilities and define its relationships to others; and Citizens as consumers expect to be involved in the process of securing services to suit their needs, and to receive a higher standard of 'customer care' from government.

Most governments in the developed world have moved towards some form of implementation of Information and Communication Technologies (ICTs) to deliver services to the public and better administer their internal programmes. In many countries, there are varying attempts to engage the citizen in the process of government electronically.

The increasing use of Information and Communication Technology (ICT) in a variety of activities has been changing the way business is conducted, the way people live, and the way government functions all over the world. The benefits of using this technology (*e.g.* the Internet and computer networks) to improve democratic systems are being recognized by an increasing number of international organizations, governments and citizens.

Access to information is both a consequence, and a driver of, the digital revolution.

International debate has recently highlighted the centrality and importance of "good governance" for sustainable development.

Information and communication technologies ("ICTs") have always influenced the evolution of society and, as a consequence, the nature of government. Historically, they have enhanced existing social, economic and political interactions, and even introduced new forms of interactivity.

This interactivity is, in both a social and technical sense, the unfastened cork that allows the informational genie to escape from the bottle. It leads to the emergence of new relationships, connections and expectations that are difficult to control or predict, and which can bring about fundamental, even revolutionary change.

The development of human language in prehistoric times, for example, surely among the most innovative of communications technologies, is considered by most sociologists to have been a prerequisite for the emergence of organized human culture. Less dramatically, the telegraph, telephone, radio, television and even photocopier for their part have all effected a greater or lesser measure of change in the instruments of governance.

There are at least three basic needs, apart from the potentials of e-commerce, that ask for instituting "e-governance" both in developing and developed countries.

First, the essentiality of electronic governance emanates from emerging "participatory models" in management systems. The argument lays stress on shared visions for strategies both at the horizontal and vertical levels of planning and management. Therefore, in order to involve citizens in dialogue and decision-making at the public policy and practice levels, there is a great need for making government departments reachable to stakeholders through harnessing the potentials of new technologies and media.

Second, there it is a need to bridge information-data gaps and lapses which lead to inappropriate planning and decision making divorced from sharable scientific statistical data amongst the government departments and planning agencies.

Third, the emerging new models of good governance which stress to involve governments, civil society and business community at appropriate levels of planning and implementation makes it imperative to let decision making bodies, personnel and debates electronically accessible to public with the rapid diffusion of ICTs in societies.

"The Rapid Diffusion Argument" is supported by the fact, "if 50 million is taken as a measure to make a technology ubiquitous, then the automobile took some 30-odd years to reach this level and television twenty. The Internet, however, has taken only five, and is well on its way to doubling that number in less than two years more."

In today's speedy and accelerative world passing through a phase of transition like all previous times in which not only means of communication but the very living patterns and norms of societies are in the melting pot, there is an unprecedented urgency for making bureaucracies and state governments responding to social needs.

Notwithstanding, the needs not only qualify to subsistence level facilities but new and adjusted laws which govern the means of wealth creation and its distribution along with access to tangible and intangible resources. In this context the patterns of living in information societies going for "e-governance" don't expect to let files move at the speed they are moving with tags of "through proper channel". They ask for problems simultaneously worked out in both horizontal and vertical manner of bureaucratic management.

Do we want to reciprocate emerging social and economic realities with new laws or old laws tinkered at faster speed? Yes, is the unanimous answer while looking at stereotype bureaucratic hurdles that do nothing but impede the smooth transition of societies from underdeveloped to developed and from stagnant to dynamic ones. Sequentially, it can be said without fear of contradiction that the ICTs have potential to help engineer such an enabling atmosphere where the prevailing governance paradigms meet shifts in the command and control mechanisms both at the policy and implementation level.

Good Governance rests on the pillars of knowledge and recognition of this set of knowledge by the decision-makers. Digitization of this entire set of knowledge within a network which links every individual including the decision-makers, gives freedom to everyone to access and make use of this knowledge—paving the way for Digital Governance.

Digital Governance therefore includes ICT induced changes in delivery of governance services and more importantly changes induced in the way citizens interact and participate in the governance sphere.

Governments can respond to the need to be more open by adopting a number of principles of information management, using a 'mix' of technologies.

Convergence of governance forms that integral part of the needs of each individual with the wider interests of the community.

Information and Communication Technologies (ICT) are changing the power equations based on access and control to information and knowledge. They are leading to a fundamental shift in way information and knowledge flows, is stored and gets used. ICT will change the old ways of Governance.

A more informed civil society is in a better position to understand and exercise its rights, and ICT will lead to reduction in Knowledge Gaps on issues concerning governance.

ICT can help Governance create avenues and opportunities to enable people participate in the Governance processes through :

— Issues and agendas would be a part of the larger public debate before any decision is taken on them.
— Expanding policy debates beyond the confines of dominant individuals and groups, and enriching the stock of policy knowledge in the process.
— Greater Transparency in actions and decisions.
— Creation of Public Watch guards.
— Creation of strong virtual communities.
— Online polls.
— Greater representation of un-represented communities-women, aged, children who are otherwise kept marginalised out of democratic processes.

In the context of global economy and competitive markets, new technological developments in information and communication technologies (ICTs) such as, satellite television broadcasting, radio, long-distance telephony, computers, Internet and telecommunications, have sparked optimism about their potential to accelerate the pace of social and economic development in developing countries. ICTs can be harnessed to meet basic human needs of the poor and marginalised communities in rural and remote areas, and create new structures for governance and commerce.

Recent strides in ICT present tremendous opportunities for human developments achieving that potential depends on how the technology is used.

— Making fundamental rights, laws and legalisation online.
— Fighting corruption—Central Vigilance Committee website to have names of Government Officials allegedly involved in corrupt practices.

Digital Governance is a term to focus on the new and evolving forms of governance in which ICTs have a substantial role to play.

Introduction of Digital Governance is a way to ensure that common citizens have equal right to be a part of decision-making processes which affect them directly or indirectly, and influence them in a manner which best improves their conditions and the quality of lives.

The new form of Governance will ensure that citizens are no longer passive consumer of governance services offered to them, and instead would have the potential to play a decisive role in deciding the kind of services they want and the structure which could best provide the same.

As seen above the use of Digital Governance transforms governance from "representative" to a more "individual based" form, and from "passive" to being "pro-active". Further as use of digital governance leads to closer contact of individuals with decision-makers/officials in the government, the impact is immediate. On the whole, it puts greater access and control over governance mechanism in the hands of individuals, and in process leads to better transparent, accountable and efficient governance.

Quite obviously, the objective of achieving Electronic Governance (EG) goes far beyond mere computerization of stand alone back office operations. It means to fundamentally change how Government operates and this implies a new set of responsibilities for the executive, legislature and the citizenry.

While the transformation of how government operates promises the most direct benefits for business, it is the transformation of governance-reexamining what a global, networked economy will mean to how democratic institutions work, to the relationship between the citizen and the state, and to the future of the nation-state itself-that seems to hold the most interest for everyone.

The intriguing part of research being done is what does it mean to be an e-state, an e-government or an e-citizen? The reason that some analysts think e-citizens (the better educated, more affluent people who now regularly use the Web) are so important is because they are the ones who will force governments to change.

E-citizens are e-consumers who are going online and ordering their computers and their books and getting them within a couple of days, and they are expecting the same kind of fulfillment from their legislators and their government officials. That's a real challenge to government. It's not just good enough to put in the systems; you have to figure out a way to respond to people in a timely fashion.

The information technology governance structures must leverage the expertise of faculty and staff in decision making and policy setting and help to make timely and appropriate institutional decisions on major IT strategies and investments.

The country's IT success is largely dependent on a governance framework that defines roles, responsibilities and expectations. Without governance, the alignment of IT and business strategies will fall victim to turf wars, service gaps and lack of coordination. The role of IT policy is to provide clear guidance as to how IT decisions are to be made and who can make them. Useful governance must be future-directed.

Information and Communication Technologies (ICTs) are not only a significant factor in the performance and growth of economies—the importance of which is continuously growing—but they also represent a novel and effective tool to help advance sustainable human development.

There is an old saying to the effect that people with weak stomachs shouldn't watch either sausages or legislation being made. Some IT pundits think a truly digital government will change at least the legislation part of that by giving people input to government in a way no one, not even today's much-derided special interest groups, has had before. It is possible that as government processes become more transparent to the average citizen, they will also become more palatable, with fewer quid pro quo deals.

Governments—central or local, national or regional—from around the world are or should be cognizant of the critical roles they can play and the key responsibilities they can hold in transforming the emerging digital convergence into creative divergence through initiatives aimed to create knowledge societies.

Knowledge societies may be perceived as societies that are able to exploit knowledge, limited only by their imagination (creative divergence), to derive comparative as well as competitive advantage using the opportunities rendered possible by the emergence of digital convergence.

Right now most citizens see policy decisions and how legislation gets made and so on as something of a black box that exists in government. Governments are accustomed to holding all the cards in lots of ways, certainly the trump card.

Governments think that they will have all these conversations but we'll go away and make the decision and tell you what it was. In an e-government, citizens will be able to argue for their own causes, not just the well-heeled lobbying groups. It is likely that the stateless Internet will radically change the governments under which people live. It is important to keep in perspective that the nation-state is a relatively recent development.

While the key focus in governments in developed countries has been on information and services delivery through a networked environment, single contacts that link into a range of government departments, and the use of electronic information-age services, these governments have recognized that application of information technology to all levels of government is an important part of public sector reform.

Format for an ICT Infrastructure

As people communicate differently, they're looking at different forms of governance from this relatively modern thing that was developed in Europe a couple of centuries ago. We are starting the next evolution and where it will end, is unpredictable.

While there is much discussion about what digital government can or will do, the process is still in its infancy. Few governments or agencies have anything even as elemental as EDS's Form, linking three databases together. And that may be all to the good. Even before you get to the people who think government is just one giant conspiracy, there are many people with deep concerns about hyperefficient governments.

Given the dangerous excesses that non-digital governments have been capable of, it is indeed sobering to think about what tomorrow's e-government might do with unfettered access to the digital information of its citizenry. But that is not the only risk. There are also concerns about individuals and businesses having too much input in the day-to-day business of government, creating a hyper-responsive government. Will it move us toward a direct democracy, where people vote on whatever hot-button issue they see on the evening news.

The first step in using ICTs as a tool is to improve governance is to ignore ICTs altogether and focus on selecting and prioritizing improvement goals that are urgent or important. Once the most important goals are established, senior level policymakers must establish milestones that will indicate that the activities designed to meet these goals are on track. The next step is to review alternative ICT solutions that support the activities designed to achieve the goals, given constraints on financing, infrastructure, literacy and skills. Each solution must be associated with (financial and opportunity) costs — of infrastructure, training, etc. — and benefits.

Once the ICT solution is accepted based on the planners' estimation of its merits and costs, a detailed workplan must be developed, with provisions for adequate training and capacity building. Again the key is to focus on strategic goals and user constraints. The final step in the process is to lay the groundwork for monitoring and evaluation (M&E) and to incorporate M&E as an ongoing integral part of the process of adapting ICTs to meet needs.

Build capacities in people to absorb information and knowledge and use it for improvement in their quality of life. Basic education enhances people's capacity to learn and to interpret information. Knowledge about technology asserts a belief in people that they can be a part of the ICT revolution. (Education, Computer Literacy, Exposure Visits, Creation of Innovative Models of people centered governance).

Simplify information to suit the capacity of the end users. (Language Barriers etc.):

- Efficient Judiciary to enforce amendments and abiding to people's decisions.
- Low Literacy rate.
- Fostering intermediary organizations and strong civil society groups to force changes.
- Transformation from information and knowledge deprivation to easy access to the same—Capacities to Absorb and Understand.

There are several stumbling blocks for an effective implementation of an ICT policy, which are as follows:

— Undermining of Political Control?
— Governance will become accountable to not just opposition parties but to individuals.
— Public Policies that hinder the spread of ICT's.
— Lack of understanding about the technology and its potential.
— High Cost of setting up ICT infrastructure for inclusion of all but not higher than the cost of inclusion incurred so far and to be incurred in the future.
— Greater use of ICT can influence the process of Governance in several ways.
— Technical—in terms of automation of tedious or repetitive governance tasks and thereby improving efficiency of governance processes. For instance, automated filing of tax forms, checking the status of an application online etc. Through technology it enhances the productivity effectively of response and grievance handling on part of the governments.
— To a Facilitating / Supportive role— in terms of using ICT to complement existing efforts/methods to improve governance. For instance, putting government information on a website, or opening avenues for people to communicate with government officials through e-mail.
— To a completely innovative role— which involves initiating new services and new mechanisms to improve governance. For instance, the potential for any individual to access the same information instantly as and when it becomes available in the public domain is useful to fighting corruption and reducing information monopoly of traditional power bearers etc. In other cases, rapid access to information from sources other than government sources can improve decision-making capacity of an individual.

E-governance is not just about government web site and e-mail. It is not just about service delivery over the Internet. It is not just about digital access to government information or electronic payments. *It will change how citizens relate to governments as much as it changes how citizens relate to each other.* It will bring forth new concepts of citizenship, both in terms of needs and responsibilities.

E-governance will allow citizens to communicate with government, participate in the governments' policy-making and citizens to communicate each other. The governance will truly allow citizens to participate in the government decision-making process, reflect their true needs and welfare by utilizing e-government as a tool.

Different organizations seek to integrate ICT in their governance infrastructures to achieve different motives

UNDP is using ICT to :

— Raise awareness, build vision and advise on policies to capture information and knowledge for development;

— Promote and build connectivity and necessary infrastructure for access to information and development;

— Build required human and social capacities and institutions and provide training and education to impart requisite skills;

— Empower communities and disadvantaged groups, reinforce participatory approaches and good governance and foster networking;

— Help create new livelihood and employment opportunities;

— Conduct pilot projects to demonstrate the feasibility, suitability and impact of ICTs for SHD through electronic community centres;

— Promote partnerships between the public sector, the private sector and civil society.

2

Policy Initiatives in India

Minimum Agenda for E-Governance in the Ministries/ Departments of the Central Government (Government of India).

— Each Ministry / Department must set up LANs and provide PCs with necessary software up to the Section Officer level.

— 100% training of all staff who have access to and need to use computers for their office work should be ensured.

— Each Ministry/Department would start using the Office Procedure Automation software developed by NIC with a view to keeping a record of receipt of dak, issue of letters, as well as movement of files in the department.

— Pay roll accounting and other house-keeping software should be put to use in day-to-day operations.

— Notices for internal meeting should be sent by e-mail to the officers and also put up on online notice boards of the Ministry / Department.

— Ministries/Departments should use the Web-enabled Grievance Redressal Software developed by Department of AR & PG.

— Each Ministry/Department should have its own web-site.

— All Acts, Rules, Circulars should be converted into electronic form and along with other published material of interest or relevance to the public, should be made available on the internet and be accessible from the Information and Facilitation Counter.

- The websites of Ministries/Departments/Organisations should specifically contain a section in which various forms to-be used by citizens/customers are available. The forms should be available for being printed out or for being completed on the computer itself and then printed out for submission. Attempts should also be made to enable completion and submission of forms online.
- The Hindi version of the content of the websites should be developed simultaneously, as far as possible.
- Each Ministry/Department would also make efforts to develop packages so as to begin electronic delivery of services to the public.
- Each Ministry/Department should have an overall IT version or strategy for a five year period, within which it could do detail specific action plans and targets (including the minimum agenda) to be implemented within one year.

IT Policy Mission in India

Development with Equity

One of the prime policy consideration of a democratic government is the need to ensure that the benefits of its initiatives spread evenly and reach the under privileged population groups as well. While the benefits of citizen services projects reach the rich and the poor equally, IT projects aimed at improving the internal efficiencies benefit the poor indirectly through better planning and targeting of weaker section programmes and superior enforcement of law. Apart from this, the IT should percolate to the middle class and people below the poverty line. This can be achieved by taking latent to the villages, promoting IT-enabled education, tele-medicine and socially relevant extension and outreach programmes.

Economic Development

The Information Technology should be used as a vehicle

for the economic development of the islands and thus the upgradation of the standard of living of the people. It should be used as a tool to enhance the productivity, efficiency and optimum utilization of resources. It could be used for:

* Creation of employment potential.
* Full exploitation of employment potential of the IT sector.
* Creation of IT industry.
  * Data entry centers.
  * Transcription centers.
  * Software development (by attracting companies located on mainland through different incentives).
* Attracting investment from outside the State.
* Improvement of the employment of educated youth in the IT sector through academic & training programme.

Human Resource Development

Economic development leads to improved quality of life of citizens and this includes:

* Quality education.
* Access to quality health care.
* Elevation of academic institutions as centers of excellence in knowledge (ex. Establishment of IIT at Port Blair).

Good Governance

Good governance is a *sine qua non* for the orderly functioning of the society. IT is being used as an enabling fool for the delivery of services in the public sector (Government sector) in many countries. The following facets of the governance can be significantly improved with the use of IT:

* Government—Citizen Interface
* Government—Business Interface
* Government—Government Interface
* Intra—Government—Process

The Objective of achieving Electronic—Governance (e-governance) goes far beyond mere computerization of stand alone back office operation. It should not be merely used to automate process but as a strategic tool to simplify procedures and revamp processes. The e-governance should aim to bring in the following benefits:

* Any—where, any—time services to citizens;
* One-stop shop for all transactions in the Government—citizen interface;
* Better accountability, responsiveness and transparency of all systems;
* Highly efficient government machinery and systems.

IT Education of All

The IT Education has remained confirmed to the urban centers and thus one of the objectives is to take IT education to rural areas as well. This can be done by setting up Community Information Centers in all islands, which will:

* Serve as backbone for communication;
* Provide internet access to remote areas;
* internet access at block level;
* Information exchange through e-mail for the effective implementation of the socio-economic development programmes in the region;
* Access to the database/development information of national importance such as;
    * Population
    * Village Amenities
    * North East Resource Database
    * Judgement of Supreme Court and High Courts;
* Training through Distance Learning Technique;
* Connectivity to all leading Education & Research institutions in the country;
* Computer awareness training programme at the block level.

Establishment of State Information Infrastructure (SII)

State Information Infrastructure comprising of high speed broad band communication backbone, nodes, access network, distributed data warehouses and service locations to cater to the needs of trade, commerce, industry and tourism and also to enhance the delivery of Government Services to the people, is required as the base on which IT related services can be built.

National e-Governance Initiative—
Government of India

Agenda for the X 5-Year Plan
(Revised on March *15*, 2002)

1. e-Governance and e-Government

There is a lot of discussion and interest generated globally on the concepts of e-Governance and e-Government. Though both these terms are used interchangeably, 'e-Government' refers to the larger process of using IT for improving both the Internal operations of the Govt. as well as its external interface in several forms, while the term 'e-Government' relates mostly to improving the Govt. interface with the citizens and the business.

2. Components of the National Agenda for the X Five-year Plan

The National Agenda for the X Five-year Plan may consist of the following components:

- Defining a **vision** for the National e-Governance
- Designing appropriate **architectures** that enable realization of the vision
- Creating the **Infrastructure** in conformity with the architectures
- Developing appropriate **frameworks** for resource mobilization and implementation
- Implementing a set of **core initiatives**
- **Capacity building**

This approach paper attempts to outline the above components.

3. e-Governance Vision

The e-Governance vision differs from country to country, state to state and region to region, as it should reflect the needs and aspirations of those countries states and regions. However, a certain commonality exists in the expectations of the stakeholders, namely, the Govt. on one hand and the citizen/ business on the other. The following table brings out these expectations as viewed from the Government's point and as viewed from the citizen/business point.

Government's View	Citizen/Business View
Efficiency	Speedy service
Transparency	Fair trial / audit-ability
Equity/Social justice / Inclusion	Accessibility / Spread / Regional language
Cost effectiveness	Affordability, value proposition
Simplicity	User-friendliness, self-service
Responsiveness	Interactivity
Participating	Consultations, democratic
Security	Trust
Consistency	Expect-ability
Integration / Collaboration	Convenience, cost and time saving, citizen centric

It is necessary to involve all the stakeholders in developing the vision. The stakeholders should cover a good cross section of citizens, NGO's, politicians, professional groups, farmers, students, artisans, organizations of weaker sections, employees, representatives of local bodies like municipal councils & Gram Panchayats etc. The exercise should be based on the concept of inclusion and specifically address issues of digital divide.

The vision and the implementation plans that emerge out of this exercise should be reviewed periodically to reflect the dynamic changes that occur on both the demand and supply sides of e-governance.

4. Varying degrees of development of e-Governance among the states

Within India, there is a tremendous divergence in the extent of implementation of the concept of e-Governance. It is, therefore, not possible to come up with a framework for implementation of e-Governance which is straightaway applicable to all states and the Central Government. In this context, it is necessary to develop a simple diagnostic tool for assessing the 'e-readiness' of different states or different departments of Goi. The table below indicates a suitable diagnostic framework:

Parameter	Weightage	Readiness index			Measure of
		Poor	*Medium*	*Good*	
Computer to employee ratio (No of computers per 1000 employees)	15	<10 (0-6)	10-20 (7-14)	>20 (15)	Competency
Statewide WAN up to district level	15	NA	<2 yr	>2 yr	Connectivity
Enterprise-wise applications running Successfully for 1 year	20	<50-9 prorata)	5-10--10-19 prorata)	>10-20	Content
Investment in e-G over 3 years (Public+Pvt.) cumulative	20	75< (0-9) (prorata)	75-200 (10-19) (prorata)	>200 (20)	Capital
Portal containing Info on Depts/ providing citizen Services	10	NA (0)	In pipeline (5)	Operational *(10)*	Citizen interface
Overall e-Gov architecture	20	NA (0)	Partly avails (10)	Comprehensive (20)	Planning

The states/Goi departments may be ranked using the following scale:

0-40 — poor
41-70 — medium
>70 —good

The above assessment will be useful not only for adopting the appropriate strategies but also in regulating the plan assistance to the various states. The formula for plan assistance in e-Government programme should be designed such that there is sufficient encouragement for the states which are in the 'medium' and 'good' categories while the states in the 'poor' category will be persuaded to take sufficient initial steps using their own funds till the time they get into the 'medium' or 'good' category. States with situational disadvantage like the NE States, will be treated on a different footing.

5. Priorities at national level: Frameworks have to be built at the national level on the following lines on top priority.

- **Architectures**
  - Technology Architecture
  - Infrastructure Architecture
  - Security Architecture
  - Functional Architecture

- **BPR**
  - Admn. Reforms
  - Legal Reforms
- **People**
  - Change Mgt.
  - Training
- **Implementation**
  - Resources
    - Public Private Partnership
    - Public-NGO Partnership
  - Project Development & Mgt.

6. Consultancy on developing the architectures

- It is necessary to appoint globally renowned consultancy firms through a competitive evaluation process for designing the architectures referred to above. The benefit of evolving these architectures are:
  - Adopting open global standards in various technology areas
  - Development of Scalable and inter-operable systems
  - Avoidance of duplication across departments
  - Developing the 'big picture of e-Government' at the national level
  - Establishing linkages between various IT projects ***a priori***
  - Ensuring adequate security at each level
  - Preparation of a blue print for e-Governance at Goi / State levels, which indicates the "as is" and "to be" status, identifies global best practices in each sector and suggests a business model to be adopted in each sector.

7. Giving a quick start to the core initiatives

There are certain **core initiatives** (policies, infrastructure and projects) the implementation of which is critical to an all round and rapid progress. These initiatives cut across departments and agencies and are applicable throughout the country.

The Core initiatives are depicted below:

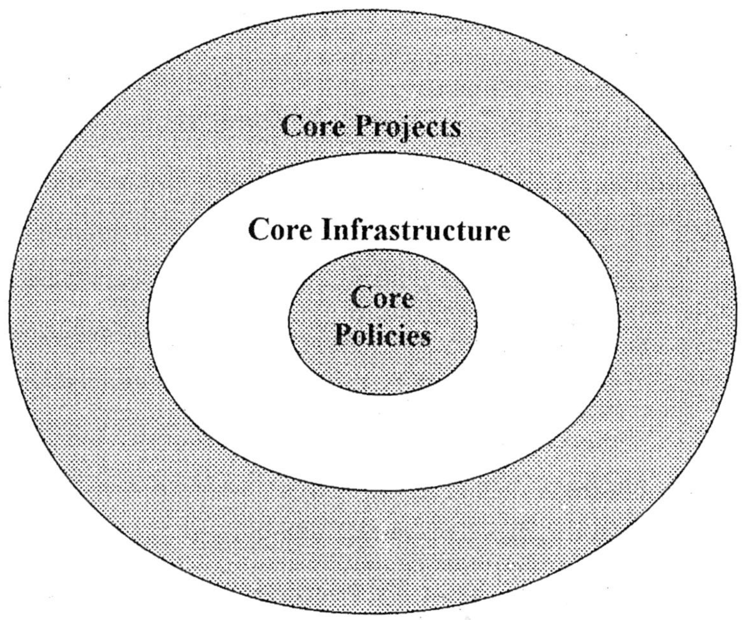

Examples of the core initiatives are given below:

- **Core Policies**
  - National e-Governance Architecture
  - Security Policy
  - Policy of Standardization of data definitions
  - Change management among employees
  - National language interface
  - e-Learning
  - Inter-State protocol for data communication and sharing EDI & EFT policies
  - Promotion of entrepreneurship at all levels
  - Policy on financial support to NGO's implementing e-gov. projects
  - Policy on User Charges
  - Policy on PPP
    - Public Private Partnership
    - Public-NGO Partnership

- **Core Infrastructure for e-Governance**
  - National e-Government Intranet
    - State-wide Intranets
  - National e-Government Data Centre
    - State Data Centres
  - Network of R&D & Training Institutions
    - NISG
    - Centre for Good Governance AP
    - E-Gov. units of IIM's/ IIT's
    - State Institutes of Administration
    - LBSNAA
  - Public Key Infrastructure
  - Service Delivery Infrastructure at State, District, Block & Village levels
    - Citizen/Business Service Centres
    - Information Kiosks

- **Core Projects**
  - SMART CARD/National ID Card
  - Computerization of Revenue earning departments
    - Income tax, Customs, Excise etc., at the Central level
    - VAT, Registration, Transport at the State level
  - Generic office management systems for Central & State Govt. departments
  - India portal
  - e-Procurement
  - Human Resource Management System

8. The Big Picture of National e-Governance

It is necessary to paint the big picture of National e-Governance as it would bring the following advantages:

- Relative importance of various initiatives
- Inter-linkages of various projects
- Development of re-usable projects/components
- Feasibility of sharing of best practices across states
- Attracting private investments into e-governance sector
- Faster roll-out

Based on the exercise made in Andhra Pradesh, where such a Big Picture has been evolved for the State, an attempt has been made at painting the big picture at the national level. It is shown in the Annexure. There is scope for a several-fold improvement to this, which can be achieved through a global consultancy. The Big Picture should incorporate all the core initiatives — policies, infrastructure and projects in one frame.

9. The e-Governance Blue Print

Simultaneous with the development of the Big Picture, an attempt should be made to survey the 100 largest Ministries/departments/agencies of GOI that have a significant place in the process of governance. This can be done in a relatively short time frame by engaging external consultants. The purpose of this exercise is to prepare a set of documents that bring out the following aspects:

- Mission / objectives of each organization
- State of computerization
- Global best practices in use of ICT in that sector
- Gap analysis
- Suggested business model for implementation
- Linkages with other organizations of GOI/States/external agencies and standards to be maintained for each interface.

Such a blue print would enable the departments to proceed fast on the path of government while maintaining interoperability and scalability. The headway made in AP in this regard should be made widely known.

10. Suggested structure of CSS for e-Governance

It is necessary to infuse investments from the GOI to give a thrust to the e-Gov. initiative. This is essential because e-Gov. can not be developed in isolation by the GOI since there is an organic link between the developments in the Centre and states in this area. It should be a mix of GOI schemes and shared schemes as indicated in the table at next page.

The above is an illustrative list and can be refined considerably.

The guidelines on implementation of the various schemes under the CSS should be flexible enough to take care of the regional variations, but rigid enough in areas like enforcement of standards and architectures.

GOI Schemes	100 % GOI funded but implemented by States	50% GOI 50% State funded	100% funded by the states
Architecture	e-learning	State IT architecture	State Intranet
Core initiatives at national level	Change management and incentivization	State level core initiatives	Departmental IT projects (non-core)
GOI departments	Administrative reforms	Delivery mechanism (Kiosks, Service centers)	
Inter-state protocols		State Portal	

Simple but reliable tools should be designed and built into the schemes and projects for monitoring and metrics.

Cost-effective solutions shall be encouraged.

An approximate assessment of the requirement of financial resources for implementation of e-Gov. at the State and central govt. levels yields a figure of Rs. 40,000 crores. However, by adopting appropriate architectures and policies, it is possible to eliminate duplication of efforts and optimize the requirement to about Rs. 20,000 crores. It is possible to tap 60% resources from the private sector by structuring appropriate PPP frameworks. The following is estimated requirement of funds during the plan period:

- Total requirement on a conventional implementation model — Rs. 40,000cr.
- Optimized requirement — Rs. 20,000cr.
- Government share (40%) — Rs. 8,000cr.
- Private sector share (60%) — Rs. 12,000 cr.
- GOI share — Rs. 4000cr.
- Share of States (all states put together) — Rs. 4,000 cr.

It is necessary to refine and validate the above model and superimpose the sharing model suggested in the above table so that the CSS can be administered accordingly.

It is necessary to provide extra allocations for the NE States and certain special areas.

11. Role of NIC

It is absolutely essential to rethink the role of NIC in the scheme of things. If the dream of National e-Governance is to be realized, we must create and rely on institutions that are suitably equipped with the right skill-sets and operating flexibilities.

12. Concluding framework

'The question is not ***whether*** e-Government is to be implemented, but ***when*** and ***how***'. We have to design appropriate architectures and frameworks, create the necessary institutional structures, partner with the private sector and implement certain core initiatives, always remembering that focus on ***customer*** and ***content*** is the key to success. After the approach paper is internally approved, a few workshops may be held at the national, state and district levels to elicit the views of all the stakeholders before finalizing the schemes.

3

Ministry of Law, Justice and Company Affairs (Legislative Department)

New Delhi. the 9th June, 2000/Jyaistha 19, 1922 (Saka)

The following Act of Parliament received the assent of the President on the 9th June, 2000, and is hereby published for general information:

THE INFORMATION TECHNOLOGY ACT, 2000 (No. 21 OF 2000)

[9th June. 2000]

An Act to provide legal recognition for transactions carried out by means of electronic data interchange and other means of electronic communication, commonly referred to as "electronic commerce", which involve the use of alternatives to paper-based methods of communication and storage of information, to facilitate electronic filing of documents with the Government agencies and further to amend the Indian Penal Code, the Indian Evidence Act, 1872, the Bankers' Books Evidence Act, 1891 and the Reserve Bank of India Act, 1934 and for matters connected therewith or incidental thereto.

WHEREAS the General Assembly of the United Nations by resolution A/RES/51/162, dated the 30th January, 1997 has adopted the Model Law on Electronic Commerce adopted by the United Nations Commission on International Trade Law;

AND WHEREAS the said resolution recommends *inter alia* that all States give favourable consideration to the said Model Law when they enact or revise their laws, in view of the need for uniformity of the law applicable to alternatives to paper-cased methods of communication and storage of information;

AND WHEREAS it is considered necessary to give effect to the said resolution and to promote efficient delivery of Government services by means of reliable electronic records.

BE it enacted by Parliament in the Fifty-first Year of the Republic of India as follows:

Chapter 1
PRELIMINARY

I. Short title, extent, commencement and application

(1) This Act may be called the Information Technology Act, 2000.

(2) It shall extend to the whole of India and, save as otherwise provided in this Act, it applies also to any offence or contravention thereunder committed outside India by any person.

(3) It shall come into force on such date as the Central Government may, by notification, appoint and different dates may be appointed for different provisions of this Act and any reference in any such provision to the commencement of this Act shall be construed as a reference to the commencement of that provision.

(4) Nothing in this Act shall apply to—

(a) a negotiable instrument as defined in section 13 of the Negotiable Instruments Act, 1881;

(b) a power-of-attorney as defined in section 1A of the Powers-of-Attorney Act, 1882;

(c) a trust as defined in section 3 of the Indian Trusts Act, 1882;

(d) a will as defined in clause *(h)* of section 2 of the Indian Succession Act, 1925 including any other testamentary disposition by whatever name called;

(e) any contract for the sale or conveyance of immovable property or any interest in such property;

(f) any such class of documents or transactions as may be notified by the Central Government in the Official Gazette.

2. Definitions

(1) In this Act, unless the context otherwise requires,—

(a) "access" with its grammatical variations and cognate expressions means gaining entry into, instructing or communicating with the logical, arithmetical, or memory function resources of a computer, computer system or computer network;

(b) "addressee" means a person who is intended by the originator to receive the electronic record but does not include any intermediary;

(c) "adjudicating officer" means an adjudicating officer appointed under subsection (1) of section 46;

(d) "affixing digital signature" with its grammatical variations and cognate expressions means adoption of any methodology or procedure by a person for the purpose of authenticating an electronic record by means of digital signature;

(e) "appropriate Government" means as respects any matter,—

(i) Enumerated in List II of the Seventh Schedule to the Constitution;

(ii) relating to any State law enacted under List III of the Seventh Schedule to the Constitution;

The State Government and in any other case, the Central Government;

(f) "asymmetric crypto system" means a system of a secure key pair consisting of a private key for creating a digital signature and a public key to verify the digital signature;

(g) "Certifying Authority" means a person who has been granted a licence to issue a Digital Signature Certificate under section 24;

(h) "certification practice statement" means a statement issued by a Certifying Authority to specify the practices that the Certifying Authority employs in issuing Digital Signature Certificates;

(i) "computer" means any electronic magnetic, optical or other high-speed data processing device or system which performs logical, arithmetic, and memory functions by manipulations of electronic, magnetic or optical impulses, and includes all input, output, processing, storage, computer software, or communication facilities which are connected or related to the computer in a computer system or computer network;

(j) "computer network" means the interconnection of one or more computers through;

   (i) the use of satellite, microwave, terrestrial line or other communication media; and

   (ii) terminals or a complex consisting of two or more interconnected computers whether or not the interconnection is continuously maintained;

(k) "computer resource" means computer, computer system, computer network, data, computer data base or software;

(l) "computer system" means a device or collection of devices, including input and output support devices and excluding calculators which are not programmable and capable of being used in conjunction with external files, which contain computer programmes, electronic instructions, input data and output data, that performs logic, arithmetic, data storage and retrieval, communication control and other functions;

(m) "Controller" means the Controller of Certifying Authorities appointed under sub-section **(1)** of section 17;

(n) "Cyber Appellate Tribunal" means the Cyber Regulations Appellate Tribunal established under sub-section (1) of section 48;

(o) "data" means a representation of information, knowledge, facts, concepts or instructions which are being prepared or have been prepared in a formalised manner, and is intended to be processed, is being processed or has been processed in a computer system or computer network, and may be in any form (including computer printouts magnetic or optical storage media, punched cards, punched tapes) or stored internally in the memory of the computer;

(p) "digital signature" means authentication of any electronic record by a subscriber by means of an electronic method or procedure in accordance with the provisions of section 3;

(q) "Digital Signature Certificate" means a Digital Signature Certificate issued under subsection (4) of section 35;

(r) "electronic form" with reference to information means any information generated, sent, received or stored in media, magnetic, optical, computer memory, micro film, computer generated micro fiche or similar device;

(s) "Electronic Gazette" means the Official Gazette published in the electronic form;

(t) "electronic record" means data, record or data generated, image or sound stored, received or sent in an electronic form or micro film or computer generated micro fiche;

(u) "function", in relation to a computer, includes logic, control arithmetical process, deletion, storage and retrieval and communication or telecommunication from or within a computer;

(v) "information" includes data, text, images, sound, voice, codes, computer programmes, software and databases or micro film or computer generated micro fiche;

(w) "intermediary" with respect to any particular electronic message means any person who on behalf of another person receives, stores or transmits that message or provides any service with respect to that message;

(x) "key pair", is an asymmetric crypto system, means a private key and its mathematically related public key, which are so related that the public key can verify a digital signature created by the private key;

(y) "law" includes any Act of Parliament or of a State Legislature, Ordinances promulgated by the President or a Governor, as the case may be. Regulations made by the President under article 240, Bills enacted as President's Act under sub-clause (a) of clause (1) of article 357 of the Constitution and includes rules, regulations, bye-laws and orders issued or made thereunder;

(z) "licence" means a licence granted to a Certifying Authority under section 24;

(za) "originator" means a person who sends, generates, stores or transmits any electronic message or causes any electronic message to be sent, generated, stored or transmitted to any other person but does not include an intermediary;

(zb) "prescribed" means prescribed by rules made under this Act;

(zc) "private key" means the key of a key pair used to create a digital signature;

(zd) "public key" means the key of a key pair used to verify a digital signature and listed in the Digital Signature Certificate;

(ze) "secure system" means computer hardware, software and procedure that—

(a) are reasonably secure from unauthorised access and misuse;

(b) provide a reasonable level of reliability and correct operation;

(c) are reasonably suited to performing the intended functions; and

(d) adhere to generally accepted security procedures;

(zf) "security procedure" means the security procedure prescribed under section 16 by the Central Government;

(zg) "subscriber" means a person in whose name the Digital Signature Certificate is issued;

(zh) "verify" in relation to a digital signature, electronic record or public key, with its grammatical variations and cognate expressions means to determine whether—

(a) the initial electronic record was affixed with the digital signature by the use of private key corresponding to the public key of the subscriber;

(b) the initial electronic record is retained intact or has been altered since such electronic record was so affixed with the digital signature.

(2) Any reference in this Act to any enactment or any provision thereof shall, in relation to an area in which such enactment or such provision is not in force, be construed as a reference to the corresponding law or the relevant provision of the corresponding law, if any, in force in that area.

Chapter II
DIGITAL SIGNATURE

3. Authentication of electronic records

(1) Subject to the provisions of this section any subscriber may authenticate an electronic record by affixing his digital signature.

(2) The authentication of the electronic record shall be effected by the use of asymmetric crypto system and hash function which envelop and transform the initial electronic record into another electronic record.

Explanation.—For the purposes of this sub-section, "hash function" means an algorithm mapping or translation of one sequence of bits into another, generally smaller, set known as "hash result" such that an electronic record yields the same hash result every time the algorithm is executed with the same electronic record as its input making it computationally infeasible—

(a) to derive or reconstruct the original electronic record from the hash result produced by the algorithm;

(b) that two electronic records can produce the same hash result using the algorithm.

(3) Any person by the use of a public key of the subscriber can verify the electronic record.

(4) The private key and the public key are unique to the subscriber and constitute a functioning key pair.

Chapter III
ELECTRONIC GOVERNANCE

4. Legal recognition of electronic records

Where any law provides that information or any other matter shall be in writing or in the typewritten or printed form, then, notwithstanding anything contained in such law, such requirement shall be deemed to have been satisfied if such information or matter is —

(a) rendered or made available in an electronic form; and

(b) accessible so as to be usable for a subsequent reference.

5. Legal recognition of digital signatures

Where any law provides that information or any other matter shall be authenticated by affixing the signature or any document shall be signed or bear the signature of any person then, notwithstanding anything contained in such law, such requirement shall be deemed to have been satisfied, if such information or matter is authenticated by means of digital signature affixed in such manner as may be prescribed by the Central Government.

Explanation—For the purposes of this section, "signed", with its grammatical variations and cognate expressions, shall, with reference to a person, mean affixing of his hand written signature or any mark on any document and the expression "signature" shall be construed accordingly.

6. Use of electronic records and digital signatures in Government and its agencies

(1) Where any law provides for—

(a) the filing of any form, application or any other document with any office, authority, body or agency owned or controlled by the appropriate Government in a particular manner;

(b) the issue or grant of any licence, permit, sanction or approval by whatever name called in a particular manner;

(c) the receipt or payment of money in a particular manner,

then, notwithstanding anything contained in any other law for the time being in force, such requirement shall be deemed to have been satisfied if such filing, issue, grant, receipt or payment, as the case may be, is effected by means of such electronic form as may be prescribed by the appropriate Government.

(2) The appropriate Government may, for the purposes of sub-section (1), by rules, prescribe—

(a) the manner and format in which such electronic records shall be filed, created or issued;

(b) the manner or method of payment of any fee or charges for filing, creation or issue any electronic record under clause *(a)*.

7. Retention of electronic records

(1) Where any law provides that documents, records or information shall be retained for any specific period, then, that requirement shall be deemed to have been satisfied if such documents, records or information are retained in the electronic form, if—

(a) the information contained therein remains accessible so as to be usable for a subsequent reference;

(b) the electronic record is retained in the format in which it was originally generated, sent or received or in a format which can be demonstrated to represent accurately the information originally generated, sent or received;

(c) the details which will facilitate the identification of the origin, destination, date and time of despatch or receipt of such electronic record are available in the electronic record;

Provided that this clause does not apply to any information which is automatically generated solely for the purpose of enabling an electronic record to be despatched or received.

(2) Nothing in this section shall apply to any law that expressly provides for the retention of documents, records or information in the form of electronic records.

8. Publication of rule, regulation, etc., in Electronic Gazette

Where any law provides that any rule, regulation, order, bye-law, notification or any other matter shall be published in the Official Gazette, then, such requirement shall be deemed to have been satisfied if such rule, regulation, order, bye-law, notification or any other matter is published in the Official Gazette or Electronic Gazette:

Provided that where any rule, regulation, order, bye-law, notification or any other matter is published in the Official Gazette or Electronic Gazette, the date of publication shall be deemed to be the date of the Gazette which was first published in any form.

9. Sections 6,7 and 8 not to confer right to insist document should be accepted in electronic form

Nothing contained in sections 6, 7 and 8 shall confer a right upon any person to insist that any Ministry or Department of the Central Government or the State Government or any authority or body established by or under any law or controlled or funded by the Central or State Government should accept, issue, create, retain and preserve any document in the form of electronic records or effect any monetary transaction in the electronic form.

10. Power to make rules by Central Government in respect of digital signature

The Central Government may, for the purposes of this Act, by rules, prescribe- —

(a) the type of digital signature;

(b) the manner and format in which the digital signature shall be affixed;

(c) the manner or procedure which facilitates identification of the person affixing the digital signature;

(d) control processes and procedures to ensure adequate integrity, security and confidentiality of electronic records or payments; and

(e) any other matter which is necessary to give legal effect to digital signatures.

Chapter IV
ATTRIBUTION, ACKNOWLEDGMENT AND DESPATCH OF ELECTRONIC RECORDS

11. Attribution of electronic records

An electronic record shall be attributed to the originator—

(a) if it was sent by the originator himself;

(b) by a person who had the authority to act on behalf of the originator in respect of that electronic record; or

(c) by an information system programmed by or on behalf of the originator to operate automatically.

12. Acknowledgment of receipt.

(1) Where the originator has not agreed with the addressee that the acknowledgment of receipt of electronic record be given in a particular form or by a particular method, an acknowledgment may be given by——

(a) any communication by the addressee, automated or otherwise; or

(b) any conduct of the addressee, sufficient to indicate to the originator that the electronic record has been received.

(2) Where the originator has stipulated that the electronic record shall be binding only on receipt of an acknowledgment of

such electronic record by him, then unless acknowledgment has been so received, the electronic record shall be deemed to have been never sent by the originator.

(3) Where the originator has not stipulated that the electronic record shall be binding only on receipt of such acknowledgment, and the acknowledgment has not been received by the originator within the time specified or agreed or, if no time has been specified or agreed to within a reasonable time, then the originator may give notice to the addressee stating that no acknowledgment has been received by him and specifying a reasonable time by which the acknowledgment must be received by him and if no acknowledgment is received within the aforesaid time limit he may after giving notice to the addressee, treat the electronic record as though it has never been sent.

13. Time and place of despatch and receipt of electronic record

(1) Save as otherwise agreed to between the originator and the addressee, the dispatch of an electronic record occurs when it enters a computer resource outside the control of the originator.

(2) Save as otherwise agreed between the originator and the addressee, the time of receipt of an electronic record shall be determined as follows, namely—

(a) if the addressee has designated a computer resource for the purpose of receiving electronic records,—

(i) receipt occurs at the time when the electronic, record enters the designated computer resource; or

(ii) if the electronic record is sent to a computer resource of the addressee that is not the designated computer resource, receipt occurs at the time when the electronic record is retrieved by the addressee;

(b) if the addressee has not designated a computer resource along with specified timings, if any, receipt occurs when the electronic record enters the computer resource of the addressee.

(3) Save as otherwise agreed to between the originator and the addressee, an electronic record is deemed to be dispatched at the place where the originator has his place of business, and

is deemed to be received at the place where the addressee has his place of business.

(4) The provisions of sub-section (2) shall apply not with standing that the place where the computer resource is located may be different from the place where the electronic record is deemed to have been received under sub-section (3).

(5) For the purposes of this section—

(a) if the originator or the addressee has more than one place of business, the principal place of business, shall be the place of business;

(b) if the originator or the addressee does not have a place of business, his usual place of residence shall be deemed to be the place of business;

(c) "usual place of residence", in relation to a body corporate, means the place where it is registered.

Chapter V
SECURE ELECTRONIC RECORDS AND SECURE DIGITAL SIGNATURES

14. Secure electronic record

Where any security procedure has been applied to an electronic record at a specific point of time, then such record shall be deemed to be a secure electronic record from such point of time to the time of verification.

15. Secure digital signature

If, by application of a security procedure agreed to by the parties concerned, it can be verified that a digital signature, at the time it was affixed, was—

(a) unique to the subscriber affixing it;

(b) capable of identifying such subscriber;

(c) created in a manner or using a means under the exclusive control of the subscriber and is linked to the electronic record to which it relates in such a manner that if the electronic record was altered the digital signature would be invalidated,

then such digital signature shall be deemed to be a secure digital signature.

16. Security procedure

The Central Government shall for the purposes of this Act prescribe the security procedure having regard to commercial circumstances prevailing at the time when the procedure was used, including—

(a) the nature of the transaction;

(b) the level of sophistication of the parties with reference to their technological capacity;

(c) the volume of similar transactions engaged in by other parties;

(d) the availability of alternatives offered to but rejected by any party;

(e) the cost of alternative procedures; and

(f) the procedures in general use for similar types of transactions or communications.

Chapter VI
REGULATION OF CERTIFYING AUTHORITIES

17. Appointment of Controller and other officers

(1) The Central Government may, by notification in the Official Gazette, appoint a Controller of Certifying Authorities for the purposes of this Act and may also by the same or subsequent notification appoint such number of Deputy Controllers and Assistant Controllers as it deems fit.

(2) The Controller shall discharge his functions under this Act subject to the general control and directions of the Central Government.

(3) The Deputy Controllers and Assistant Controllers shall perform the functions assigned to them by the Controller under the general superintendence and control of the Controller.

(4) The qualifications, experience and terms and conditions of service of Controller, Deputy Controllers and Assistant Controllers shall be such as may be prescribed by the Central Government.

(5) The Head Office and Branch Office of the office of the Controller shall be at such places as the Central Government may specify and these may be established at such places as the Central Government may think fit.

(6) There shall be a seal of the Office of the Controller.

18. Functions of Controller

The Controller may perform all or any of the following functions, namely:——

(a) exercising supervision over the activities of the Certifying Authorities;

(b) certifying public keys of the Certifying Authorities;

(c) laying down the standards to be maintained by the Certifying Authorities;

(d) specifying the qualifications and experience which employees of the Certifying Authorities should possess;

(e) specifying the conditions subject to which the Certifying Authorities shall conduct their business;

(f) specifying the contents of written, printed or visual materials and advertisements that may be distributed or used in respect of a Digital Signature Certificate and the public key;

(g) specifying the form and content of a Digital Signature Certificate and the key.

(h) specifying the form and manner in which accounts shall be maintained by the Certifying Authorities;

(i) specifying the terms and conditions subject to which auditors may be appointed and the remuneration to be paid to them;

(j) facilitating the establishment of any electronic system by a Certifying Authority either solely or jointly with other Certifying Authorities and regulation of such systems;

(k) specifying the manner in which the Certifying Authorities shall conduct their dealings with the subscribers;

(l) resolving any conflict of interests between the Certifying Authorities and the subscribers;

(m) laying down the duties of the Certifying Authorities;

(n) maintaining a data base containing the disclosure record of every Certifying Authority containing such particulars as may be specified by regulations, which shall be accessible to public.

19. Recognition of foreign Certifying Authorities

(1) Subject to such conditions and restrictions as may be specified by regulations, the Controller may with the previous

approval of the Central Government, and by notification in the Official Gazette, recognise any foreign Certifying Authority as a Certifying Authority for the purposes of this Act.

(2) Where any Certifying Authority is recognised under sub-section (1), the Digital Signature Certificate issued by such Certifying Authority shall be valid for the purposes of this Act.

(3) The Controller may, if he is satisfied that any Certifying Authority has contravened any of the conditions and restrictions subject to which it was granted recognition under subsection (1) he may, for reasons to be recorded in writing, by notification in the Official Gazette, revoke such recognition.

20. Controller to act as repository

(1) The **Controller** shall be the repository of all Digital Signature Certificates issued under this Act.

(2) The Controller shall—

(a) make use of hardware, software and procedures that are secure .i/m Intrusion and misuse;

(b) observe such other standards as may be prescribed by the Central Government,

to ensure that the secrecy and security of the digital signatures are assured.

(3) The Controller shall maintain a computerised data base of all public keys in such a manner that such data base and the public keys are available to any member of the public.

21. Licence to issue Digital Signature Certificates

(1) Subject to the provisions of sub-section (2), any person may make an application, to the Controller, for a licence to issue Digital Signature Certificates.

(2) No licence shall be issued under sub-section (1), unless the applicant fulfills such requirements with respect to qualification, expertise, manpower, financial resources and other infrastructure facilities, which are necessary to issue Digital Signature Certificates as may be prescribed by the Central Government.

(3) A licence granted under this section shall—

(a) be valid for such period as may be prescribed by the Central Government;

(b) not be transferable or heritable;

(c) be subject to such terms and conditions as may be specified by the regulations.

22. Application for licence

(1) Every application for issue of a licence shall be in such form as may be prescribed by the Central Government.

(2) Every application for issue of a licence shall be accompanied by

(a) a certification practice statement;

(b) a statement including the procedures with respect to identification of the applicant;

(c) payment of such fees, not exceeding twenty-five thousand rupees as may be prescribed by the Central Government;

(d) such other documents, as may be prescribed by the Central Government.

23. Renewal of licence

An application for renewal of a licence shall be—

(a) in such form;

(b) accompanied by such fees, not exceeding five thousand rupees,

as may be prescribed by the Central Govern-ment and shall be made not less than forty-five days before the date of expiry of the period of validity of the licence.

24. Procedure for grant or rejection of licence—

The Controller may, on receipt of an application under sub-section (1) of section 21, after considering the documents accompanying the application and such other factors, as he deems fit, grant the licence or reject the application:

Provided that no application shall be rejected under this section unless the applicant has been given a reasonable opportunity of presenting his case.

25. Suspension of licence—

(1) The Controller may, if he is satisfied after making such inquiry, as he may think fit, that a Certifying Authority has,—

(a) made a statement in, or in relation to, the application for the issue or renewal of the licence, which is incorrect or false in material particulars;

(b) failed to comply with the terms and conditions subject to which the licence was granted;

(c) failed to maintain the standards specified under clause *(h)* of sub-section (2) of section 20;

(d) contravened any provisions of this Act, rule, regulation or order made there under,

revoke the licence:

Provided that no licence shall be revoked unless the Certifying Authority has been given a reasonable opportunity of showing cause against the proposed revocation.

(2) The Controller may, if he has reasonable cause to believe that there is any ground for revoking a licence under sub-section (1), by order suspend such licence pending the completion of any inquiry ordered by him:

Provided that no licence shall be suspended for a period exceeding ten days unless the Certifying Authority has been given a reasonable opportunity of showing cause against the proposed suspension.

(3) No Certifying Authority whose licence has been suspended shall issue any Digital Signature Certificate during such suspension.

26. Notice of suspension or revocation of licence

(1)Where the licence of the Certifying Authority is suspended or revoked, the Controller shall publish notice of such suspension or revocation, as the case may be, in the database maintained by him.

(2)Where one or more repositories are specified, the Controller shall publish notices of such suspension or revocation, as the case may be, in all such repositories:

Provided that the data base containing the notice of such suspension or revocation, as the case may be, shall be made available through a web site which shall be accessible round the clock:

Provided further that the Controller may, if he considers necessary, publicise the contents of database in such electronic or other media, as he may consider appropriate.

27. Power to delegate

The Controller may, in writing, authorise the Deputy Controller. Assistant Controller or any officer to exercise any of the powers of the Controller under this Chapter.

28. Power to investigate contraventions

(1) The Controller or any officer authorised by him in this behalf shall take up for investigation any contravention of the provisions of this Act, rules or regulations made thereunder.

(2) The Controller or any officer authorised by him in this behalf shall exercise the like powers which are conferred on Income-tax authorities under Chapter XIII of the Income-tax Act, 1961 and shall exercise such powers, subject to such limitations laid down under that Act.

29. Access to computers and data

(1) Without prejudice to the provisions of sub-section (1) of section 69, the Controller or any person authorised by him shall, if he has reasonable cause to suspect that any contra-vention of the provisions of this Act, rules or regulations made thereunder has been committed, have access to any computer system, any apparatus, data or any other material connected with such system, for the purpose of searching or causing a search to be made for obtaining any information or data contained in or available to such computer system.

(2) For the purposes of sub-section (1), the Controller or any person authorised by him may, by order, direct any person incharge of, or otherwise concerned with the operation of, the computer system, data apparatus or material, to provide him with such reasonable technical and other assistance as he may consider necessary.

30. Certifying Authority to follow certain procedures

Every Certifying Authority shall—

(a) make use of hardware, software and procedures that are secure from intrusion and misuse,

(b) I provide a reasonable level of reliability in its services which are reasonably suited to the performance of intended functions;

(c) adhere to security procedures to ensure that the secrecy and privacy of the digital signatures are assured; and

(d) observe such other standards as may be specified by regulations.

31. Certifying Authority to ensure compliance of the Act, etc.

Every Certifying Authority shall ensure that every person employed or otherwise engaged by it complies, in the course of his employment or engagement, with the provisions of this Act, rules, regulations and orders made thereunder.

32. Display of licence

Every Certifying Authority shall display its licence at a conspicuous place of the premises in which it carries on its business.

33. Surrender of licence

(1) Every Certifying Authority whose licence is suspended or revoked shall immediately after such suspension or revocation, surrender the licence to the Controller.

(2) Where any Certifying Authority fails to surrender a licence under sub-section (1). the person in whose favour a licence is issued, shall be guilty of an offence and shall be punished with imprisonment which may extend upto six months or a fine which may extend upto ten thousand rupees or with both.

34. Disclosure

(1) Every Certifying Authority shall disclose in the manner specified by regulations—

(a) its Digital Signature Certificate which contains the public key corresponding to the private key used by that Certifying Authority to digitally sign another Digital Signature Certificate;

(b) any certification practice statement relevant thereto;

(c) notice of the revocation or suspension of its Certifying Authority certificate, if any; and

(d) any other fact that materially and adversely affects either the reliability of a Digital Signature Certificate, which that Authority has issued, or the Authority's ability to perform its services.

(2) Where in the opinion of the Certifying Authority any event has occurred or any situation has arisen which may materially and adversely affect the integrity of its computer system or the conditions subject to which a Digital Signature

Certificate was granted, then, the Certifying Authority shall—

(a) use reasonable efforts to notify any person who is likely to be affected by that occurrence; or

(b) act in accordance with the procedure specified in its certification practice statement to deal with such event or situation.

Chapter VII
DIGITAL SIGNATURE CERTIFICATES

35. Certifying Authority to issue Digital Signature Certificate

(1) Any person may make an application to the Certifying Authority for the issue of a Digital Signature Certificate in such form as may be prescribed by the Central Government.

(2) Every such application shall be accompanied by such fee not exceeding twenty-five thousand rupees as may be prescribed by the Central Government, to be paid to the Certifying Authority:

Provided that while prescribing fees under sub-section (2) different fees may be prescribed for different classes of applicants'.

(3) Every such application shall be accompanied by a certification practice statement or where there is no such statement, a statement containing such particulars, as may be specified by regulations.

(4) On receipt of an application under sub-section (1), the Certifying Authority may, after consideration of the certification practice statement or the other statement under sub-section (3) and after making such enquiries as it may deem fit, grant the Digital Signature Certificate or for reasons to be recorded in writing, reject the application:

Provided further that no Digital Signature Certificate shall be granted unless the Certifying Authority is satisfied that—

(a) the applicant holds the private key corresponding to the public key to be listed in the Digital Signature Certificate;

(b) the applicant holds a private key, which is capable of creating a digital signature,

(c) the public key to be listed in the certificate can be used to verify a digital signature affixed by the private key held by the applicant:

Provided further that no application shall be rejected unless the applicant has been given a reasonable opportunity of showing cause against the proposed rejection.

36. Representations upon issuance of Digital Signature Certificate

A Certifying Authority while issuing a Digital Signature Certificate shall certify that—

(a) it has complied with the provisions of this Act and the rules and regulations made thereunder;

(b) it has published the Digital Signature Certificate or otherwise made it available to such person relying on it and the subscriber has accepted it;

(c) the subscriber holds the private key corresponding to the public key, listed in the Digital Signature Certificate;

(d) the subscriber's public key and private key constitute a functioning key pair;

(e) the information contained in the Digital Signature Certificate is accurate; and

(f) it has no knowledge of any material fact, which if it had been included in the Digital Signature Certificate would adversely affect the reliability of the representations made in clauses (a) to (d).

37. Suspension of Digital Signature Certificate

(1) Subject to the provisions of sub-section (2), the Certifying Authority which has issued a Digital Signature Certificate may suspend such Digital Signature Certificate,-

(a) on receipt of a **request** to that effect *from*—

(i) the subscriber listed in the Digital Signature Certificate; or

(ii) any person duly authorised to act on behalf of that subscriber;

(b) if it is of opinion that the Digital Signature Certificate should be suspended in public interest.

(2) A Digital Signature Certificate shall not be suspended

for a period exceeding fifteen days unless the subscriber has been given an opportunity of being heard in the matter.

(3) On suspension of a Digital Signature Certificate under this section, the Certifying Authority shall communicate the same to the subscriber.

38. Revocation of Digital Signature Certificate

(1) A Certifying Authority may revoke a Digital Signature Certificate issued by it—

(a) where the subscriber or any other person authorised by him makes a request to that effect; or

(b) upon the death of the subscriber; or

(c) upon the dissolution of the firm or winding up of the company where the subscriber is a firm or a company.

(2) Subject to the provisions of sub-section (3) and without prejudice to the provisions of sub-section (1), a Certifying Authority may revoke a Digital Signature Certificate which has been issued by it at any time, if it is of opinion that—

(a) a material fact represented in the Digital Signature Certificate is false or has been concealed;

(b) a requirement for issuance of the Digital Signature Certificate was not satisfied;

(c) the Certifying Authority's private key or security system was compromised in a manner materially affecting the Digital Signature Certificate's reliability;

(d) the subscriber has been declared insolvent **or** dead or where a subscriber is a firm or a company, which has been dissolved, wound-up **or** otherwise ceased to exist.

(3) A Digital Signature Certificate shall not be revoked unless the subscriber has been given an opportunity of being heard in the matter.

(4) On revocation of a Digital Signature Certificate under this section, the Certifying Authority shall communicate the same to the subscriber.

39. Notice of suspension or revocation

(1) Where a Digital Signature Certificate is suspended or revoked under section 37 or section 38, the Certifying Authority

shall publish a notice of such suspension or revocation, as the case may be, in the repository specified in the Digital Signature Certificate for publication of such notice.

(2) Where one or more repositories are specified, the Certifying Authority shall publish notices of such suspension or revocation, as the case may be. In all such repositories.

Chapter VIII
DUTIES OF SUBSCRIBERS

40. Generating key pair

Where any Digital Signature Certificate, the public key of which corresponds to the private key of that subscriber which is to be listed in the Digital Signature Certificate has been accepted by a subscriber, then, the subscriber shall generate the key pair by applying the security procedure.

41. Acceptance of Digital Signature Certificate

(1) A subscriber shall be deemed to have accepted a Digital Signature Certificate if he publishes or authorises the publication of a Digital Signature Certificate——

(a) to one or more persons;

(b) in a repository, or otherwise demonstrates his approval of the Digital Signature Certificate in any manner.

(2) By accepting a Digital Signature Certificate the subscriber certifies to all who reasonably rely on the information contained in the Digital Signature Certificate that—

(a) the subscriber holds the private key corresponding to the public key listed in the Digital Signature Certificate and is entitled to hold the same;

(b) all representations made by the subscriber to the Certifying Authority and all material relevant to the information contained in the Digital Signature Certificate are true;

(c) all information in the Digital Signature Certificate that is within the knowledge of the subscriber is true.

42. Control of private key

(1) Every subscriber shall exercise reasonable care to retain control of the private key corresponding to the public key listed

in his Digital Signature Certificate and take all steps to prevent its disclosure to a person not authorised to affix the digital signature of the subscriber.

(2) If the private key corresponding to the public key listed in the Digital Signature Certificate has been compromised, then, the subscriber shall communicate the same without any delay to the Certifying Authority in such manner as may be specified by the regulations.

Explanation.—For the removal of doubts, it is hereby declared that the subscriber shall be liable till he has informed the Certifying Authority that the private key has been compromised.

Chapter IX
PENALTIES AND ADJUDICATION

43. Penalty for damage to computer, computer system, etc.

If any person without permission of the owner or any other person who is incharge of a computer, computer system or computer network—

(a) accesses or secures access to such computer, computer system or computer network;

(b) downloads, copies or extracts ay data, computer data base or information from such computer, computer system or computer network including information or data held or stored in any removable storage medium;

(c) introduces or causes to be introduced any computer contaminant or computer virus into any computer, computer system or computer network;

(d) damages or causes to be damaged any computer, computer system or computer network, data, computer data base or any other programmes residing in such computer, computer system or computer network;

(e) disrupts or causes disruption of any computer, computer system or computer network;

(f) denies or causes the denial of access to any person authorised to access any computer, computer system or computer network by any means;

(g) provides any assistance to any person to facilitate

access to a computer, computer system or computer network in contravention of the provisions of this Act, rules or regulations made thereunder;

(h) charges the services availed of by a person to the account of another person by tampering with or manipulating any computer, computer system, or computer network,

he shall be liable to pay damages by way of compensation not exceeding one crore rupees to the person so affected.

Explanation.—For the purposes of this section,— -

(i) "computer contaminant" means any set of computer instructions that are designed—

(a) to modify, destroy, record, transmit data or programme residing within a computer, computer system or computer network; or

(b) by any means to usurp the normal operation of the computer, computer system, or computer network;

(ii) "computer data base" means a representation of information, knowledge, facts, concepts or instructions in text, image, audio, video that are being prepared or have been prepared in a formalised manner or have been produced by a computer, computer system or computer network and are intended for use in a computer, computer system or computer network;

(iii) "computer virus" means any computer instruction, information, data or programme that destroys, damages, degrades or adversely affects the performance of a computer resource or attaches itself to another computer resource and operates when a programme, data or instruction is executed or some other event takes place in that computer resource;

(iv) "damage" means to destroy, alter, delete, add, modify or rearrange any computer resource by any means.

44. Penalty for failure to furnish information return, etc.

If any person who is required under this Act or any rules or regulations made thereunder to—

(a) furnish any document, return or report to the Controller or the Certifying Authority fails to furnish the same, he shall be liable to a penalty not exceeding one lakh and fifty thousand rupees for each such failure;

(b) file any return or furnish any information, books or other documents within the time specified therefore in the regulations fails to file return or furnish the same within the time specified therefore in the regulations, he shall be liable to a penalty not exceeding five thousand rupees for every day during which such failure continues;

(c) maintain books of account or records, fails to maintain the same, he shall be liable to a penalty not exceeding ten thousand rupees for every day during which the failure continues.

45. Residuary penalty

Whoever contravenes any rules or regulations made under this Act, for the contravention of which no penalty has been separately provided, shall be liable to pay a compensation not exceeding twenty-five thousand rupees to the person affected by such contravention or a penalty not exceeding twenty-five thousand rupees.

46. Power to adjudicate

(1) For the purpose of adjudging under this Chapter whether any person has committed a contravention of any of the provisions of this Act or of any rule, regulation, direction or order made thereunder the Central Government shall, subject to the provisions of sub-section (3), appoint any officer not below the rank of a Director to the Government of India or an equivalent officer of a State Government to be an adjudicating officer for holding an inquiry in the manner prescribed by the Central Government.

(2) The adjudicating officer shall, after giving the person referred to in sub-section (1) a reasonable opportunity for making representation in the matter and if, on such inquiry, he is satisfied that the person has committed the contravention, he may impose such penalty or award such compensation as he thinks fit in accordance with the provisions of that section.

(3) No person shall be appointed as an adjudicating officer unless he possesses such experience in the field of Information Technology and legal or judicial experience as may be prescribed by the Central Government.

(4) Where more than one adjudicating officers are appointed, the Central Government shall specify by order the matters and places with respect to which such officers shall exercise their jurisdiction.

(5) Every adjudicating officer shall have the powers of a civil court which are conferred on the Cyber Appellate Tribunal under sub-section (2) of section 58, and—

(a) all proceedings before it shall be deemed to be judicial proceedings within the meaning of sections 193 and 228 of the Indian Penal Code;

(b) shall be deemed to be a civil court for the purposes of sections 345 and 346 of the Code of Criminal Procedure, 1973.

47. Factors to be taken into account by the adjudicating officer

While adjudging the quantum of compensation under this Chapter, the adjudicating officer shall have due regard to the following factors, namely:—

(a) the amount of gain of unfair advantage, wherever quantifiable, made as a result of the default;

(b) the amount of loss caused to any person as a result of the default;

(c) the repetitive nature of the default.

Chapter X
THE CYBER REGULATIONS APPELLATE TRIBUNAL

48. Establishment of Cyber Appellate Tribunal

(1) The Central Government shall, by notification, establish one or more appellate tribunals to be known as the Cyber Regulations Appellate Tribunal.

(2) The Central Government shall also specify, in the notification referred to in subsection (1), the matters and places in relation to which the Cyber Appellate Tribunal may exercise jurisdiction.

49. Composition of Cyber Appellate Tribunal

A Cyber Appellate Tribunal shall consist of one person only

(hereinafter referred to as the Residing Officer of the Cyber Appellate Tribunal) to be appointed, by notification, by the Central Government.

50. Qualifications for appointment as Presiding Officer of the Cyber Appellate Tribunal

A person shall not be qualified for appointment as the Presiding Officer of a Cyber Appellate Tribunal unless he—

(a) is, or has been, or is qualified to be, a Judge of a High Court; or

(b) is or has been a member of the Indian Legal Service and is holding or has held a post in Grade I of that Service for at least three years.

51. Term of office

The Presiding Officer of a Cyber Appellate Tribunal shall hold office for a term of five years from the date on which he enters upon his office or until he attains the age of sixty-five years, whichever is earlier.

52. Salary, allowances and other terms and conditions of service of Presiding Officer

The salary and allowances payable to, and the other terms and conditions of service including pension, gratuity and other retirement benefits of the Presiding Officer of a Cyber Appellate Tribunal shall be such as may be prescribed:

Provided that neither the salary and allowances nor the other terms and conditions of service of the Presiding Officer shall be varied to his disadvantage after appointment.

53. Filling up of vacancies

If, for reason other than temporary absence, any vacancy occurs in the office of the Presiding Officer of a Cyber Appellate Tribunal, then the Central Government shall appoint another person in accordance with the provisions of this Act to fill the vacancy and the proceedings may be continued before the Cyber Appellate Tribunal from the stage at which the vacancy is filled.

54. Resignation and removal

(1) The Presiding Officer of a Cyber Appellate Tribunal

may, by notice in writing under his hand addressed to the Central Government, resign his office:

Provided that the said Presiding Officer shall, unless he is permitted by the Central Government to relinquish his office sooner, continue to hold office until the expiry of three months from the date of receipt of such notice or until a person duly appointed as his successor enters upon his office or until the expiry of his term of office, whichever is the earliest.

(2) The Presiding Officer of a Cyber Appellate Tribunal shall not be removed from his office except by an order by the Central Government on the ground of proved misbehaviour or incapacity after an inquiry made by a Judge of the Supreme Court in which the Presiding Officer concerned has been informed of the charges against him and given a reasonable opportunity of being heard in respect of these charges.

(3) The Central Government may, by rules, regulate the procedure for the investigation of misbehaviour or incapacity of the aforesaid Presiding Officer.

55. Orders constituting Appellate Tribunal to be final and not to invalidate its proceedings

No order of the Central Government appointing any person as the Presiding Officer of a Cyber Appellate Tribunal shall be called in question in any manner and no act or proceeding before a Cyber Appellate Tribunal shall be called in question in any manner on the ground merely of any defect in the constitution of a Cyber Appellate Tribunal.

56. Staff of the Cyber Appellate Tribunal

(1) The Central Government shall provide the Cyber Appellate Tribunal with such officers and employees as that Government may think fit.

(2) The officers and employees of the Cyber Appellate Tribunal shall discharge their functions under general superintendence of the Presiding Officer.

(3) The salaries, allowances and other conditions of service of the officers and employees or the Cyber Appellate Tribunal shall be such as may be prescribed by the Central Government.

57. Appeal to Cyber Appellate Tribunal

(1) Save as provided in sub-section (2), any person aggrieved by an order made by Controller or an adjudicating officer under this Act may prefer an appeal to a Cyber Appellate Tribunal having jurisdiction in the matter.

(2) No appeal shall lie to the Cyber Appellate Tribunal from an order made by an adjudicating officer with the consent of the parties.

(3) Every appeal under sub-section (1) shall be filed within a period of twenty-five days from the date on which a copy of the order made by the Controller or the adjudicating officer is received by the person aggrieved and it shall be in such form and be accompanied by such fee as may be prescribed:

Provided that the Cyber Appellate Tribunal may entertain an appeal after the expiry of the said period of twenty-five days if it is satisfied that there was sufficient cause for not filing it within that period.

(4) On receipt of an appeal under sub-section (1), the Cyber Appellate Tribunal may, after giving the parties to the appeal, an opportunity of being heard, pass such orders thereon as it thinks fit, confirming, modifying or setting aside the order appealed against.

(5) The Cyber Appellate Tribunal shall send a copy of every order made by it to the parties to the appeal and to the concerned Controller or adjudicating officer.

(6) The appeal filed before the Cyber Appellate Tribunal under sub-section (1) shall be dealt with by it as expeditiously as possible and endeavour shall be made by it to dispose of the appeal finally within six months from the date of receipt of the appeal.

58. Procedure and powers of the Cyber Appellate Tribunal

(1) The Cyber Appellate Tribunal shall not be bound by the procedure laid down by the Code of Civil Procedure, 1908 but shall be guided by the principles of natural justice and, subject to the other provisions of this Act and of any rules, the Cyber Appellate Tribunal shall have powers to regulate its own procedure including the place at which it shall have its sitting.

(2) The Cyber Appellate Tribunal shall have, for the purposes of discharging its functions under this Act, the same powers as are vested in a civil court under the Code of Civil Procedure, 1908, while trying a suit, in respect of the following matters, namely:—

(a) summoning and enforcing the attendance of any person and examining him on oath;

(b) requiring the discovery and production of documents or other electronic records;

(c) receiving evidence on affidavits;

(d) issuing commissions for the examination of witnesses or documents;

(e) reviewing its decisions;

(f) dismissing an application for default or deciding it *ex pane;*

(g) any other matter which may be prescribed.

(3) Every proceeding before the Cyber Appellate Tribunal shall be deemed to be a judicial proceeding within the meaning of sections 193 and 228, and for the purposes of section 196 of the Indian Penal Code and the Cyber Appellate Tribunal shall be deemed to be a civil court for the purposes of section 195 and Chapter XXVI of the Code of Criminal Procedure, 1973.

59. Right to legal representation

The appellant may either appear in person or authorise one or more legal practitioners or any of its officers to present his or its case before the Cyber Appellate Tribunal.

60. Limitation

The provisions of the Limitation Act, 1963, shall, as far as may be, *apply* to an appeal made to the Cyber Appellate Tribunal.

61. Civil court not to have jurisdiction

No court shall have jurisdiction to entertain any suit or proceeding in respect of any matter which an adjudicating officer appointed under this Act or the Cyber Appellate Tribunal constituted under this Act is empowered by or under this Act to determine and no injunction shall be granted by any court or other authority in respect of any action taken or to be taken in pursuance of any power conferred by or under this Act.

62. Appeal to High Court.

Any person aggrieved by any decision or order of the Cyber Appellate Tribunal may file an appeal to the High Court within sixty days from the date of communication of the decision or order of the Cyber Appellate Tribunal to him on any question of fact or law arising out of such order :

Provided that the High Court may, if it is satisfied that the appellant was prevented by sufficient cause from filing the appeal within the said period, allow it to be filed within a further period not exceeding sixty days.

63. Compounding of contraventions

(1) Any contravention under this Chapter may, either before or after the institution of adjudication proceedings, be compounded by the Controller or such other officer as may be specially authorised by him in this behalf or by the adjudicating officer, as the case may be, subject to such conditions as the Controller or such other officer or the adjudicating officer may specify:

Provided that such sum shall not, in any case, exceed the maximum amount of the penalty which may be imposed under this Act for the contravention so compounded.

(2) Nothing in sub-section (1) shall apply to a person who commits the same or similar contravention within a period of three years from the date on which the first contravention, committed by him, was compounded.

Explanation.—For the purposes of this sub-section, any second or subsequent contravention committed after the expiry of a period of three years from the date on which the contravention was previously compounded shall be deemed to be a first contravention.

(3) Where any contravention has been compounded under sub-section (1), no proceeding or further proceeding, as the case may be, shall be taken against the person guilty of such contravention in respect of the contravention so compounded.

64. Recovery of penalty

A penalty imposed under this Act, if it is not paid, shall be recovered as an arrear of land revenue and the licence or the Digital Signature Certificate, as the case may be, shall be suspended till the penalty is paid.

Chapter XI
OFFENCES

65. Tampering with computer source documents

Whoever knowingly or intentionally conceals, destroys or alters or intentionally or knowingly causes another to conceal, destroy or alter any computer source code used for a computer, computer programme, computer system or computer network, when the computer source code is required to be kept or maintained by law for the time being in force, shall be punishable with imprisonment upto three years, or with fine which may extend upto two lakh rupees, or with both.

Explanation. —For the purposes of this section, "computer source code" means the listing of programmes, computer commands, design and layout and programme analysis of computer resource in any form.

66. Hacking with computer system

(1) Whoever with the intent to cause or knowing that he is likely to cause wrongful loss or damage to the public or any person destroys or deletes or alters any information residing in a computer resource or diminishes its value or utility or affects it injuriously by any means, commits hack:

(2)Whoever commits hacking shall be punished with imprisonment upto three years, or with fine which may extend upto two lakh rupees, or with both.

67. Publishing of information which is obscene in electronic form

Whoever publishes or transmits or causes to be published in the electronic form, any material which is lascivious or appeals to the prurient interest or if its effect is such as to tend to deprave and corrupt persons who are likely, having regard to all relevant circumstances, to read see or hear the matter contained or embodied in it, shall be punished on first conviction with imprisonment of either description for a term which may extend to five years and with fine which may extend to one lakh rupees and in the event of a second or subsequent conviction with imprisonment of either description for a term which may extend to ten years and also with fine which may extend to two lakh rupees.

68. Power of Controller to give directions

(1) The Controller may, by order, direct a Certifying Authority or any employee of such Authority to take such measures or cease carrying on such activities as specified in the order if those are necessary to ensure compliance with the provisions of this Act, rules or any regulations made thereunder.

(2) Any person who fails to comply with any order under sub-section (1) shall be guilty of an offence and shall be liable on conviction to imprisonment for a term not exceeding three years or to a Fine not exceeding two lakh rupees or to both.

69. Directions of Controller to a subscriber to extend facilities to decrypt information

(1) If the Controller is satisfied that it is necessary or expedient so to do in the interest of the sovereignty or integrity of India, the security of the State, friendly relations with foreign States or public order or for preventing incitement to the commission of any cognizable offence, for reasons to be recorded in writing, by order, direct any agency of the Government to intercept any information transmitted through any computer resource.

(2) The subscriber or any person incharge of the computer resource shall, when called upon by any agency which has been directed under sub-section (1), extend all facilities and technical assistance to decrypt the information.

(3) The subscriber or any person who fails to assist the agency referred to in sub-section (2) shall be punished with an imprisonment for a term which may extend to seven years.

70. Protected system

(1) The appropriate Government may, by notification in the Official Gazette, declare that any computer, computer system or computer network to be a protected system.

(2) The appropriate Government may, by order in writing, authorise the persons who are authorised to access protected systems notified under sub-section (1).

(3) Any person who secures access or attempts to secure access to a protected system in contravention of the provisions of this section shall be punished with imprisonment of either description for a term which may extend to ten years and shall also be liable to fine.

71. Penalty for misrepresentation

Whoever makes any misrepresentation to, or suppresses any material fact from, the Controller or the Certifying Authority for obtaining any licence or Digital Signature Certificate, as the case may be, shall be punished with imprisonment for a term which may extend to two years, or with fine which may extend to one lakh rupees, or with both.

72. Penalty for breach of confidentiality and privacy

Save as otherwise provided in this Act or any other law for the time being in force, any person who, in pursuance of any of the powers conferred under this Act, rules or regulations made thereunder. Has secured access to any electronic record, book, register, correspondence, information, document or other material without the consent of the person concerned discloses such electronic record, book, register, correspondence, information, document or other material to any other person shall be punished with imprisonment for a term which may extend to two years, or with fine which may extend to one lakh rupees, or with both.

73. Penalty for publishing Digital Signature Certificate false in certain particulars

(1) No person shall publish a Digital Signature Certificate or otherwise make it available to any other person with the knowledge that—

(a) the Certifying Authority listed in the certificate has not issued it; or

(b) the subscriber listed in the certificate has not accepted it; or

(c) the certificate has been revoked or suspended,

unless such publication is for the purpose of verifying a digital signature created prior to such suspension or revoca-tion.

(2) Any person who contravenes the provisions of sub-section (1) shall be punished with imprisonment for a term which may extend to two years, or with fine which may extend to one lakh rupees, or with both.

74. Publication for fraudulent purpose

Whoever knowingly creates, publishes or otherwise makes available a Digital Signature Certificate for any fraudulent or unlawful purpose shall be punished with imprisonment for a term which may extend to two years, or with fine which may extend to one lakh rupees, or with both.

75. Act to apply for offence or contravention committed outside India

(1) Subject to the provisions of sub-section (2), the provisions of this Act shall apply also to any offence or contravention committed outside India by any person irrespective of his nationality.

(2) For the purposes of sub-section (1), this Act shall apply to an offence or contravention committed outside India by any person if the act or conduct constituting the offence or contravention involves a computer, computer system or computer network located in India.

76. Confiscation

Any computer, computer system, floppies, compact disks, tape drives or any other accessories related thereto, in respect of which any provision of this Act, rules, orders or regulations made thereunder has been or is being contravened, shall be liable to confiscation:

Provided that where it is established to the satisfaction of the court adjudicating the confiscation that the person in whose possession, power or control of any such computer, computer system, floppies, compact disks, tape drives or any other accessories relating thereto is found is not responsible for the contravention of the provisions of this Act, rules, orders or regulations made thereunder, the court may, instead of making an order for confiscation of such computer, computer system, floppies, compact disks, tape drives or any other accessories related thereto, make such other order authorised by this Act against the person contravening of the provisions of this Act, rules, orders or regulations made thereunder as it may think fit.

77. Penalties or confiscation not to interfere with other punishments

No penalty imposed or confiscation made under this Act shall prevent the imposition of any other punishment to which the person affected thereby is liable under any other law for the time being in force.

78. Power to investigate offences.

Notwithstanding anything contained in the Code of Criminal Procedure, 1973, a police officer not below the rank of Deputy Superintendent of Police shall investigate any offence under this Act.

Chapter XII
NETWORK SERVICE PROVIDERS NOT TO BE LIABLE IN CERTAIN CASES

79. Network service providers not to be liable in certain cases.

For the removal of doubts, it is hereby declared that no person providing any service as a network service provider shall be liable under this Act, rules or regulations made thereunder for any third party information or data made available by him if he proves that the offence or contravention was committed without his knowledge or that he had exercised all due diligence to prevent the commission of such offence or contravention.

Explanation.—For the purposes of this section, —

(a) "network service provider" means an intermediary;

(b) "third party information" means any information dealt with by a network service provider in his capacity as an intermediary,

Chapter XIII
MISCELLANEOUS

80. Power of police officer and other officers to enter, search, etc.

(1) Notwithstanding anything contained in the Code of Criminal Procedure, 1973, any police officer, not below the rank of a Deputy Superintendent of Police, or any other officer of the Central Government or a State Government authorised by the Central Government in this behalf may enter any public place and search and arrest without warrant any person found therein who is reasonably suspected or having committed or of committing or of being about to commit any offence under this Act

Explanation.—For the purposes of this sub-section, the expression "public place" includes any public conveyance, any hotel, any shop or any other place intended for use by, or accessible to the public.

(2) Where any person is arrested under sub-section (1) by an officer other than a police officer, such officer shall, without unnecessary delay, take or send the person arrested before a magistrate having jurisdiction in the case or before the officer-in-charge of a police station.

(3) The provisions of the Code of Criminal Procedure, 1973 shall, subject to the provisions of this section, apply, so far as may be, in relation to any entry, search or arrest, made under this section.

81. Act to have overriding effect

The provisions of this Act shall have effect notwithstanding anything inconsistent therewith contained in any other law for the time being in force.

82. Controller, Deputy Controller and Assistant Controllers to be public servants

The Presiding Officer and other officers and employees of a Cyber Appellate Tribunal, the Controller, the Deputy Controller and the Assistant Controllers shall be deemed to be public servants within the meaning of section 21 of the Indian Penal Code.

83. Power to give directions

The Central Government may give directions to any State Government as to the carrying into execution in the State of any of the provisions of this Act or of any rule, regulation or order made thereunder.

84. Protection of action taken in good faith

No suit, prosecution or other legal proceeding shall lie against the Central Government, the State Government, the Controller or any person acting on behalf of him, the Presiding Officer, adjudicating officers and the staff of the Cyber Appellate Tribunal for anything which is in good faith done or intended to be done in pursuance of this Act or any rule, regulation or order made thereunder.

85. Offences by companies

(1) Where a person committing a contravention of any of the provisions of this Act or of any rule, direction or order made thereunder is a company, every person who, at the time the contravention was committed, was in charge of, and was responsible to, the company for the conduct of business of the company as well as the company, shall be guilty of the contravention and shall be liable to be proceeded against and punished accordingly:

Provided that nothing contained in this sub-section shall render any such person liable to punishment if he proves that the contravention took place without his knowledge or that he exercised all due diligence to prevent such contravention.

(2) Notwithstanding anything contained in sub-section (1), where a contravention of any of the provisions of this Act or of any rule, direction or order made thereunder has been committed by a company and it is proved that the contravention has taken place with the consent or connivance of, or is attributable to any neglect on the part of, any director, manager, secretary or other officer of the company, such director, manager, secretary or other officer shall also be deemed to be guilty of the contravention and shall be liable to be proceeded against and punished accordingly.

Explanation. —For the purposes of this section,—

(i) "company" means any body corporate and includes a firm or other association of individuals; and

(ii) "director", in relation to a firm, means a partner in the firm.

86. Removal of difficulties

(1) If any difficulty arises in giving effect to the provisions of this Act, the Central Government may, by order published in the Official Gazette, make such provisions not inconsistent with the provisions of this Act as appear to it to be necessary or expedient for removing the difficulty:

Provided that no order shall be made under this section after the expiry of a period of two years from the commencement of this Act.

(2) Every order made under this section shall be laid, as soon as may be after it is made, before each House of Parliament.

87. Power of Central Government to make rules

(1) The Central Government may, by notification in the Official Gazette and in the Electronic Gazette make rules to carry out the provisions of this Act.

(2) In particular, and without prejudice to the generality of the foregoing power, such rules may provide for all or any of the following mailers, namely:—

(a) the manner in which any information or matter may be authenticated by means of digital signature under section 5;

(b) the electronic form in which filing, issue, grant or payment shall be effected under sub-section (1) of section 6;

(c) the manner and format in which electronic records shall be filed, or issued and the method of payment under sub-section (2) of section 6;

(d) the matters relating to the type of digital signature, manner and format in which it may be affixed under section 10;

(e) the security procedure for the purpose of creating secure electronic record and secure digital signature under section 16;

(f) the qualifications, experience and terms and conditions of service of Controller, Deputy Controllers and Assistant Controllers under section 17;

(g) other standards to be observed by the Controller under clause (b) of sub-section (2) of section 20;

(h) the requirements which an applicant must fulfil under sub-section (2) of section 21;

(i) the period of validity of licence granted under clause (a) of sub-section (3) of section 21;

(j) the form in which an application for licence may be made under sub-section (1) of section 22;

(k) the amount of fees payable under clause (c) of sub-section (2) of section 22;

(l) such other documents which shall accompany an application for licence under clause (a) of sub-section (2) of section 22;

(m) the form and the fee for renewal of a licence and the fee payable there of under section 23;

(n) the form in which application for issue of a Digital Signature Certificate may be made under sub-section (1) of section *35;*

(o) the fee to be paid to the Certifying Authority for issue of a Digital Signature Certificate under sub-section (2) of section *35;*

(p) the manner in which the adjudicating officer shall hold inquiry under sub-section (1) of section 46:

(q) the qualification and experience which the adjudicating officer shall possess under sub-section *(3) of* section 46;

(r) the salary, allowances and the other terms and conditions of service of the Presiding Officer under section 52;

(s) the procedure for investigation of misbehaviour or incapacity of the Presiding Officer under sub-section *(3)* of section 54;

(t) the salary and allowances and other conditions of service of other officers and employees under sub-section *(3)* of section 56;

(u) the form in which appeal may be filed and the fee thereof under sub -section (3) of section 57;

(v) any other power of a civil court required to be prescribed under clause (g) of sub-section (2) of section 58; and

(w) any other matter which is required to be, or may be, prescribed.

(3) Every notification made by the Central Government under clause *(f)* of sub-section (4) of section 1 and every rule made by it shall be laid, as soon as may be after it is made, before each House of Parliament, while it is in session, for a total period of thirty days which may be comprised in one session or in two or more successive sessions, and if, before the expiry of the session immediately following the session or the successive sessions aforesaid, both Houses agree in making any modification in the notification or the rule or both Houses agree that the notification or the rule should not be made, the notification or the rule shall thereafter have effect only in such modified form or be of no effect, as the case may be; so, however, that any such modification or annulment shall be without prejudice to the validity of anything previously done under that notification or rule.

88. Constitution of Advisory Committee

(1) The Central Government shall, as soon as may be after the commencement of this Act, constitute a Committee called the Cyber Regulations Advisory Committee.

(2) The Cyber Regulations Advisory Committee shall consist of a Chairperson and such number of other official and non-official members representing the interests principally affected or having special knowledge of the subject-matter as the Central Government may deem fit.

(3) The Cyber Regulations Advisory Committee shall advise—

(a) the Central Government either generally as regards any rules or for any other purpose connected with this Act;

(b) the Controller in framing the regulations under this Act.

(4) There shall be paid to the non-official members of such Committee such travelling and other allowances as the Central Government may fix.

89. Power of Controller to make regulations

(1) The Controller may, after consultation with the Cyber Regulations Advisory Committee and with the previous approval of the Central Government, by notification in the Official Gazette, make regulations consistent with this Act and the rules made thereunder to carry out the purposes of this Act.

(2) In particular, and without prejudice to the generality of the foregoing power, such regulations may provide for all or any of the following matters, namely: —

(a) the particulars relating to maintenance of data-base containing the disclosure record of every Certifying Authority under clause (m) of section 18;

(b) the conditions and restrictions subject to which the Controller may recognise any foreign Certifying Authority under sub-section (1) of section 19;

(c) the terms and conditions subject to which a licence may be granted under clause (c) of sub-section *(3)* of section 21;

(d) other standards to be observed by a Certifying Authority under clause *(d)* of section 30;

(e) the manner in which the Certifying Authority shall disclose the matters specified in sub-section (1) of section 34;

(f) the particulars of statement which shall accompany an application under sub-section (3) of section 35,

(g) the manner in which the subscriber shall communicate the compromise of private key to the certifying Authority under sub-section (2) of section 42.

(3) Every regulation made under this Act shall be laid, as soon as may be after it is made, before each House of Parliament, while it is in session, for a total period of thirty days which may be comprised in one session or in two or more successive sessions, and if, before the expiry of the session immediately following the session or the successive sessions aforesaid, both Houses agree in making any modification in the regulation or both Houses agree that the regulation should not be made, the regulation shall thereafter have effect only in such modified form or be of no effect, as the case may be; so, however, that any such modification or annulment shall be without prejudice to the validity of anything previously done under that regulation.

90. Power of State Government to make rules

(1) The State Government may, by notification in the Official Gazette, make rules to carry out the provisions of this Act.

(2) In particular, and without prejudice to the generality of the foregoing power, such rules may provide for all or any of the following matters. namely:—

(a) the electronic form in which filing, issue, grant receipt or payment shall be effected under sub-section (1) of section 6;

(b) for matters specified in sub-section (2) of section 6;

(c) any other matter which is required to be provided by rules by the State Government.

(3) Every rule made by the State Government under this section shall be laid, as soon as may be after it is made, before each House of the State Legislature where it consists of two Houses, or where such Legislature consists of one House, before that House.

91. Amendment of Act 45 of 1860

The Indian Penal Code shall be amended in the manner specified in the First Schedule to this Act.

92. Amendment of Act 1 of 1872

The Indian Evidence Act, 1872 shall be amended in the manner specified in the Second Schedule to this Act.

93. Amendment of Act 18 of 1891

The Bankers' Books Evidence Act, 1891 shall be amended in the manner specified in the Third Schedule to this Act.

94. Amendment of Act 2 of 1834

The Reserve Bank of India Act, 1934 shall be amended in the manner specified in the Fourth Schedule to this Act.

THE FIRST SCHEDULE

(See section 91)

AMENDMENTS TO THE INDIAN PENAL CODE (*45* OF 1860)

1. After section 29, the following section shall be inserted, namely:—

Electronic record.

"29A. The words "electronic record" shall have the meaning assigned to them in clause (t) of sub-section (1) of section 2 of the Information Technology Act, 2000".

2. In section 167, for the words "such public servant, charged with the preparation or translation of any document, frames or translates that document", the words "such public servant, charged with the preparation or translation of any document or electronic record, frames, prepares or translates that document or electronic record" shall be substituted.

3. In section 172, for the words "produce a document in a Court of Justice", the words "produce a document or an electronic record in a Court of Justice" shall be substituted.

4.In section 173, for the words "to produce a document in a Court of Justice", the words "to produce a document or electronic record in a Court of Justice" shall be substituted.

5. In section *175,* for the word "document" at both the places where it occurs, the words "document or electronic record" shall be substituted.

6. In section 192, for the words "makes any false entry in any book or record, or makes any document containing a false statement", the words "makes any false entry in any book or record, or electronic record or makes any document or electronic record containing a false statement" shall be substituted.

7. In section 204, for the word "document" at both the places where it occurs, the words "document or electronic record" shall be substituted.

8. In section 463, for the words "Whoever makes any false documents or part of a document with intent to cause damage or injury", the words "Whoever makes any false documents or false electronic record or part of a document or electronic record, with intent to cause damage or injury" shall be substituted.

9. In section 464,—

(a) for the portion beginning with the words "A person is said to make a false document" and ending with the words "by reason of deception practised upon him, he does not know the contents of the document or the nature of the alteration", the following shall be substituted. namely:

"A person is said to make a false document or false electronic record—-

First-—Who dishonestly or fraudulently—-

(a) makes, signs, seals or executes a document or part of a document;

(b) makes or transmits any electronic record or part of any electronic record;

(c) affixes any digital signature on any electronic record;

(d) makes any mark denoting the execution of a document or the authenticity of the digital signature,

with the intention of causing it to be believed that such document or part of document, electronic record or digital signature was made, signed, sealed, executed, transmitted or affixed by or by the authority of a person by whom or by whose authority he knows that it was not made, signed, sealed, executed or affixed; or

Secondly—Who, without lawful authority, dishonestly or fraudulently, by cancellation or otherwise, alters a document or an electronic record in any material part thereof, after it has been made, executed or affixed with digital signature either by himself or by any other person, whether such person be living or dead at the time of such alteration; or

Thirdly—Who dishonestly or fraudulently causes any person to sign, seal, execute or alter a document or an electronic record or to affix his digital signature on any electronic record knowing that such person by reason of unsoundness of mind or intoxication cannot, or that by reason of deception practised upon him, he does not know the contents of the document or electronic record or the nature of the alteration."

(b) after *Explanation* 2, the following *Explanation* shall be inserted at the end, namely:–

'*Explanation* 3.—For the purposes of this section, the expression "affixing digital signature" shall have the meaning assigned to it in clause *(d)* of sub-section (1) of section 2 of the Information Technology Act, 2000.'.

10. In section 466,—

(a) for the words "Whoever forges a document", the words "Whoever forges a document or an electronic record" shall be substituted;

(b) the following *Explanation* shall be inserted at the end, namely:—

'**Explanation.**——For the purposes of this section, "register" includes any list, data or record of any entries maintained in the electronic form as defined in clause (r) of sub-section (1) of section 2 of the Information Technology Act, 2000.'.

11. In section 468, for the words "document forged", the words "document or electronic record forged" shall be substituted.

12. In section 469, for the words "intending that the document forged", the words "intending that the document or electronic record forged" shall be substituted.

13. In section 470, for the word "document" in both the places where it occurs, the words "document or electronic record" shall be substituted.

14. In section 471, for the word "document" wherever it occurs, the words "document or electronic record" shall be substituted.

15. In section 474, for the portion beginning with the words

"Whoever has in his possession any document" and ending with the words "if the document is one of the description mentioned in section 466 of this Code", the following shall be substituted, namely:—

> "Whoever has in his possession any document or electronic record, knowing the same to be forged and intending that the same shall fraudulently or dishonestly be used as a genuine, shall, if the document or electronic record is one of the description mentioned in section 466 of this Code.".

16. In section 476, for the words "any document", the words "any document or electronic record" shall be substituted.

17. In section 477A, for the words "book, paper, writing" at both the places where they occur, the words "book, electronic record, paper, writing" shall be substituted.

THE SECOND SCHEDULE

(See section 92)

AMENDMENTS TO THE INDIAN EVIDENCE ACT, 1872
(1 OF 1872)

1.In section 3,——

(a) in the definition of "Evidence", for the words "all documents produced for the inspection of the Court", the words "all documents including electronic records produced for the inspection of the Court" shall be substituted;

(b) after the definition of "India", the following shall be inserted, namely:—'the expressions "Certifying Authority", "digital signature", "Digital Signature Certificate", "electronic form", "electronic records", "information". "secure electronic record", "secure digital signature" and "subscriber" shall have the meanings respectively assigned to them in the Information Technology Act, 2000.'.

2. In section 17, for the words "oral or documentary", the words "oral or documentary or contained in electronic form" shall be substituted.

2. After section 22, the following section shall be inserted, namely:——

When oral admission as to contents of electronic records are relevant.

"22A. Oral admissions as to the contents of electronic records are not relevant, unless the genuineness of the electronic record produced is in question.".

4. In section 34, for the words "Entries in the books of account", the words "Entries in the books of account, including those maintained in an electronic form" shall be substituted.

5. In section *35,* for the word "record", in both the places where it occurs, the words "record or an electronic record" shall be substituted.

6. For section 39, the following section shall be substituted, namely:—

What evidence to be given when statement forms part of a conversation, document, electronic record, hook or series of letters or papers.

"39. When any statement of which evidence is given forms part of a longer statement, or of a conversation or pan of an isolated document, or is contained in a document which forms part of a book, or is contained in part of electronic record or of a connected series of letters or papers, evidence shall be given of so much and no more of the statement, conversation, document, electronic record, book or series of letters or papers as the Court considers necessary in that particular case to the full understanding of the nature and effect of the statement, and of the circumstances under which it was made.".

7. After section 47, the following section shall be inserted, namely:—

Opinion as to digital signature where relevant.

"47A. When the Court has 10 form an opinion as to the digital signature of any person, the opinion of the Certifying Authority which has issued the Digital Signature Certificate is a relevant fact."

8.In section *59,* for the words "contents of documents" the words "contents of documents or electronic records" shall be substituted.

9. After section *65,* the following sections shall be inserted, namely: —

Special provisions as to evidence relating to electronic record.

'*65A.* The contents of electronic records may be proved in accordance with the provisions of section 65B.

Admissibility of electronic records

65B. (1) Notwithstanding anything contained in this Act, any information contained in an electronic record which is printed on a paper, stored, recorded or copied in optical or magnetic media produced by a computer (hereinafter referred to as the computer output) shall be deemed to be also a document, if the conditions mentioned in this section are satisfied in relation to the information and computer in question and shall be admissible in any proceedings, without further proof or production of the original, as evidence of any contents of the original or of any fact stated therein of which direct evidence would be admissible.

(2) The conditions referred to in sub-section (1) in respect of a computer output shall be the following, namely: —

(a) the computer output containing the information was produced by the computer during the period over which the computer was used regularly to store or process information for the purposes of any activities regularly carried on over that period by the person having lawful control over the use of the computer;

(b) during the said period, information of the kind contained in the electronic record or of the kind from which the information so contained is derived was regularly fed into the computer in the ordinary course of the said activities;

(c) throughout the material part of the said period, the computer was operating properly or, if not, then in respect of any period in which it was not operating properly or was out of operation during that part of the period, was not such as to affect the electronic record or the accuracy of its contents; and

(d) the information contained in the electronic record reproduces or is derived from such information fed into the computer in the ordinary course of the said activities.

(3) Where over any period, the function of storing or processing information for the purposes of any activities regularly

carried on over that period as mentioned in clause (a) of sub-section (2) was regularly performed by computers, whether—

(a) by a combination of computers operating over that period; or

(b) by different computers operating in succession over that period; or

(c) by different combinations of computers operating in succession over that period; or

(d) in any other manner involving the successive operation over that period, in whatever order, of one or more computers and one or more combinations of computers, all the computers used for that purpose during that period shall be treated for the purposes of this section as constituting a single computer; and references in this section to a computer shall be construed accordingly,

(4) In any proceedings where it is desired to give a statement in evidence by virtue of this section, a certificate doing any of the following things, that is to say—

(a) identifying the electronic record containing the statement and describing the manner in which it was produced;

(b) giving such particulars of any device involved in the production of that electronic record as may be appropriate for the purpose of showing that the electronic record was produced by a computer;

(c) dealing with any of the matters to which the conditions mentioned in sub-section (2) relate,

and purporting to be signed by a person occupying a responsible official position in relation to the operation of the relevant device or the management of the relevant activities (whichever is appropriate) shall be evidence of any mattler stated in the certificate: and for the purposes of this sub-section it shall be sufficient for a matter to be stated to the best of the knowledge and belief of the person stating it.

(5) For the purposes of this section,—

(a) information shall be taken to be supplied to a computer if it is supplied thereto in any appropriate form and whether it is so supplied directly or (with or without human intervention) by means of any appropriate equipment;

(b) whether in the course of activities carried on by any

official, information is supplied with a view to its being stored or processed for the purposes of those activities by a computer operated otherwise than in the course of those activities, that information, if duly supplied to that computer, shall be taken to be supplied to it in the course of those activities,

(c) a computer output shall be taken to have been produced by a computer whether it was produced by it directly or (with or without human intervention) by means of any appropriate equipment.

Explanation.—For the purposes of this section any reference to information being derived from other information shall be a reference to its being derived therefore by calculation, comparison or any other process.

10. After section 67, the following section shall be inserted, namely:—

Proof as to digital signature.

"67A. Except in the case of a secure digital signature, if the digital signature of any subscriber is alleged to have been affixed to an electronic record the fact that such digital signature is the digital signature of the subscriber must be proved.".

11. After section 73, the following section shall be inserted, namely: —

Proof as to verification of digital signature.

'73A. In order to ascertain whether a digital signature is that of the person by whom it purports to have been affixed, the Court may direct—

(a) that person or the Controller or the Certifying Authority to produce the digital Signature Certificate;

(b) any other person to apply the public key listed in the Digital Signature Certificate and verify the digital signature purported to have been affixed by that person.

Explanation.—For the purposes of this section, "Controller" means the Controller appointed under sub-section (1) of section 17 of the Information Technology Act, 2000'.

12. Presumption as to Gazettes in electronic forms

After section 81, the following section shall be inserted, namely:—

"81 A. The Court shall presume the genuineness of every

electronic record purporting to be the Official Gazette, or purporting to be electronic record directed by any law to be kept by any person, if such electronic record is kept substantially in the form required by law and is produced from proper custody.".

13. Presumption as to electronic agreements

After section *85,* the following sections shall be inserted, namely:—

"*85A.* The Court shall presume that every electronic record purporting to be an agreement containing the digital signatures of the parties was so concluded by affixing the digital signature of the parties.

Presumption as to electronic records and digital signatures.

85B. (1) In any proceedings involving a secure electronic record, the Court shall presume unless contrary is proved, that the secure electronic record has not been altered since the specific point of time to which the secure status relates.

(2) In any proceedings, involving secure digital signature, the Court shall presume unless the contrary is proved that—

(a) the secure digital signature is affixed by subscriber with the intention of signing or approving the electronic record;

(b) except in the case of a secure electronic record or a secure digital signature, nothing in this section shall create any presumption relating to authenticity and integrity of the electronic record or any digital signature.

Presumption as to Digital Signature Certificates.

85C. The Court shall presume, unless contrary is proved, that the information listed in a Digital Signature Certificate is correct, except for information specified as subscriber information which has not been verified, if the certificate was accepted by the subscriber.".

14. Presumption as to electronic messages.

After section 88, the following section shall be inserted, namely:—

'88A. The Court may presume that an electronic message forwarded by the originator through an electronic mail server to the addressee to whom the message purports to be addressed corresponds with the message as fed into his computer for transmission; but the Court shall not make any presumption as to the person by whom such message was sent.

Explanation.—For the purposes of this section, the expressions "addressee" and "originator" shall have the same meanings respectively assigned to them in clauses (b) and (za) of sub-section (1) of section 2 of the Information Technology Act, 2000.'.

15. Presumption as to electronic records five years old. After section 90, the following section shall be inserted, namely:—

"90A. Where any electronic record, purporting or proved to be five years old, is produced from any custody which the Court in the particular case considers proper, the Court may presume that the digital signature which purports to be the digital signature of any particular person was so affixed by him or any person authorised by him in this behalf.

Explanation:—Electronic records are said to be in proper custody if they are in the place in which, and under the care of the person with whom, they naturally be; but no custody is improper if it is proved to have had a legitimate origin, or the circums-tances of the particular case are such as to render such an origin probable.

This *Explanation* applies also to section 81A.".

16. **For section 131, the following section shall be substituted, namely: —**

Production of documents or electronic records which another person, having possession, could refuse to produce.

"131. No one shall be compelled to produce documents in his possession or electronic records under his control, which any other person would be entitled to refuse to produce if they were in his possession or control, unless such last-mentioned person consents to their production.".

THE THIRD SCHEDULE

(See *section 93)*

AMENDMENTS TO THE BANKERS' BOOKS EVIDENCE ACT' 891

(18 OF *1891)*

1. In section 2—

(a) for clause (3), the following clause shall be substituted, namely:—

'(3) "bankers' books" include ledgers, day-books, cash-books, account-books and all other books used in the ordinary business of a bank whether kept in the written form or as printouts of data stored in a floppy, disc, tape or any other form of electro-magnetic data storage device;

(h) for clause *(8)*. The following clause shall be substituted, namely: — '*(8)* "certified copy" means when the books of a bank—

(a) are maintained in written form, a copy of any entry in such books together with a certificate written; the foot of such copy that it is a true copy of such entry, that such entry is contained in one of the ordinary books of the bank and was made in the usual and ordinary course of business and that such book is still in the custody of the bank, and where the copy was obtained by a mechanical or other process which in itself ensured the accuracy of the copy, a further certificate to that effect, but where the book from which such copy was prepared has been destroyed in the usual course of the bank's business after the date on which the copy had been so prepared, a further certificate to that effect, each such certificate being dated and subscribed by the principal accountant or manager of the bank with his name and official title; and

(b) consist of printouts of data stored in a floppy, disc, tape or any other electro-magnetic data storage device, a printout of such entry or a copy of such printout together with such statements certified in accordance with the provisions of section 2A.'.

2. After section 2, the following section shall be inserted, namely: —

Conditions in the printout

"2A. A printout of entry or a copy of printout referred to in sub-section *(8) of* section 2 shall be accompanied by the following, namely: —

(a) a certificate to the effect that it is a printout of such entry or a copy of such printout by the principal accountant or branch manager; and

(b) a certificate by a person in-charge of computer system containing a brief description of the computer system

and the particulars of—

(A) the safeguards adopted by the system to ensure that data is entered or any other operation performed only by authorised persons;

(B) the safeguards adopted to prevent and detect unauthorised change of data;

(C) the safeguards available to retrieve data that is lost due to systemic failure or any other reasons;

(D) the manner in which data is transferred from the system to removable media like floppies, discs, tapes or other electro-magnetic data storage devices;

(E) the mode of verification in order to ensure that data has been accurately transferred to such removable media;

(F) the mode of identification of such data storage devices;

(G) the arrangements for the storage and custody of such storage devices;

(H) the safeguards to prevent and detect any tampering with the system; and

(I) any other factor which will vouch for the integrity and accuracy of the system.

(c) a further certificate from the person in-charge of the computer system to the effect that to the best of his knowledge and belief, such computer system operated properly at the material time, he was provided with all the relevant data and the printout in question represents correctly, or is appropriately derived front, the relevant data.".

THE FOURTH SCHEDULE

(See *section 94)*

AMENDMENT TO THE RESERVE BANK OF INDIA ACT, 1934 (2 OF 1934)

In the Reserve Bank of India Act, 1934, in section 58, in sub-section (2), after clause (p), the following clause shall be inserted, namely:—

"*(pp)* the regulation of fund transfer through electronic means between the banks or between the banks and other financial institutions referred to in clause (c) of section 45-I, including the laying down of the conditions subject to which banks and other financial institutions shall participate in such fund transfers, the manner of such fund transfers and the rights and obligations of the participants in such fund transfers;".

SUBHASH C. JAIN,
Secy. to the Govt. of India.

4

E-Governance in Indian States

I. The Vision

The Government of Andhra Pradesh has a clear vision for the all round development of the State. This is reflected in the form of a well-conceptualized and cogent blueprint called Vision 2020. The Vision 2020 document sets the goals and milestones and suggests the strategies and plans necessary to realize the vision. The constantly inspiring and overreaching goal is to build **Swarna Andhra Pradesh**—the ideal society of the future. The vision of the State for the IT sector is embodied in the following statement:—

> *"Andhra Pradesh will leverage Information Technology to attain a position of leadership and excellence in the information age and to transform itself into a knowledge society."*

—***Vision 2020***

(A collaborative effort of GOAP & Mckinsey & Co.)

The vision on the IT front is also nicely paraphrased in the following statement of Sri N. Chandrababu Naidu, Honourable Chief Minister of Andhra Pradesh:

> "My Vision is to make AP the foremost State in ten years time in terms of standard of living of my people... through adoption of Information Technology in all aspects of development and governance."

The IT policy for Andhra Pradesh is so formulated as to create the right environment for realizing the above vision.

Objectives of IT policy

The policy objectives for the IT sector flow from the vision of the Government of Andhra Pradesh described in the foregoing section. The policy shall act as the beacon light for guiding the actions of all those interested in reaching the goal of the over all development of the State using IT as the major vehicle. The set of such interested parties includes the State consisting of the legislative, executive and judicial arms, IT entrepreneurs, citizens, businesses, academicians, students, intelligentsia, association of professionals etc. The policy contains guidance for each of these stakeholders. The objectives of the IT policy are enunciated below :

· **Economic development:** The first and foremost objective is to use IT as an instrument to foster the economic development of the State. This translates to specific action in the following areas :

- Growth of IT industry in the state.
- Growth of software exports.
- Creation of employment potential.
- Attracting investments from outside the state.
- Providing high quality services in all spheres.
- Promoting knowledge as the key resource for economic progress of individuals & institutions.

One of the prime policy considerations of a democratic government is the need to ensure that the economic benefits that flow out of its initiatives spread evenly and reach the underprivileged population groups as well. While the benefits of citizen services projects reach the rich and the poor equally, IT projects aimed at improving the internal efficiencies benefit the poor indirectly through better planning and targeting of weaker section programmes and superior enforcement of law. Apart from this, the Government intends to make conscious efforts to see that IT percolates to the middle class and people below the poverty line. This translates to goals such as :

- Taking Internet to the villages,
- Promoting IT-enabled education,
- Promoting Local Language interface, and
- Taking up socially relevant extension and outreach programmes.

Human Resource Development : Together with economic development, an improved quality of life to the citizens has to be assured. These include the following:

- Quality, standards and universalization of education.
- Access to quality health care for all.
- Availability of nutritious food for all.
- Development of centers of excellence in knowledge.

- **Good Governance** : Good governance is a *sine qua non* for the orderly functioning of the society. IT can significantly impact on the quality of governance. The following facets of governance can be significantly improved with the use of IT:
  - Government- Citizen Interface
  - Government-Business interface
  - Intra-Governmental processes

IT shall be used not merely to automate processes but as a strategic tool to simplify procedures and revamp processes. Electronic governance will bring in the following benefits:

- Any-where, any-time services to citizens.
- One-stop shop for all transactions in the G-C interface.
- Better accountability, responsiveness and transparency of all systems.
- Highly efficient government machinery & systems.
- Reduced discretion and arbitrariness.

This document on the IT policy 2000 makes an endeavour to put in place the overall framework necessary for achieving the above objectives.

The IT policy 2000 is not a static document. The nature and pace of development of Information Technology dictates that such a policy document has to be dynamic and evolutionary, to take into its fold emerging technologies and trends. It is, therefore, proposed to update the document as frequently as required.

II STRATEGIES

The Harvard Business School defines entrepreneurship as *'the relentless pursuit of opportunity with no regard to the available resources'*. This definition, however, is in the context of an individual entrepreneur. This definition has to be suitably tempered in the context of a State policy and a State initiative. In the context of the State, the policy objectives, however laudable, have to be assessed for their feasibility against the background of the socio-economic conditions prevalent in the State, the financial and human resources available with the Government, the conduciveness of the fiscal environment for growth of capital and entrepreneurship in the IT sector and, above all, the will of the people to support and encourage achievements in this sector. Given the fact that many of the above requisites are not available to the desirable degree in any State at any point, **the Governments have to design and adopt a suitable set of strategies to derive optimum benefit from the available set of resources** and mould the circumstances to advantage for achieving the policy objectives.

The set of strategies most appropriate for the overall development of the IT sector in the State are discussed below :

1. Putting the enablers in place

One strategy that is extremely relevant in the circumstances is to identify and put in place the enablers, which catalyse and foster a rapid growth of IT on all fronts. It is necessary for us to study the factors that were responsible for such rapid growth of IT sector in areas like the Silicon Valley, Route 128 , Singapore, Taiwan and China. The following are believed to be the set of enablers that would be required in the Andhra Pradesh context :

- **Apex policy-making bodies :** The key to the design and development of a successful IT policy and monitoring its implementation is the existence of a high-powered policy making body that forms a think tank capable of drawing a large yet manageable canvas and that which can take quick decisions. This assumes special significance in the context of the IT sector, given the traditionally slow decision-making process associated with Governments and in contrast, the speedy decision making required to keep pace with the developments in this internet age. In view of this, the Government of Andhra Pradesh has created a suitable institutional mechanism in the form of the following bodies :
- **AP FIRST:** This is the apex body with the responsibility for the design of suitable IT policies, strategies and plans and reviewing their implementation. It is

chaired by the Chief Minister and consists of Ministers for Finance and Revenue besides experts of the Indian IT industry. This IT Board meets on a fixed day of every alternate month.

- **ITPC** : (Information Technology Promotion Committee). This Committee, headed by the Chief Secretary and consisting of Senior Secretaries of the Government, is responsible for evaluation of major IT projects besides implementing the IT policy and reviewing its progress.
- **C-IT** : (Departmental Committee on Information Technology). These Department-level Committees headed by the respective ministers are responsible for drawing up suitable IT plan for the department and its implementation and review.

The structure described above has been created through GOMs 4, Finance & Planning (Plg. IT&C) Department dated 24-1-2000, a copy of which can be seen at **Annexure I.**

- **The Technology Think Tank** : When the policy objective is to develop IT within the Government and outside in a ubiquitous way, it is necessary to be clear about the technology options available so that the state has the advantage of keeping itself on par with the best in the world. It is equally important to forge technical standards so that we do not create islands of excellence which can not communicate with each other ! These standards could cover simple things like the way we define data to complex things like communication and networking standards. For considering these matters, a Technical Advisory Board (TAB) is to be constituted.
- **The Right Regulatory Regime:** Efforts shall be made to ensure that starting and running of businesses in the State in general and IT industries in particular, is fast and smooth and to see that the interface with Government is required to be minimal and positive. Efforts shall be made to put in place a regulatory regime that regulates the least! The G2B interface shall be through electronic means within 3 years. The areas identified to be reformed in this regard are:

- Licensing & registration of a business
- Declaratory & filing requirements under:
  - *Income Tax Act*
  - *Customs & Central Excise*
  - Sales Tax
  - *FERA*
- Compliance requirements under various Acts like:
  - Water & Air Pollution Act
  - Factories Act
  - Employment Exchange (Notification of Vacancies) Act
  - Payment of Wages Act
  - Minimum Wages Act
  - Contract Labour (Regulation & Abolition) Act
  - Workmen Compensation Act
  - A P Shops & Establishments
  - Employees State Insurance Act
- Facilitating regulatory regime conducive to formation of capital, under the:
  - *SEBI Act*
  - *RBI Act*

While some of the Acts are under the purview of the State Government, the items shown in italics are under the purview of the Central Government. In respect of a majority of the State laws requiring liberalization at the hands of the State Government, suitable orders have already been issued through GOMs 114 dated 25-5-1999 (Copy at **Annexure II**). It shall be the endeavour of the Government of Andhra Pradesh to use its good offices to bring about desired reforms in the legal, taxation and regulatory matters relating to the Central Government also.

CCITI : The Government has constituted a Consultative Committee on IT Industry through GOMs No 3, IT &C Dept dated 25-5-2000, (copy at **Annexure III**) under the Secretary IT&C, to create a forum for coordination between the various agencies under the Central & State Governments and the IT industry. The committee is supposed to meet once in 2 months and resolve the problems faced by the industry. The issues relating to grant of Incentives to IT industry are also under the purview of the CCITI.

2. Building Infrastructure

One of the most important pre-requisites for fostering the growth of IT industry is the building up of the required infrastructure in the government sector to the extent necessary and in the private sector to the extent desirable. The infrastructure for IT is broadly in the form of the following:

- **Hi-tech Habitat :** Ready availability of Hi-tech space with the required amenities like built-in electrical and communication ducts, data ports, central air-conditioning etc. will be a great incentive for IT companies to set up shop on a fast track. It is the endeavour of the Government to facilitate creation of large extents of hi-tech space not only in and around Hyderabad but in the important cities and towns in the state.

  The first major effort at this is the Hitec City at Madhapur, 7 km. from the heart of the city. It is a 1 million square-feet of world class lTspace. The phase 2 of the Hitec city is fully booked already. It is noteworthy that the Hitec city has come up in a mere 11 months through a Joint venture, L&T Infocity, between the AP Industrial Infrastructure Corporation and Larsen & Toubro Ltd. in keeping with the strategy of leveraging the best private sector strengths. This JV is actively engaged in developing phase II of the Project to create about 860,000 sqft. of high tech space in blocks of 250,000 sqft . The first block will be available by December 2000.

  In addition to developing Phase II of the Hitec city, the Government has also enabled IT majors to develop space of their own by allotting plots of land adjacent to the Hitec city, at a concessional rate. Wipro, Baan, SoftSol, Infotech have already brought up their development centers in this area. An extent of about 100 acres of land is available in the vicinity of the Hitec city, for allotment to IT companies, as of January 2000.

  The Government has issued a set of guidelines to facilitate allotment of land to the IT units at the concessional rates in terms of the IT policy. These guidelines contain the format of application for land and other incentives, the eligibility criteria, the procedure for evaluation of the requests etc. A copy of the guidelines can be seen at **Annexure IV (GOMs 5, IT&C dept. dated 16-6-2000).**

Given the policy objective of developing all parts of the state using IT as the instrument, it is imperative that hitec space is built in and around all the major cities and towns in the districts. Such space would be extremely useful to spawn the growth of IT-enabled services — a sector that has the promise of providing jobs to millions. It is the policy of the Government to encourage and promote the building of mini-hitec cities in this hinterland at medium to low rates within the reach of start-up IT entrepreneurs. A suitable framework for promoting such efforts will soon be brought in place.

The Government has cleared a proposal to construct a Hitec city at Vizag. A plot of 10 acres of land has been set apart for this purpose in an important part of the city, abutting the National Highway 5.

- **Cyber City:** The march towards a knowledge society requires the establishment of intelligent cities which are planned and constructed with all features conducive to give a free play to the explosive development of IT. These features include a suitable city plan, energy-conserving and environment-friendly building architectures, in-built connectivity with bandwidths on futuristic scales, recreational facilities that induce innovative thoughts and entrepreneurship, excellent transportation facilities and logistics, education and healthcare of international standards with highly focused IT education and an ideal networking environment for entrepreneurs, investors and academics.

  The services of an international consultant have to be hired for the prepation of a blueprint for the Cyber-city. The AP industrial Infrastructure Corporation has been requested to initiate work in this regard.

- **Band-width:** Bandwidth is to IT what oxygen is to human existence. Bandwidth is an electronic highway, which is critical for the conduct of all human interactions in the new millennium. However, by international standards, the State is still way behind . Viewed in the above perspective, Andhra Pradesh must take the lead in creating this mission-critical infrastructure by designing an attractive model for acquiring bandwidth in an economically viable manner, quite like constructing other IT infrastructure.

Optical Fibre Connectivity

Government will facilitate and promote the establishment of broadband digital networks in the State. For example, the existing transmission and distribution network of the Electricity utilities and the highways could be used to establish a digital backbone network in association with the private sector.

Policy on Right of Way

The Government has announced its policy on right of way along all the highways of the state, for the telecommunications sector. The salient features of this policy are given below :

- The policy is modelled after that of the Ministry of Surface Transport, Govt. of India in respect of National Highways.
- Any entrepreneur holding the necessary licenses from Department of Telecommunications, can apply for permission to lay optic fibre along the State Highways, forest roads, district roads, Municipal and Panchayati Raj roads, along with a set of plans.
- Permission will be accorded by the respective Engineer-in-Chief within 14 days.
- The applicant has to enter into a license agreement with the concerned department agreeing to restore the road margin/road to its original standard after laying the cable.
- The right of way is given free of any charges or license fee.

A copy of the GOMS 5 Fin. & Planning (IT&C) department dated 11-2-2000 can be seen at Annexure V.

Satellite communications

The Government will promote the use of satellite communication systems to provide connectivity, especially to the remote locations in the State. The Government has two proposals on hand in this area.

The Government will also promote the use of wireless communication technologies to provide better communication services especially in the last mile. The Government will ensure the efficient management of the radio frequency spectrum to maximize convenience to users. An integrated approach to wireless communications to meet governmental requirements will be developed.

The use of CORDECT technology is being experimented to connect the villages in Kuppam constituency, in Chittoor district. It is being implemented by the Telecom Department.

The other approaches for bandwidth creation being explored currently are—

- Getting permission for a landing point for fibre carriers on the East Coast.
- Promoting the building of sub-marine OF link with the US West Coast *via* Singapore and Japan.
- Broadband high speed links with the metropolitan centers of the country.
- Early implementation of Sankhya Vahini Project—a joint venture of lUnet, DoT and IIIT which envisages laying down optical fibre backbone touching all major cities in India. This project has received the approval of the Union Government in January 2000.

- **A Modern International Airport**: International Airport is essential for speedy and convenient travel and cargo movement to international IT centers. It facilitates:—
    - Travel of IT professionals to Silicon Valley and to other IT hubs of the world;
    - Quick cargo movement of computer hardware produced by Hardware manufacturers to the International markets; and
    - Importing IT equipment required for research and development.

The Government of Andhra Pradesh is promoting an international airport at Shamshabad, about 40 KM from Hyderabad. In pursuance of a notification issued calling for expressions of interest, 7 major international consortia have expressed interest in the project. RFP is about to be issued (as of July 2000).

Following are some of the salient features of the Hyd

International Airport project:—

- Suitable site admeasuring 2000 acres is being acquired.
- Tata Consultancy Services with Speedwing UK (British Airways) were appointed as consultants.
- Bids invited for expression of interest under Design, Finance, Build, Operate and Maintain basis.
- 50 year planning horizon—
  - World class International Convention Centre Complex
  - Engineering & Maintenance Centre
  - Airport Management & Aviation Academy
  - World Class Export Promotion Zone
  - Cargo Complex
- Airport to be positioned as Regional Hub in the domestic and International sectors.
- **International Convention Centre :** Another piece of essential infrastructure is the establishment of an International Convention Centre with facilities to host International IT exhibitions, Seminars and Conferences. Hyderabad with its multifarious advantages like availability of quality manpower, central geographic location, competitive real estate prices, good social and civic infrastructure, decent quality of life and a facilitating proactive Government is perceived to be an ideal investment destination in India.

The State Government offers 5 hectares of picturesque land in the Central Business District, where other tourism and leisure development projects are envisaged, for establishment of the Convention Centre. The Government intends to establish it through a partnership between the AP Industrial Infrastructure Corporation and the private sector.

3. Creating the right social environment

The development of IT industry in a region is an evolutionary process. It happens over a period of time — typically a decade or two. This continuous process of evolution needs a continuity also in the policy environment, which, in turn, depends on the socio-economic milieu. A climate conducive to the development of IT has, fortunately, emerged in India in general and in Andhra Pradesh in particular. It is the firm intention of the Government to exploit these climatic conditions fully on one hand and take steps that would ensure its consolidation on the other.

The creation of confidence in society in the capability of IT to manage its day to day affairs and the generation of the wide spread belief that IT can be an effective instrument for the economic well being of a people are essential in this context. Fortunately for the State, such a confidence and belief have already begun to take root due to the successful and visible effects of some of the projects taken up or promoted by the State. Examples are the Hitec city, the IIIT, CARD and TWINS projects, which have fired the imagination of not only the citizens of the state but also of the other States and countries. This is an excellent and highly conducive situation.

Building public awareness

However good the objectives of the IT policy may be, its successful implementation depends to a large extent on the extent to which the citizens in general and the benefit groups in particular appreciate its usefulness and derive the fruit it provides. Very well implemented IT projects could not achieve the desired objectives due to the disinterest—bordering on apathy — and ignorance of what benefit the project could offer to the citizen. A well designed campaign to continually enhance the public awareness of the benefits of the various programmes is quite relevant and essential in this context. This campaign could be in several forms like:—

- Advertisements through press and media
- Electronic Display Boards
- Project-specific seminars and workshops
- Press conferences
- Web-sites
- Mega IT Events
- Road shows
- Participation in exhibitions

The cost and effort required to create the right degree of awareness among the user groups — be it the citizens, the entrepreneurs, the employees — has to be built into the design of all IT projects.

4. Leverage private sector Initiative

One other strategy critical to drive massive investments into the IT sector that it rightly needs at this point, is to leverage the financial, managerial and technological strengths of the private sector. For such a strategy to take root and work, it is necessary for the Government to spell out the areas in which such investments are invited and to spell out the ground rules for private initiatives. Some of these areas are :—

- Creation of IT infrastructure
- Implementation of e-Governance Projects on BOO and BOOT basis
- Development of software for e-governance projects
- Facilities Management
- Distance education & healthcare
- Community Internet Infrastructure
- E-commerce

While it is not possible in this document to detail the ground rules required for participation of the private sector, it is necessary to lay down the principles governing the same. The Government intends to be guided by the following principles in this regard:

- Transparency of procedures adopted for selection of private parties
- Designing a suitable scheme for creation of a stream of revenue linked to the transactions, in relation to implementation of governance projects on BOO, BOOT basis, before throwing a project to the process of open bidding.
- **An institutional mechanism for empanelling players in the IT sector who intend to work on Government IT projects,** and awarding projects based on pre-determined eligibility criteria on a fast-track basis. The range of IT players include system designers, developers, system integrators, facility managers, ISP's, IT training institutes, internet companies, web-site developers & hosts etc.

The Government believes that the adoption of such a strategy would have three advantages. Firstly, it will pave the way for pumping in large amount of investments into the priority areas of IT, which Government can not hope to do at the required pace. Secondly, it would give a fillip to the development of a variety of IT skills locally and create job opportunities. Thirdly, it will give the required experience to the local IT players and give them enough confidence and credentials to compete globally.

5. Strategic alliances and partnerships

One of the key objectives of the policy is to make the State globally competitive in the IT sector. This requires emulation of global best practices. Strategic alliances and partnerships with global leaders in specific thrust areas of IT, especially in IT infrastructure and IT education, is ideally suited to achieve this end. This strategy will have several distinct advantages. Firstly, the global player would bring to the table the state-of-the-art technology and skill set. The Government need not invest its resources on a technology hunt. Secondly, the financial and managerial resources of the State are not put to undue strain. This strategy has already been successfully used in the development of Hi-tec city, IIIT and the international IT schools around IIIT and the Indian School of Business. The government intends to take up more such projects through the alliance/partnership route in diverse areas. While it is not possible to straight-jacket the policy or the norms for arriving at and concluding such alliances/partnerships, it is certainly possible to indicate the areas in which proposals are welcome. The following is the list of priority areas in which the government intends to follow the alliance/partnership route :—

(i) IT-enabled education.
(ii) Data centers /server farms.
(iii) Digital libraries.
(iv) Smart cards.
(v) Electronic Payment systems.

6. Collaboration

The Government intends to foster strategic collaborations with other countries to derive the synergies in bringing the best practices of the world into the State. An MOU has been signed with Singapore in 1997.

7. International consultancies

It is crucial to design an overall **architecture** for the development of IT in the State and for assessing global trends and the competitive advantages of the State. Though such an architecture is likely to be dynamic due to the very nature and pace of advancement of information technology, it is felt desirable to have an initial blue print, which can be updated at yearly intervals. Putting such an architecture in view would benefit the State immensely by eliminating redundancies and enabling interoperable solutions to be developed in all sectors of e-Governance. To this end, the Government proposes to retain the services of an International consultancy firm in designing large systems. **The Government has sought Expression of Interest (EOI) from 6 international consultancy firms for the purpose in June 2000. The work may be entrusted by mid-August 2000.**

8. Thrust areas

It would be strategically important to identify and focus on the thrust areas in IT based on the strengths of Andhra Pradesh. This would give visible results in the medium and long run. The Government considers that the focus of Andhra Pradesh should be on **IT-enabled education, e-Governance and IT-enabled Services.**

III. e-GOVERNANCE

The Government of Andhra Pradesh firmly believes that e-Governance is one of the pillars of the edifice of IT. The Government exists for the people. All the efforts and initiatives of the Government should, therefore, be directed to the goal of providing good governance. It is well recognized principle of public administration that a good government is that which governs the least ! Hence, fundamental to the concept of good governance is a process of administrative and legal reforms aimed at reducing State controls and regulations to the barest minimum and developing a system that can administer the minimum required controls in the most efficient manner. The Government cherishes the vision of establishing a Simple, Moral,

Accountable, Responsive and Transparent Government — **SMART** government.

e-Governance is one of the vehicles that can be gainfully used in reaching the goal of **SMART** governance. The Government is aware of the fact that transition to e-Governance is a difficult exercise, which can be costly, time-consuming and fraught with several organizational and behavioural impediments. In the face of these constraints, the Government desires to adopt a pragmatic and graded approach to the issue.

1. Ground gained so far

Andhra Pradesh has already gained the pride of place in the area of e-Governance owing to the efforts made over the last five years. Several major projects are on ground and beginning to yield good results. A brief survey of these efforts is made below:

o **APSWAN:** Connectivity is perceived to be the backbone of all efforts at e-Governance. A 2Mbps optical fibre connectivity has, therefore, been established between Hyderabad and all the District Headquarters plus two other major towns (Vijayawada & Tirupati). The network has been operational from 1-11-99. It has been implemented under the BOO concept.

The Government has the following policy perspective for the APSWAN:—

- Putting an alternative backbone in position with higher capacities and better technologies.
- Taking the connectivity to the next logical levels of the mandal and village levels in one and 2 years. The vision of the Government to take to its villages, the benefits of access to the internet can be thereby achieved.
- The WAN infrastructure already created and planned in future is proposed to be optimally used by the government departments and agencies to translate the concept of e-Governance into a reality. Detailed technical guidelines have been issued to all the departments of the Government for connecting to APSWAN through leased lines & on dial up basis.

- **Video-conferencing Facility** : A video-conferencing facility between Hyderabad and the 25 cities/towns has been operational from 1-11-99. It rides on the APSWAN. The facility has to be eventually extended to all major departments at Hyderabad and their officers at the district level. It should be used also as a tool for specialized professional education and extension activities.

- **CARD (Computer-aided Administration of Registration Department):** This is one of the major success stories of e-Governance in India. 214 registration offices have been completely computerized from 4-11-98. The process of registration of deeds is completed in one hour and several other miscellaneous services like issue of Encumbrance Certificates and valuation certificates are accomplished in 15 minutes. The government is seriously contemplating provision of registration services on a remote access basis as it would promote public convenience tremendously. **About 950,000 documents have been registered under CARD till end of June 2000.**
- **COMPACT (Computer-aided Administration of Commercial Taxes):** 220 offices of Commercial Taxes Department, including 16 checkposts have been computerized from 1-4-96. The database of the details of over 350,000 registered dealers has been built up. Over 1 million returns are fed annually into the computers at 182 CTO offices for processing and analysis. About 5,000,000 transactions are captured online in the computers at 16 checkposts annually and the data is analysed and used for taking up investigations to detect evasion of sales tax.
- **TWINS ((TWIN cities Network Services)** : A pilot project to provide one-stop services to the citizens has been launched in December 1999. It provides an initial set of 18 services to the citizens of ward 8 of Hyderabad. These include payments of utility bills, issue of certificates, licenses and provision of information useful to the citizens.

Road Ahead — on integrated citizen services

The Government proposes to:—

o Replicate the TWINS pilot to all parts of the twin cities

initially and to all other areas of the State eventually.

- o Add more citizen services to the project.
- o Introduce electronic payment systems.
- o Provide some of the services on the internet.

The extension of the concept to several other locations in the State is sought to be achieved adopting BOOT model, involving the private sector. This model is expected to provide cost-effective services to the citizens in a speedy way. It is planned to extend the project to entire twin cities by October 2000 and to all major cities and towns subsequently.

A comprehensive RFP to extend expanded services of TWINS to 24 more Service Centres covering the light and breadth of twin cities, on BOOT basis, has been issued in June 2000. The Government is keen to implement the project by December 2000.

An experiment in providing such single-window services in the rural areas is being currently planned.

- **SKIMS (Secretariat Knowledge and Information Management System):** This project is designed to develop a generic product that efficiently manages the information and knowledge of a large organization like the secretariat. Secretariat being the seat of the Government, is a repository of a fund of information and knowledge. Public interest lies in efficiently managing this pool. The Government feels that IT holds the key to this delicate management exercise. The Government intends to implement the SKIMS project in a phased manner over 12 months (FY 2000-01) to achieve the following goals:—
  - Increase employee productivity & satisfaction.
  - Create a Knowledge Bank.
  - Exploit the power of the network.
  - Automate the work flows in the secretariat.
  - Prioritize areas of work.
  - Provide effective tools for performance evaluation.

The functional requirements have been arrived at and the RFP has been released in June 2000 for outsourcing the mammoth work of developing application software for the Central Information System and for each of the 40 departments.

At the end of Phase I of the bidding, TCS, Intelligroup and NIIT are in the fray for the final selection in Stage II.

The product to be developed can be customized to be deployed in any major Govt. organization that deals with files, like the following:—

- Other State Secretariats
- Central Secretariat
- Departments of Govt of India
- Pubic Sector Undertakings

- **FAST (Fully Automated Services of Transport department) :** The Fully Automated Services of Transport project is another e-governance project that aims at providing all transport department services like Issue of learner's licenses, driving licenses and registration of vehicles through a comprehensive, networked solution. A pilot project has been launched (on 12-5-2000) at 3 sites in the State — Secunderabad, Vijayawada and Tirupati. It is being implemented on a BOO basis. The Government intends to implement it at 34 more sites across the State on a BOO basis with participation of the private sector.
- **Computerization of Treasuries** : This is one of the oldest e-governance projects taken up in the State. All the accounting needs of the Treasuries Department are taken care of under this project. 23 District Treasuries and 300 sub treasuries have been computerized under this project. It is possible to know the receipts and expenditure of the Government on a dynamic basis.
- **MPHS (Multi-Purpose Household Survey project):** This is one of the largest IT projects undertaken by the Government. It aims to create the database of the socio-economic data of all the citizens of the state. The project is proposed to be implemented at all the 1122 mandals, which are the pivotal administrative units of the Government at the cutting edge level. The package of applications implemented under this project include — creation and maintenance of a citizen database that can be used in a variety of ways like for the public distribution system, issue of individual identity cards,

in ensuring better targeting in all the poverty alleviation programmes, land records, land acquisition and grievance redressal system. The MPHS project has been implemented so far in 320 mandals. The remaining mandals are likely to be covered by July 2000. The Government proposes to use the infrastructure created under this project for being used as the nucleus of all efforts aimed at taking the benefits of IT to the common man.

- **APDMS** : The Andhra Pradesh Development Monitoring System is a GIS-based system that has been launched on 26-1-2000. It has created the base maps of all the 1122 mandals and the constituent revenue villages and habitations together with a suite of applications which superimpose the thematic data on the road network, the community infrastructure, basic demographic data, soil and geomorphological data etc. This information is accessible on the web and provides a tremendous support to research, analysis, project design and monitoring in the area of development planning.

2. Approach to Computerization of all departments

Given the resource constraint, it is not possible for the Government to attempt computerization of all the departments and agencies at one time. A thin spread of the resources is likely to result in a large number of failures and non-starters. The government, therefore, considers it a better strategy to prioritize its departments and agencies on rational criteria and focus on the priority areas so as to computerize all of them over the next 3 years. The objective of an e-governance project could be any or all of the following:—

- Improve the quality of citizen services
- Improve the internal efficiencies of the Govt. dept. or agency
- Better enforcement of law
- Promotion & Outreach activities
- Education & Information

It is necessary to identify and prioritize the IT projects in different departments along the above lines. An exercise has already been started in this direction.

The next step is to impart the necessary skills to the senior functionaries of the Government like the Secretaries and the Heads of the Departments and to draw up plans of action that identify the clear objectives of each IT project, the resources required, the HRD and change management required and the phasing.

• Local Language initiative

All the major IT projects have adopted English as the medium. However, for administration to be effective and for the benefits of computerization to reach the common man, it is desirable to adopt Telugu as the medium. The Government of AP has appointed a Committee headed by the Chairman of the Official Language Commission to design and develop standards for use of the Telugu Font on computers, development of Internet content in Telugu, translation of English content to Telugu and suggest the steps necessary to promote the use of Telugu in computers.

The Committee has submitted its recommendations to the Government in June 2000. **The consequential action to notify the standards and implement the other recommendations of the Committee would be taken in July 2000.**

• Security Policy

Security of the data is of paramount importance for a reliable and stable administration. The Government of AP intends to develop a security policy by engaging an international consultancy firm for the purpose and implement firewalls around all major databases.

• Computerization of Collectorates

The Collectorates are still the pivotal units for maintaining and improving the standards of administration. The computerization of collectorates is one of the major components of e-Governance as this is an institution that has a large citizen interface and the common man sees the collectorate as the enduring symbol of governance. The Government intends to computerize all the 23 collectorates by developing common software with the following objectives:—

- Provide a computerized interface to the citizen for all his needs.
- Workflow automation of all standard licensing and permit procedures.
- Dissemination of Information useful to the citizens
- Monitoring of all developmental activities.

A number of programmes have been developed in different Districts over a period of time. Some of them have registered stable and useful operations over the last 2 years. It is proposed to integrate all such packages into the proposed comprehensive system so as to save time and effort.

• Mandal level horizontal integration of departments

There are 1122 mandals in the state. All the mandal offices are going to be provided with computers under the MPHS project. Computerized systems are available at 214 sub-registrar offices and the 300 sub-treasuries also. It is envisaged that major IT projects would be taken up in at least 25 departments over the next 5 years, out of which around 10 will extend to mandal level administrative units as well. Examples are police, agriculture, education, health, panchayati raj, engineering, welfare, cooperation, veterinary and self-help groups etc.

It is necessary to network these institutions horizontally so that we derive optimum synergy from the efforts of various departments. By integrating thus, we add to the citizen's convenience as he need not go to several government institutions but can get things done at a single location. We also add to the efficiency and effectiveness of administration by eliminating duplication of work in several departments.

It is proposed to undertake a pilot project at one representative mandal initially to gauge the technicalities and complexities involved in this proposal. The pilot project, once perfected, can then be extended to all other mandals in a phased manner.

• Internet & e-mail policy

The entire secretariat workplace comprising of 2000 nodes has been brought on to a LAN with a bandwidth of 10 Mbps to 622 Mbps over optic fibre. Internet facility has been provided to all the users of the rank of Deputy Secretary and above.

Simultaneously internet facility through dial up is in the process of being extended to all the Heads of Department at Hyderabad. Similarly all the Dist. Collectors, Heads of different offices in district level will also have internet facility through APSWAN. To provide quality internet facility, it is proposed to provide 2 MBPS internet leased circuit connecting APSCAN to VSNL. The feasibility of securing a 2 Mbps satellite connectivity through NIC is also under consideration.

E-Mail:

E-mail has caught the imagination of one and all and going to be the most effective way of communication from end to end. Realizing the importance of E-mail communication, Govt. Of Andhra Pradesh has extended this facility to all its employees in Secretariat and the facility is also being extended to HoDs through dial up to start with. This facility will also be available to all the Offices at District level very soon.

Datawarehouse:

The Data Warehouse project jointly implemented by the Andhra Pradesh State Government and C-DAC, Pune has two core objects. *i.e.* (i) Person object and (ii) Land object. The main source of data for these core objects is MPHS data and Land Records data. The data will be cleansed and loaded into PARAM Super computer which has been installed at Secretariat, Hyderabad in June 2000. The web-enabled data will be made available to all Govt. Agencies for planning and analysis.

The person object has information like name, father's name, sex, religion, caste, occupation and land object contains name of the owner, extent of land, nature of land, nature of crops raised, type of irrigation source. Different types of analysis can be made on both the objects with different permutations and combinations. **The pilot level implementation of project is planned to be achieved by August, 2000.**

Electronic Kiosks:

To enable the citizens to have access to Government information and development activities and to bring transparency in the administration it is proposed to commission 10 electronic kiosks in the State on a pilot basis. The Government intends to encourage setting up the internet kiosks on the lines of public telephone booths not only to serve the information needs of the citizens but also to provide employment to a large number of educated youth. For the kiosk to be viable, it has to handle several.

• CIO's

Can there be an institutionalized programme to produce champions who understand Government and Information technology? A fund of officers who can make many e-governance projects bloom. That was the idea which inspired the Government of Andhra Pradesh, Indian Institute of Management-Ahmedabad and Satyam School of Applied Information Systems, IIIT-Hyderabad to conceptualize and design a unique Advanced Management Programme (AMP) in Information Systems and Electronic Governance. What makes the programme unique is not just its first-class pedigree but also the fact that it envisages a direct linkage with a live e-governance project implementation in the field in AP. Thus, the programme would juxtapose theory and practice, academic rigour and pragmatic realism so that one can have several more e-governance projects happen in myriad spheres of interface between government, business and citizens in AP. We believe that initially individuals produce institutions. Later Institutions produce individuals. This is the touchstone if any, to judge the Chief Information Officer Programme of Andhra Pradesh.

The training programme for the first batch of 25 CIO's starts at IIM Ahmedabad from 10th July 2000. It is proposed to continue the efforts and train a total of 100 CIO's in the next 4 years.

• Centre for Good Governance

It is proposed to start a Centre for Good Governance to be a focal point for IIRD required for the purpose. It includes a component for showcasing all successful e-Governance projects and conducting research and training on the methodologies and technologies appropriate for these projects. This project will be useful to all other Governments also. The project is being implemented with assistance from DFID at the Dr. MCR Human Resource Development Centre, Hyderabad.

- **Financing e-Governance projects**

In a world of increasing fiscal deficits, it is inappropriate for Governments to think of finding financial resources for implementation and maintenance of major IT projects in the area of e-Governance.

Many good IT projects decline in performance for want of timely availability of funds for maintenance of systems, consumable and upgradation. These gaps are much more devastating as the technologies change by the month.

At the same time, the Government's firm intention is to use IT in all aspects of development and governance. In this context, it was felt essential to put in place a framework to create local equilibrium within each IT project that matches the need for funds with a source of revenue from the transactions.

The Government intends to create sources of income to each major IT projects in the area of e-Governance within the framework of the functioning of the department. The policy allows the departments to fix service charges after ensuring that quality of service is defined precisely and that the solution offered is the most cost-effective one.

- **Cyber Laws:** Andhra Pradesh is committed to ensuring that the overall legal regime is in consonance with the requirements of transactions and interactions in the electronic medium. The State Government shall examine all the state level legislation and statutes so as to ensure the necessary harmonizations with the above objective in mind. The overall objective is to provide a transparent, simple and enforceable set of laws, which shall facilitate e-business and all other IT-enabled activities.

- **Reorganization and strengthening of IT&C department:** The Information Technology & Communications department has functioned as a thin organization deriving strengths from sister organizations like the AP Industrial Infrastructure Corporation, APTS etc. However, sustained efforts are not possible unless the Department has adequate human resources to drive the ambitious initiatives. An organizational structure consisting of the following wings is proposed to be established for this purpose—
  - Policy formulation & Planning
  - Promotion of IT

- E-Governance
- HRD in IT
- Infrastructure
- Administration

Private sector talent is proposed to be drawn in areas like promotion and Infrastructure planning.

IV. HUMAN RESOURCE DEVELOPMENT

The spectacular growth of software industry all over the world has generated a huge demand for highly skilled Information Technology manpower resulting in projections of a long-term global demand-supply gap for such manpower. Unlike the traditional industries, human resource constitutes the single most important resource in the Information Technology industry and the finest companies in Information Technology funnel their growth into areas that have the richest availability of skilled IT manpower.

Tremendous potential exists in Andhra Pradesh for generating such skilled software professionals. Among the states of India, Andhra Pradesh contributes the highest percentage of IT professionals. The IT industry in Andhra Pradesh has been consistently registering a growth of more than 100% per year for the last several years, necessitating rapid increase in the number of highly skilled IT professionals to sustain such growth.

There has been a significant increase in the academic institutions, such as engineering, MCA and BCA colleges and polytechnics that offer IT education in the state. The state now has 102 engineering colleges with an annual intake of 24,135 students (out of which 4,750 students pursue computer science and 2,200 are in IT programmes). Colleges offering MCA number 118 and enroll 3730 students annually and there are 413 BCA colleges that enroll 16520 students annually. In addition, there are 103 Polytechnics with an annual intake of 17,100 out of which 3,500 students are enrolled in IT related courses. This educational infrastructure will generate a significant number of IT professionals to fuel the growth of IT industry in the state. In order to generate highly skilled IT professionals, the areas that need attention are:

1. Addressing problems that colleges face in attracting and retaining high calibre faculty;
2. Getting high bandwidth access to the internet and thereby to resources available from other institutions; and
3. Providing students and faculty members with state-of-the-art technologies on a continuing basis.

It is also relevant to note that generation of highly skilled IT professionals requires high initial as well as ongoing investment to provide access to state-of-the-art-technology. In view of the rapid developments in Information Technology, keeping pace with the requirements of the Industry calls for regular and frequent changes in curriculum, provision of access to new technologies, new hardware as well as software, along with highly qualified researchers and academicians. Competition in IT industry is not confined within traditional geographical boundaries. The compensation offered by the Industry for persons holding high qualifications and experience in Information Technology is very high as compared to what is offered by conventional academic institutions.

Certain strengths have been built in the recent past that can be tapped to address some of these issues.

Indian Institute of Information Technology

The Government of Andhra Pradesh has played a lead role in the establishment of Indian Institute of Information Technology (IIIT) at Hyderabad. The Institute is established with the active participation, support and contribution of the finest global and Indian IT companies. The aim is to pool the strengths and resources of the best companies with facilitation and support of the Government to create an institution designed to play the role that Stanford University has played for Silicon Valley. IIIT commenced its main academic programme in the year 1998 with a four-year Undergraduate Programme in Information Technology.

While the Government has provided land and initial infrastructure on a long-term lease, major global IT companies like IBM, Oracle, Microsoft, Metamor & Satyam are directly participating in the establishment of this Institution and have signed agreements with the Government of Andhra Pradesh to set up Schools of Excellence within IIIT, which would focus on IT education and training in their respective areas of core competence. Three of the schools *viz.* "IBM School of Enterprise Wide Computing", "Metamor School of Excellence in Software Development Methodologies" and "Oracle School of Advance Software Technology" have already commenced operations. The conceptual model of IIIT has emerged as an embodiment of industry-academia interaction across a spectrum of academic, research and training activities.

IIIT plans to conduct interdisciplinary research and development in IT. Research centres of international standards are planned that will focus on areas and problems of most significance to IT and the nation. The first research centre of IIIT, Language Technologies Research Centre (LTRC), has already become operational. Its research activity focuses on language translation especially among Indian languages and from English to Indian languages, search engines for Indian languages, information extraction from text, summarisation, information retrieval, speech recognition/generation for Indian languages, and optical character recognition for Indian scripts.

Networked Universities and Colleges within the state

With the rich pool of technology, research and faculty resources at IIIT, the institute can spearhead the process of networking universities, colleges and research centres within the state and the country. It can also serve as a resource centre for upgradation of curriculum and training of teachers of various colleges and institutions across the state. IIIT is expected to be an active participant in the establishment of Sankhya Vahini, a high bandwidth optic fibre based national network that would connect research institutions, universities and educational institutions in all the major Indian cities with each other, thereby enabling sharing of resources among all of them. Through this network, excellent multimedia educational content created by IIITs, IISc, IIIT as well as from foreign institutions like the Carnegie Mellon University is expected to become available to all the participating institutions all over the country. Coupling the A P State Wide Area Network that is now connecting 25 locations within A P with a 2 MBPS link, with the Sankhya Vahini, will provide a robust network that would bring rich academic content and resources into the entire technical education system.

Distance Education and Electronic Classrooms

High quality academic programmes can be conducted in electronic classrooms in several locations across the state to generate a high number of IT professionals. Such programmes can be tailored not only to the requirements of students of computer science or information technology but also for students in other engineering disciplines and in diverse academic streams like Medicine, Law, Economics, Commerce, Sciences, Mathematics, etc. Electronic classrooms equipped with suitable projection equipment would be set up for receiving and effectively using digital content. Existing computer labs would be strengthened and made available to students to browse content received in the form of CDs. Universities and major institutions would also be encouraged to create suitable infrastructure like classroom studio/video recording equipment etc.

Universities and their research centres & laboratories have strengths in certain areas. Each university and participating institution would be encouraged to identify areas in which it would be willing to digitize educational content to make it available for other participating institutions. Teachers and resource persons to be entrusted with the responsibility of creating content would also be identified by the respective Universities and participating institutions.

Each of the Universities and institutions would be encouraged to create significant web presence. Existing websites would be strengthened and new websites would be created by the institutions. A central website of the A.P. State Council of Higher Education would be created to serve as a portal that would catalogue the content and resources available on the websites of various universities and institutions and would provide links to all the relevant sites.

Private Computer Training Institutions

There has been a remarkable growth in the number of private training institutions offering computer-related courses. Such institutions are now available even in small towns across the state. Their offerings cover a wide spectrum of technologies and skills. There is a wide variation in the quality of infrastructure and facilities available with these institutions. The quality of instruction imparted by them ranges from very high to indifferent quality.

The Government will encourage collective efforts by the institutions engaged in computer training to define common standards and self-regulatory mechanisms, as well as the establishment of independent credible rating mechanisms for such training institutions. The Government will also support high quality institutions by involving them to meet the internal training requirements within the Government.

Use of IT in Education

Information Technology will be used in the area of school education in two distinct segments, one comprising computer literacy and skills in information technology and the other related to its use to enhance the effectiveness of teaching in other subjects. Government of Andhra Pradesh is planning various initiatives in both these segments. These would take into account the requirements in these segments in primary, secondary, higher secondary and intermediate levels of education. As a part of these initiatives, mechanisms for imparting rudimentary computer literacy as well as skills in use of various software and hardware products would be created. The latest teaching and learning technologies would be applied to increase effectiveness of teaching in other subjects.

The Government has earlier implemented the CLASS project in various schools. This project is now being implemented with appropriate changes in curriculum, software and hardware.

The Smart Schools programme taken up by the Ministry of Human Resource Development, Government of India will also be implemented in the state.

The Government will focus on early implementation of computer literacy and training in IT skills in schools. Residential schools and junior colleges run by the A P Social Welfare Residential Educational Institutions Society would be accorded high priority while implementing such programmes.

In the recent months, some projects taken up elsewhere have been studied. The Tamil Nadu Schools Project has leveraged existing infrastructure of high schools and has involved companies engaged in computer training to conduct computer literacy and IT skills programmes for high school and intermediate students. Some innovative and cost effective technologies being used in various schools have also been studied.

Appropriate implementation models suitable for schools and institutions in Andhra Pradesh are being worked out, both for creation of multimedia content in various subjects and the establishment of cost effective delivery mechanisms. The Government will encourage the participation of multiple entities in the creation of multimedia educational content for various subjects. The Government will encourage development and deployment of cost effective technologies and delivery mechanisms that can bring about a quantum jump in the number of schools and students that have access to IT-enriched education.

National Institute for Smart Government

Based on a suggestion made by the Government of Andhra Pradesh, the National IT Task Force had recommended the establishment of a National Centre for SMART Government (NISG). Here SMART is an acronym for Simple, Moral, Accountable, Responsive and Transparent.

The Institute is expected to be an independent, autonomous, non-profit, viable and self-sustaining institution, which would focus on effectively harnessing Information Technology to bring about significant improvement in the citizen services, and would at the same time use IT to create opportunities for the people while protecting them from the risks involved in these processes. The proposed Institute would serve as a think tank and resource centre with expertise on all issues related to effective use of Information Technology in governance.

The Government proposes to play the role of a lead promoter of this institution. The services of the NISG would help the Government in its endeavour to improve the efficiency of operations in its departments and improve the quality, convenience and range of services offered to the common man.

V. PROMOTION

IT INVESTMENT PROMOTION & INCENTIVES POLICY

India's software exports have been growing at a compounded annual growth rate (CAGR) of around 56% while only one state has been consistently notching up triple figures of almost 121% CAGR over the last four years. That's AP. From a mere Rs 0.2 crores in 1992 the state will be touching Rs. 1,000 crores at the end of this financial year. When Microsoft wanted to establish an Overseas Development Center it chose Hyderabad, making it the second one anywhere outside the US. General Electric is setting up a 4000-person facility here. Hyderabad is also the home to Oracle, Metamor, HSBC, Ericsson, Tata Teleservices, Aristasoft, Motorola, Toshiba, Baan, TCS, Pentafour, Satyam, Wipro, to name just a few. From software development to IT enabled services to Internet startups, to e-business companies to small and medium IT companies to logistics companies—they are all here and thriving!

The state has, as part of a unique IT Incentives Policy, incentivised software employment by subsidizing land to the extent that one can even get it completely free! Further the state has reviewed all the major Acts and rules that regulate the IT industry and in most cases has either done away with the red tape completely or else has resorted to a self-certification process.

What is even more paramount is that AP is perhaps the only state in India, which has even begun to understand the first principles of doing business with business!! Andhra Pradesh is one of the few examples of success wherein the public and private sectors have worked in mutual synergy so as to bring out the best of each. A harmonious construction of the State and Market is the ultimate mantra of economic development. Something AP has internalized in its day-to-day functioning.

The bigger underlying shift for the Government is the one from mistrust to trust. And the Government aggressively and proactively invites industry to partner in its Development Dream.

e-COMMERCE

All belief is against it, all argument is for it !- Samuel Johnson would probably forgive us for misquoting him if only he knew how e-commerce is dramatically rewriting every known relationship across the globe. E-business in India would be a market worth Rs. 400 million by 2003 say Pricewater house Coopers (PWC) in the first ever Indian E-Commerce survey, while McKinsey pegs the figure at $1.5 billion by 2004 and around $10 billion by 2020, which would be approximately 1% of the world's e-commerce business. E-Commerce is something more than just buying and selling commodities across the globe. It is more about rewiring an entire set of relationships between consumers and producers, between corporations and within them, and between government, business and civil society. In fact the Internet is like a huge business super channel and anyone who does not tap it is actually losing revenue and losing opportunities, both at once.

Andhra Pradesh has clearly recognized this opportunity and is in the process of putting in place world-class infrastructure to enable this revolution to touch every aspect of human life in AP. For e-commerce to boom, one needs bandwidth, almost as much as people need oxygen. Recognizing this truth, the state endeavours to make available adequate bandwidth with international quality of service (QoS) at competitive prices to e-businesses and IT enabled services that wish to set-up shop in the state. Further with a slew of e-governance projects happening all over the state, it is virtually an open invitation to the private sector to partner and participate in these exciting endeavours. VCs and Angels are all over the place trying to fund potential winners in the battle of ideas. Further AP is also catalysing the development of various soft issues like lifestyle, entertainment and leisure, which are critical to the creation of the correct ambience for e-commerce and Net startups in the state. To summarize, just as e-Commerce is the future of IT; So is AP. Indeed, Useless is each without the other.

- **Promotion of Venture Capital**

Venture capital is an effective answer to meet the ambitious goals set by the Govt. of India for software exports (US $ 50 billion by 2008). A number of policy initiatives are required at the GOI level, mostly, if the ambition is to be realized. A SEBI committee headed by Sri KB Chandrasekharan, Chairman, Exodus, USA has made a few recommendations in this regard.

It shall be the endeavour of the State to pursue with GOI in this regard. The initiatives required are mentioned below:

- o IT start-ups look for capital typically based on the IP they hold rather than against any physical assets they can show as security.

  The investment climate has to change suitably to recognize the value of the IP and provide 'smart capital'.
- o Implementation of the VC Committee of SEBI involving
  - Notification of SEBI as the single window for all requirements of VC's.
  - Tax- pass through benefit to avoid double taxation, irrespective of the form of VC;
  - Creation of LLP's (Limited Liability Partnership);
  - ESOP (Employee Stock Option);
  - Permitting the Banks to invest in VC's~
  - Provide flexible options for entry and exit;
  - Simplify pricing norms of Rbi;
- o Develop managers for the VC sector.
- o Conducting seminars on VC's to increase the awareness and tap the hidden potential of sources of capital for VC's.
- o Creation of incubators for startup facilitation and providing monitoring and the benefits of networking with VC's.
- o Promote the concept of angel investors.

A few of the items on the above agenda can be done at the State level itself. For Instance, developing managers for the VC sector, organizing seminars and increasing awareness on VC's and angels, establishing incubators for the benefit of start-ups, etc.

Several VC funds have been created in the recent past in India — the 100 crore Fund at the National level, a US $ 100 mil fund at the international level besides the funds created by several state governments like Andhra Pradesh (Rs. 15 cr), and Tamil Nadu, Gujarat. It is necessary to ensure that these funds are managed professionally with the least involvement of the Government.

Annexure I

GOVERNMENT OF ANDHRA PRADESH

ABSTRACT

Government of Andhra Pradesh— Establishment of Apex bodies for promotion of Information Technology and e-Governance — Orders —Issued.

Finance & Planning (Plg. I.T.&C) Department

G. O.Ms.No.4 Dated: 24-1-2000

ORDER

The vision of the Government is to substantially enhance the standard of life of the citizens of the State, among other initiatives, through the use of Information Technology in all aspects of development and governance. The Government has recognized that development of Information Technology is the key to all round economic development and prosperity in the State. Government has also identified the uses of Information Technology within Government for better Governance, particularly for providing improved citizens services. It has also been recognized very clearly that this enormous task has to be undertaken in manageable steps and that both the IT&C department and individual departments and organizations in Government have definite roles to play in achieving this goal. Government recognized very clearly the need to institutionalize a mechanism to help departments to evolve, pursue and reach clearly identified goals in I.T. usage. The Government has felt the need for establishing a suitable apex structure within Government to drive the whole process of architecturing, guiding and monitoring the overall development of Information Technology industry in the State and its deployment within the Government for achieving the desired goals of economic development and good governance. It is therefore decided that a two-tier structure would be created for this purpose with the role and constitution as suggested at para 3.I and 3.II below. Information Technology and Communications wing would play the role of the Secretariat for these bodies.

2. It has also been decided that individual departments need to work out clear plans defining their information needs and the citizen services which are of priority for improvement. Constitution of departmental IT implementation committees is also felt necessary to drive these efforts. Indicative structure of the departmental Information Technology implementation committees with their scope is given in para 3.III.

3. Government hereby constitute the following committees (I & II) and suggests the composition for the departmental committees for which separate orders will be issued by the respective departments involving all the concerned and following the procedure prescribed.

The composition and the terms of reference for each of the committees is as detailed hereunder:

I. AP FIRST

Composition

1. Chief Minister
   Chairman
2. Minister for Finance
   Member
3. Minister for Revenue
   Member
4. Minister for Home
   Member
5. Adviser to Government on IT
   Member
6. Chief Secretary
   Member
7. Sri F.C.Kohli, Vice Chairman, Tata Consultancy Services
   Member
8. Sri Azim Premji, Chairman, Wipro Infotec
   Member
9. Sri Narayana Murthy, Chairman, Infosys Technologies
   Member
10. Sri Ramalinga Raju, Chairman, Satyam Computers
    Member
11. Dr. Raj Reddy, Professor, Carnegie Mellon University, USA Member
12. Sri Dewang Mehta, Director, NASSCOM
    Member

13. Secretary, IT Member—Convenor
14. Minister, Prl. Secretary / Secretary / HOD(s) concerned will be invited as special invitees, when specific projects are discussed.

Terms of reference of AP FIRST

- Formulation of IT Policy for the State.
- Promotion of investment in IT industries in the State.
- Clearance of major IT projects to be set up in the State.
- Clearance of IT plans of Government Departments.
- Promotion of centers of excellence in IT education.
- Promotion of citizen-centric projects of e-governance.
- Coordination with the Central Government agencies as required.
- Review of the progress of major IT projects in the State.
- Any other issue(s) concerning IT as found necessary from time to time.

The committee will meet once in two months preferably on a fixed date of alternate months.

II. STATE INFORMATION TECHNOLOGY PROMOTION COMMITTEE (ITPC)

Composition

1.	Chief Secretary	Chairman
2.	Chief Commissioner Land Administration	Member
3.	Spl. CS / Prl. Secretary, G.A. (AR&T) Dept.,	Member
4.	Director General, MCR HRD Institute, A.P.	Member
5.	Prl. Secretary, Revenue	Member
6.	Prl. Secretary, Finance	Member
7.	Secretary, Law	Member
8.	Secretary, G.A. (Co-ordination) Dept.,	Member
9.	Secretary, Planning	Member
10.	Secretary, I.T. & C	Member / Convenor

11. Prl.Secretary / Secretary / HOD (s) concerned will be invited as special invitees when specific projects are discussed.

Terms of reference of ITPC

- Evolve/Design IT architecture(s) for the State.
- Examination of proposals for major investment in IT industries in the State.
- Examination of IT plans of Government Department.

- Design of centers of excellence in IT education.
- Design of citizen-centric projects of e-governance.
- Promotion of development of IT infrastructure in the State.
- Review of the progress of major IT projects in the State.
- Approval of Technical Standards for implementation of IT applications.
- Evolve guidelines for cost-effective implementation of IT projects in Government.
- Any other issue(s) concerning IT as found necessary from time to time.

The committee will meet once a month, preferably on a fixed date of a month.

III. Departmental Committees on IT (C-IT)

(To be constituted by the Departments separately according to their actual requirements)

Suggested Composition of C-IT

Minister	Chairman.
Prl. Secretary / Secretary	Vice-Chairman & Convenor.
Heads of Departments	Members
Nominee of IT Department	Member
Chief Information Officers *(CIOs)	Members

Any other member as deemed fit by the constituting authority of the committee.

* (In cases where the CIOs are so far not appointed the departments will do so under intimation to IT&C).

Proposed Terms of reference:

- Design of IT plans for the Dept(s).
- Review of the progress of ongoing IT projects.
- HRD required for e-governance.
- Approval of major IT projects relating to the Dept(s).
- Implementation of IT projects with direct funding of the Government or through involvement of private sector.
- Re-engineering the administrativo processes to suit IT implementation.
- Change management within the department.
- Individual Departments depending on their specific

requirements will be adding to the scope of the committees as and when required.

4. The Committees I & II will come into force with immediate effect.

(BY ORDER AND IN THE NAME OF THE GOVERNOR OF ANDHRA PRADESH)

V. ANANDARAU
CHIEF SECRETARY TO
GOVERNMENT

To

The Chairman and Members,
The Member- Conveners,
All Departments of Secretariat,
Secretary, Dept., of Information Technology, Government of India, New Delhi,
Secretary, Dept. of Electronics, Govt. of India, New Delhi,
The Director, STPI, Hyderabad.
The Commissioner, Information and Public Relations, Hyderabad, with a request to arrange for necessary publicity,
All Heads of Departments,
M.D.., A.P.T.S.Ltd.,, B.R.K.R. Buildings, Hyderabad,
Chairman and M.D., APIIC, Basheerbagh, Hyderabad,
Chairman and M.D. TRANSCO, Vidyutsoudha, Hyderabad,
Project Director, TWINS Project, Jubilee Hills, Hyderabad,
Project Director, M.R.O. Offices Computerization, Nampally, Hyderabad.
The President, HYSEA, Maitrivanam, HUDA Complex, Hyderabad

Annexure II
Government of Andhra Pradesh

Abstract

Information Technology (IT) Policy of the Government of Andhra Pradesh—Incentives for promoting the IT Industry and IT Enabled Services in the State—Orders—Issued.

Finance and Planning (Plg.IT&C) Department.

G.O.Ms. No. 114.

Dated *25-05-1999.*
Read the following:

1. G.O.Ms.No.506, Revenue (CT.II) Department, dated 27.6.96
2. G.O.Ms.No. 67, Energy (Power. II) Department, dated 21-07-98.
3. G.O.Ms.No.161, EFS&T (Environment) Dept, dated 15-10-98.
4. G.O.Rt.No. 58, Finance and Planning (Plg.IT&C) Dept. Dated 1-2-99.
5. T.T.O (Commercial), No.173, Transmission Corprn. of A.P. Ltd dt. 10-5-99.

ORDER

Government of Andhra Pradesh has clearly recognized the strategic importance of information technology in creating a competitive economy equipped to face the challenges and exploit the opportunities of the future. Information Technology is increasingly permeating every facet of human endeavour and has radically transformed the way societies work, play, gather and access knowledge and govern themselves. Apart from the enormous benefits accruing from usage of information technology, it is also universally well recognized now that India enjoys a unique comparative advantage globally as a natural base for the information technology industry. The primary strength of the country in this sector is the vast, highly cost-effective, highly skilled and mostly English-knowing technical personnel available in the country.

2. Within the country, it is being increasingly recognized that Andhra Pradesh in general and Hyderabad in particular, is a favoured destination for the IT industry. Surveys reveal that Andhra Pradesh is the State from which the highest percentage (23%) of Indian IT professionals worldwide originate. The quality of urban infrastructure in Hyderabad, the low cost of living in relation to other destinations in the country for the industry, and the large number of technical personnel graduating from the various institutions in the state are some of the other factors that have added to the comparative advantages of Hyderabad.

3. In order to build on these strong fundamentals, the state has embarked on certain key initiatives in order to foster the rapid growth of the industry. It has established a major state-

of-the-art IT park, the Hyderabad Information Technology and Engineering Consultancy (HITEC) city at Madhapur, on the outskirts of the city through L&T Infocity, a joint venture between the State owned AP Industrial Infrastructure Corporation and *M/s.* Larsen and Toubro, together with the Software Technology Park, Hyderabad, the HITEC City provides all requisite infrastructure for IT companies such as reliable telecommunication links, uninterrupted power, etc. Along with speedy procedural clearances. The first phase of the project has already been inaugurated and a number of IT companies are now based there. Subsequent phases of the project are expected to ensure that the availability of infrastructure is always ahead of the demand in a sector that has been consistently growing at over 100% every year.

4. Recognizing that human resource development is the key to sustained growth in the sector, the Government embarked on another major initiative, the establishment of the Indian Institute of Information Technology (IIIT), Hyderabad. This Institute has been established as an autonomous industry—led and driven institution supported by the Government. Major IT companies including several Multi National Companies (MNCs) have participated in the establishment of the institution. As a result of this joint effort, the IIIT is endowed with state-of-the-art facilities and highly competent faculty. With its emphasis on IT enabled and distance education, the Institute is expected to make a major contribution both directly and indirectly (in conjunction with the technical institutions in the state) to the continuous generation of the increasing number of skilled personnel that the industry needs. A large number of training institutions that have sprung up in the state in general and Hyderabad in particular, have seen the emergence of Hyderabad as a major IT training Centre of the country.

5. Other initiatives taken by the State include the establishment of a venture capital fund, HITVEL (Hyderabad Information Technology Venture Enterprises Limited). A special package for start-up companies, which includes venture capital, leased space (including fully furnished space) is also being worked out by APIIC, HITVEL and Software Technology Park of India (STPI), Hyderabad.

6. Another major initiative of the State Government that

has implications for the growth of the IT industry in the State is the move towards ushering in an electronic Government in the State. The primary objective of this effort is to leverage the power of modern Information and Communication Technology to provide more convenient, accessible and transparent Government services to citizens and at the same time, improve efficiency in government. As far as possible, the Government intends to utilize the capabilities and resources of the local IT software and services industry in its efforts towards ushering in an electronic government. This would also provide a strong domestic market for the IT industry, in addition to the offshore market. Some of the major computerization projects undertaken include Mandal computerization project, Treasuries, Commercial Taxes, Registration, Land Records, Employment Exchanges, Rural Development, Twin Cities Network Services project, etc. Major IT infrastructure projects namely the State Wide Area Network, Secretariat Campus Network, Video conferencing project etc. Are nearing completion and are expected to provide a sound basis for a modern Information and communication technology enabled Governance system.

7. The above initiatives together with the efforts of the Software Technology Park, Hyderabad have seen the industry reach an export turnover of nearly Rs. 600 crores in 1998-1999 with nearly 200 registered companies. This turnover is expected to touch Rs.1200 crores in 1999-2000.

8. The State Government has been actively and constantly monitoring the incentives necessary to foster the rapid growth of the industry. A major growth area identified is IT Enabled Services (ITES) or 'Remote Services'. In 1998, this segment generated more than Rs. 980 crores in revenues in India. It is estimated that by the year 2008, the ITES industry in India would generate annual revenue of US $ 20 billion (Rs. 85,000 crores) leading to opportunities for more than 10,000 full-fledged units. The ITES sector, like the software industry, requires a conducive environment and access to large pools of skilled to semi-skilled professionals. ITES affords a unique opportunity for providing employment to large numbers of qualified unemployed youth in the state as well as business opportunities for budding knowledge entrepreneurs. Keeping in view the intensely cost-competitive nature of this sector globally, the need

to have a specific set of incentives tailored to the requirements of this sector has been considered by the Government in order to attract the maximum employment potential of the industry to the state. An employment-linked incentive has accordingly been worked out to link the incentives given by the State directly to the employment generated.

9. Feedback received during deliberations with the industry also indicated that there is a need to provide certain incentives to the IT/IT infrastructure industry to ensure conditions conducive to its establishment and sustained growth in the State. A number of suggestions were also received for simplification of procedures for compliance with various regulatory Acts and Rules. Following are some of the aspects on which the industry had proposed incentives/procedural simplification:

(a) Exemption from environmental clearance;
(b) Exemption from zoning regulations for purposes of location;
(c) Fiscal incentives;
(d) Power tariff at rates applicable to industry;
(e) Exemption from sales tax;
(f) Self-certification for purposes of compliance of the following Acts:
   (i) Water and Air Pollution Act;
   (ii) Factories Act;
   (iii) Employment Exchange (Notification of Vacancies Act);
   (iv) Payment of Wages Act;
   (v) Minimum Wages Act;
   (vi) Contract Labour (Regulation and Abolition) Act;
   (vii) Workmen Compensation Act;
   (viii) Andhra Pradesh Shops and Establishments Act; and
   (ix) Employees State Insurance Act.
(g) General permission to run a three-shift operation;
(h) Rebate in land cost keeping in view the high employment potential;
(i) Relaxation of FAR for IT parks;
(j) Exemption from stamp duty, transfer of property and registration charges for all IT parks; etc.

10. Against the background narrated above, the Government of Andhra Pradesh decided to frame an appropriate

package of incentives for the IT and IT Infrastructure industry. The purpose of the package is to enable the State to leverage its resources and facilitate their optimal utilization to the best advantage of the State; provide a relative competitive edge over other competing markets; tap the massive employment potential of the global IT market in IT (software and hardware) and IT enabled Services. Accordingly, a proposal was prepared and discussed with all the departments concerned either individually or in the SIPC/ SIPB. The Cabinet Sub-Committee constituted in the orders 4th read above also considered the proposed incentives.

11. After careful consideration of all relevant aspects of the issue, Government approve the following package of incentives for the IT industry and for IT Infrastructure:

Note: 1. IT includes IT and Telecommunications.

2. IT Industry includes IT hardware and software industries; IT software industry includes IT software, IT services and IT enabled services.
3. IT Infrastructure means the physical Infrastructure built by a firm or a builder and sold to an IT Industry for its own use or the Infrastructure built by an IT Industry for its own use.
4. In case of any ambiguity in implementing/inter-preting this policy, clarifications issued from time to time by IT&C Department shall prevail.

(a) **IT Software** industry is exempted from the purview of the **AP Pollution Control Act**, except in respect of power generation sets (orders issued by Environment, Forest, Science and Technology Department *vide* reference 3rd cited);

(b) **IT industry** is exempted from the purview of statutory power cuts (orders issued by Energy department *vide* reference 2nd & 5th cited);

(c) **Industrial power tariff** and all other admissible incentives and concessions applicable to industries in respect of power shall be applicable to **the IT Industry** including those in the urban areas (orders issued by Energy Department *vide* reference 2nd & 5th cited);

- 25% concessional power tariff **shall be allowed to the** new IT Industrial units for a period of 3 years from the date of release of power or of going into actual commercial production which ever is earlier.

Note: Concessions provided by the A.P.TRANSCO, to the IT industry are elaborated in the reference 5th cited.

(d) The Government *vide* reference lst cited have totally exempted, computer software from the payment of Sales Tax payable under the provisions of *A.P. General Sales Tax Act, 1957;*

(e) IT Software Industry is exempted from zoning regulations for purposes of location;

(f) Government agree in principle to self-certification/ exemption as far as possible for the IT Software Indu-stry from the provisions of the following Acts/ Regulations (subject to issue of specific orders by the departments concerned in consultation with the I.T&C Department);

(i) Factories Act;
(ii) Employment Exchange (Notification of Vacancies Act);
(iii) Payment of Wages Act;
(iv) Minimum Wages Act;
(v) Contract Labour (Regulation and Abolition) Act;
(vi) Workmen Compensation Act;
(vii) Andhra Pradesh Shops and Establishments Act; and
(viii) Employees State Insurance Act.

(g) General permission is accorded to run a three-shift operation to the IT Software industry *(subject to issue of specific detailed order separately by the department concerned);*

(h) Rebate in the cost of land allotted to an IT industry at Rs. 20,000/-(Twenty thousand only) per job created subject to the following conditions:

(i) The rebate shall be applicable only in respect of lands allotted by Government/APIIC with prospective effect;
(ii) The rebate shall be restricted to Rs. 20,000/- per job created or the cost of the bare land (excluding development charges/cost) whichever is less subject to a ceiling computed at the rate 0.30 acres for every 100 jobs created. {Eg. If *3250* jobs

are created the limit for allotment of land at concessional price would be *9.75* acres}.

(iii) The minimum number of employees to be hired by a company in order to avail of the concession on land cost shall be 100 (corresponding to a ceiling of 0.30 acres of land).

(iv) On areas allotted in excess of the limit i.e. the ceiling of 0.30 acres for every 100 jobs created, no concessions would be applicable;

(v) The minimum gross salary! wage for an employment to be considered to have been created would be *Rs. 5000/-* per month;

(vi) The period for which such employment would have to be sustained to be eligible to be reckoned for this incentive shall be two years;

(vii) The number of employees to be considered for the purpose of this provision shall not exceed the number arrived at by the formula: [no. of computer work stations at a location × *(1.33)* × number of shifts *(of 8 hours each)* operated by the company at the location];

(viii) APIIC shall specify suitable guidelines to ensure that the benefit of this provision reaches a company only after it meets the stipulated conditions regarding job creation and that the employment figures reported are corroborated by other supporting data such as investment, turnover, returns filed with RBI, returns filed with STPI, Hyderabad, etc.;

(ix) Cost of these incentives to APIIC shall be offset against cost of Government lands alienated to APIIC;

(x) The concessions linked to employment generation will be limited to the extent of the number of persons of Andhra Pradesh origin employed by the company. A Company will be free to employ persons as per their own policies subject to conformity with local regulations as applicable. However, the concessions available under this incentive will be restricted to the number of persons of AP origin employed by the company. For the purposes of this provision, a person of AP origin is defined as a person who, at the time of employment by the company has been:

- A resident of the State of AP;
- Domiciled in the State of AP;
- Born in the State of AP;
- Studied in a school/college/university in the State of AP;
- A person either of whose parents was born or attended school/college/University in AP or was domiciled in AP.

(i) For IT infrastructure companies establishing facilities on private /APIIC/ Government lands, concessions will be in the form of rebate on registration and transfer of property charges and exemption from stamp duty on a tapering scale for sale/lease of built-up space to the IT Industry:—

(i) For facilities established and sold/leased before 1-4-2000, 90% rebate;

(ii) For facilities established and sold/leased on or after 1-4-2000 but before 1-4-2001, 70% rebate; and

(iii) For facilities established and sold/leased on or after 1-4-2001 and upto 3 1-3-2002, 50% rebate.

(iv) This concession would be available only to IT parks notified by the Department of Information Technology and Communications and which provide certain minimum facilities like uninterrupted/backup power, reliable telecom links, etc.

(v) The rebate would be applicable on the combined levy of registration fee, stamp duty and transfer of property duty and no total exemption of stamp duty would be extended.

(vi) This concession would be available only for the first transaction, when the first sale by the infrastructure company is made to an IT industry.

(vii) The above concession would also be available on the purchase of land by an IT Industry establishing an IT park for its own use provided it does not avail of the concession in para (h) above, *i.e.* rebate on cost of land linked to employment. IT&C Department would stipulate such conditions as may be necessary in this regard while notifying such IT parks.

(j) For IT Industry/IT infrastructure companies establishing facilities on private lands outside the limits of the Municipal Corporations and the nine surrounding municipalities of Hyderabad and Gaddiannaram village, relaxation of FAR to the extent of 50% of the prevailing norm will be available. For example, if the normal FAR is 1.5, the FAR allowed in such cases would be 2.25.

- This concession would be available only to IT parks notified by the Department of Information Technology and Communications and which provide certain minimum facilities like uninterrupted/backup power, reliable telecom links, etc.
- This incentive would not be available in respect of Government/APIIC lands allotted at a concessional price.

(k) District headquarters and other major economic nodes in the State like Vijayawada and Tirupathi offer highly competitive locations for siting IT parks for IT Enabled Services as skilled and semi-skilled manpower is readily available at these locations and the cost of living is very low. Government will consider providing required telecommunication linkage through the A.P. State Wide Area Network (APSWAN) to such IT parks coming up at these locations. This will also enable APSWAN to meet one of its targeted objectives of serving as a highway for jobs in ITES to flow down to the hinterland.

(l) Investment subsidy for new IT (hardware and software) industries:

Investment subsidy: 20% of the fixed capital investment but not exceeding Rs. 20.00 lakhs; however in respect of Entrepreneurs belonging to Scheduled Castes and Scheduled Tribe Categories the investment shall be 25% of Fixed Capital Cost, not exceeding Rs. 50.00 lakhs. This subsidy shall not be available to IT Industries availing of the rebate on land cost as provided in para (h) above.

(i) Fixed capital investment, wherever referred to in

this order shall always mean the original fixed capital invested in the project before depreciation.

(ii) The I.T&C Department shall prescribe a procedure for scrutiny and sanction of the claim of units involving eligible capital investment as specified from time to time. The Commissioner of Industries shall pay the sanctioned amounts to the units from the same provision and head of account from which investment subsidy is paid to industries.

(iii) The decisions of the Information Technology and Communications Department shall be final in scrutinising and deciding the eligible investment and sanctioning the incentives for eligible industries.

(m) Special Incentives for Mega Projects/Pioneering Projects:
For Mega Projects, with investment exceeding Rs. 100 crores, Government may consider Special Package of Incentives, on a case to case basis, based on the gestation period of projects, pioneer nature of projects, locational aspects, state of the art technology, profitability, scope for further related investments, etc.

(n) The above incentives will be inclusive of any similar incentives of State Government/Central Government institutions/Agencies already availed/Central incentives which may be announced from time to time by the Government of India and other such incentives extended by any other Government agency.

(o) The package of concessions will initially be valid for a period of three years and subject to review thereafter.

12. This order issues with the concurrence of the Finance wing of this department vide U.O. No.1961/P.F.S/99 dated 22.05.1999.

(BY ORDER AND IN THE NAME OF THE GOVERNOR OF ANDHRA PRADESH)

R.Chandrashekhar,
Secretary to Government.

To

All the Departments of Secretariat,
Commissioner Municipal Administration,

Commissioner and I.G Stamps and Registration,
Commissioner Industries,
Chairnnan and Managing Director APIIC,
Managing Director APIDC,
Commissioner Information and Public Relations,
Managing Director A.P.T.S. Ltd.,
Member Secretary A.P. Pollution Control Board,
Chairman GENGO/TRANSCO,
Commissioner Commercial Taxes,
Director Employment and Training,
Commissioner Labour,
Director of Factories and Boilers,
Director Employees State Insurance,
Copy to
STPI, Hyderabad,
DOE, GOI
Chief Ministers Office/Chief PRO to C.M
Secretary to C.M/Special Secretary to C.M

Annexure III

GOVERNMENT OF ANDHRA PRADESH

ABSTRACT

Committees — Information Technology & Communications Department —Consultative Committee on IT Industry (CCITI) — Constituted — Orders —Issued.

INFORMATION TECHNOLOGY & COMMUNICATIONS DEPARTMENT

G.O.Ms.No.3 Dated: 25.5.2000

Read the following:

1. G.O.Ms.No.114, Finance & Planning (Plg.IT&C) Department, dt. 25.5.1999.
2. A.P.FIRST, Information Technology Policy — 2000 (Feb.2000)
3. G.O.Ms.No. 133, GA (AR&T.I.) Department, dt.10.4.2000

Order

The Government has announced its policy of incentives for the IT Industry in reference first read above, and the IT policy has been announced in February, 2000 in reference second read above. Both these policies spell out certain incentives to the industry land place certain responsibilities on the industry as well. The speedy realization of the goals set in the policy document assumes that the commitments on either side are kept up promptly. This needs a tremendous level of coordination between the various functionaries of the Government on the one hand and the representatives of the Industry on the other, for prescribing Procedures, issue of consequent Guidelines and Notifications contemplated under the aforementioned policies, resolving difference in interpretation, etc., in several matters, such as Labour laws, power supply rates allotment of land, stamp duty rebates etc. To resolve the existing/anticipated problems in implementation of the IT policy's for speedy realization of the goals set forth in the IT Policy document, the need for a standing Committee to fulfill the objectives of efficient coordination between the functionaries of Government and representatives of Industry is highly felt.

2. In the aforementioned circumstances, Government here by constitute a standing Committee to be called Consultative Committee on IT Industry (CCITI), with the following composition:

1.	Secretary, IT&C	Chairman
2.	Chairman A.P. Transco	Member
3.	Commr., & IG Registration	Member
4.	ED, APIIC	Member
5.	GM Telecom (to be nominated by CGM)	Member
6.	Representative of Labour Dept.,	Member
7.	Representative of Commr., Customs	Member
8.	President, HYSEA (Sri J.A. Choudary)	Member
9.	Secretary, HYSEA (Sri Mallikarjuna Rao)	Member
10.	Representative of IT Industry to be nominated in consultation with HYSEA	Member
11.	Representative of L&T Infocity	Member
12.	Joint Collector, RR District	Member
13.	Director, STPI, Hyderabad	Member Secretary

3. The Committee constituted above shall meet once in two months and resolve the pending issues.

4. A copy of this order is available on the Internet land can be accessed at the address http://apts. gov.in/apgos.

(BY ORDER AND IN THE NAME OF THE GOVERNOR OF ANDHRA PRADESH)

J .SATYANARAYANA,
SECRETARY TO GOVERNMENT

To

All the Departments of Secretariat,
Commissioner, Municipal Administration,
Commissioner & I.G. Stamps and Registration,
Commissioner, Industries,
Chairman and Managing Director, APIIC,
Managing Director, APIIDC,
Commissioner, Information and Public Relations,
Managing Director, A.P.T. S. Ltd.,
Member Secretary, A.P. Pollution Control Board,
Chairman, GENCO/TRANSCO,
Commissioner, Commercial Taxes,
Director of Factories and Boilers,
Director, Employees State Insurance,

Copy to :

STPI, Hyderabad
Department of Electronics, Government of India
Chief Minister's Office/Chief PRO to C.M.
Secretary to C.M /Special Secretary to C.M.
Sri J.A. Choudary, President, HYSEA,
(Hyderabad Software Exports Association),
Sri Mallikarjuna Rao, Secretary, HYSEA,
Collector & District Magistrate, R.R. District
Jt. Collector, R.R. District, Andhra Pradesh.

Annexure IV

GOVERNMENT OF ANDHRA PRADESH

ABSTRACT

IT Incentive Policy- Issue of certain guidelines for speedy and effective implementation of IT Incentive Policy- Orders — Issued.

INFORMATION TECHNOLOGY & COMMUNICATIONS DEPARTMENT

G.O.Ms.No. 5. Dt.16-06-2000

Read the following :

1. G.O. Ms.No.114 Finance and Planning (Plg.IT&C) Department Dated 25-05-1999
2. A. P FIRST, Information Technology Policy — 2000 (Feb.- 2000)
3. G.O. Ms.No.3.IT&C Department Dated 25-05-2000
4. This Office Letter No. 263/JIT&C/2000 Dt.15-05-2000 to the CMD, APIIC
5. Letter No. 114/PM (IPU)/APIIC/2000 Dt.30-05-2000 from APIIC

ORDER

With a view to attract I.T Investments and to help in promoting the growth and sustenance of the I.T. Industry in the State, the Government announced a package of incentives to the IT industry in the orders 1st read above. In order to ensure proper coordination between the various functionaries of the Government and the representatives of the I.T. Industry, Government in the orders 3rd read above constituted a Consultative Committee on IT Industry (CCITI) under the Chairmanship of the Secretary, IT&C.

2. The package of incentives announced includes a rebate on cost of land allotted by Government or APIIC, rebate on stamp duty on transfer of land, 25 % concession in power tariff for new units upto 3 years, etc. It is considered necessary to create an institutional mechanism for determining the eligibility of the applicant industries to the various incentives and also to issue a set of guidelines for facilitating the process, as some of the

incentives need decisions to be taken at certain levels in Government. It is felt desirable to give a single window clearance for all incentives through such a mechanism. A set of guidelines for allotment of APIIC Lands on concessional rates to IT entrepreneurs was arrived at after detailed discussions with APIIC. A comprehensive set of guidelines has been prepared covering all aspects relating to the grant of incentives to IT Industries *viz.* format for application, eligibility criteria, procedure for processing the applications, the formalities to be followed by an allottee or grantee, the terms and conditions of allotment or grant etc.

3. After a careful consideration it is hereby ordered that the CCITI constituted in the orders 3rd read above will be the single window of reference for recommending grant of all the IT incentives made available under the orders 1st read above. CCITI in this connection will follow the guidelines mentioned in the annexure to this Order.

4 This order does not require the concurrence of Finance and Planning (Finance Wing) Dept.

5. Copy of this order is also available on the Internet and can be accessed at the address: http: //apts.gov.in/apgos

(BY ORDER AND IN THE NAME OF THE GOVERNOR OF ANDHRA PRADESH)

—J. SATYANARAYANA
SECRETARY TO GOVERNMENT

To,

The Principal Secretary, Ind. & Com Dept.,
The M.D, APIIC,
The Principal Secretary, Fin. & Plg. (Fin. Wing) dept.,
The Special Chief Secretary, LET&F Dept.,
The Principal Secretary, Revenue Department,
The Principal Secretary, Energy Department,
The Principal Secretary, MA&UD Dept.,
The Director, STPI, Hyderabad,
The Secretary, I& P.R.,
Commissioner Industries,
All the Members of CCITI,
The Special Secretary to Chief Minister,

The A.G., A.P., Hyderabad.
S/F
Spare

Forwarded By Order

SECTION OFFICER

Annexure to G.O. Ms. No. 5. IT&C Dept., Dated: 16-06-2000

GUIDELINES FOR GRANT OF INCENTIVES TO IT INDUSTRIES—(Under G.O. Ms. No. 114 Finance & Planning (Plg. IT&C) Department dated 25-5-99)

1. **Preamble:** The Government of Andhra Pradesh has announced a package of incentives to the IT industries through the G.O.Ms.No 114 Finance & Planning (PIg. IT&C) dept dated 25-5-99. The package of incentives includes a rebate on cost of land allotted by the Government or APIIC, rebate on Stamp duty on transfer of land, 25% concession in the rate of power tariff for new units upto 3 years, relaxations and exemptions from several Laws etc. While some of the incentives operate automatically, certain others need decisions to be taken by some agencies of the State. It is felt desirable to create an institutional mechanism for determining the eligibility of the applicant industries to the various incentives. The idea is to create a single window of reference for the IT industry in all matters relating to the grant of incentives.
2. **Application for grant of incentives:** The IT industries desirous of availing the incentives under the IT policy shall make an application to the Secretary, Department of IT & Communications, in the prescribed format shown as Annexure I. The format is common for all the incentives relating to land, power, stamp duty, FAR, connectivity through APSWAN and investment subsidy envisaged under the policy. The business plan in respect of new units and audited financial statements in respect of ongoing business, as required, shall accompany the application.

3. **Eligibility for application:** The applicants should satisfy the following eligibility criteria:

(a) The applicant shall be covered by the definition of IT Industry or IT Infrastructure Company in terms of paragraphs 11(1), 11(2) and 11(3) of G.O., Ms. No. 114 dated *25-5-99.*

(b) Application for rebate on cost of land:

(i) A Company or registered firm can apply for land under this scheme after one year of incorporation or registration either in India or abroad.

(ii) At the time of preferring the application, the applicant company or firm or its parent company or firm, should have employed at its various units, including those abroad, at least 25% of the number of employees proposed to be employed additionally during the next one year, as per the business plan.

(iii) The application shall be accompanied by a copy of the business plan indicating the overall size of operations proposed to be undertaken with yearly phasing of investment, employment and other facilities proposed to be created. The extent of land applied for should have a direct nexus to the requirements of the business plan.

(c) **Application for rebate on Stamp Duty:** The conditions specified in para 11(4) (i) shall be satis-fied. The provision of facilities like uninterrupted power/ backup and telecom link shall be certified by the APIIC.

4. **Examination of the applications:** The applications for a Committee shall consider grant of incentives under the IT Policy constituted through G.O. Ms. 3 IT&C Department Dt. 25.5.2000. The committee will examine the eligibility of the applicants for various incentives and gives its recommendations.

5. Basing on the recommendations of the Committee, the applications shall be directly referred to APIIC wherever necessary duly indicating the eligibility and the extent of land for which the applicant is eligible. APIIC in turn will report to the Government on the availability of Land and per acre price or its recommendations with in one week from the date of receiving the recommendations of CCITI, so the Government can enter into MOU and

communicate the same to APIIC for allotment of land at a rebate in terms of the IT policy. APIIC will allot Land as per the normal procedure at the earliest and in all within 6 weeks from the date of receipt of application in a complete shape in Government.

6. **Notification:** The Government shall cause a notification to be issued in terms of para 11 of the GO 114 dated *25-5-99,* wherever required.
7. **MOU:** In all cases where the Government decides on allotment of land at a concessional rate, the applicant shall enter into an MOU with the Government in the format prescribed at Annexure II. The Committee may suggest such variations to the format of the MOU as may be required in particular cases.
8. **Conditions of allotment of land:**

(i) The APIIC shall be the authority making the actual allotment based on the decision of the Government *and according to the terms and* conditions stipulated in the MOU.

(ii) The land shall not be used for any purpose other than that for which it is allotted

(iii) The allottee shall commence construction of the building within 6 months from the date of allotment by APIIC and commence commercial operations within 24 months from the date of allotment.

(iv) If the construction of the building is not completed within the stipulated time, APIIC may be directed to take over the premises on payment of assessed value to the original allottee. The premises then can be completed and allotted to other parties.

(v) **Revocation**: The APIIC may revoke the allotment in the event of violation of any of the conditions of allotment or the terms of the MOU. APIIC shall afford reasonable opportunity to the allottee before revoking the allotment. All such cases of revocation shall be reported to the Government.

9. **Bank Guarantee:** The allottee of land under this scheme shall submit a Bank Guarantee for an amount equal to the value of the incentives availed, together with interest for the period for which MOU was entered

for fulfillment of the conditions thereof, read with the relevant provisions of G.O. Ms. 114, Finance & Planning (Plg. IT&C, Wing) dated 25-5-99.

10. The registration of land shall be made in favour of the allottee after the APIIC or such other authority as may be designated by the Government, certifies compliance of the various terms and conditions of allotment, including those relating to employment. The Bank Guarantee shall be discharged thereafter. The APIIC or any other designated authority may obtain particulars of employment generated by the allottee, periodically from the company or any other competent authority.

11. **Mega Projects:** In case of mega Projects, where the proposed investment exceeds Rs 100 crores, the Committee on a case-to-case basis shall consider the grant of special incentives.

J. SATYANARAYANA
SECRETARY TO GOVERNMENT

FORWARDED BY ORDER

SECTION OFFICER

ANNEXURE. 1

Application for grant of incentives to *IT industries*

To

The Secretary to Government
Information Technology and Communications department
Government of Andhra Pradesh
A Block, A.P. Secretariat
Hyderabad

1. Name of the Applicant
   Address of the organization
   Telephone number /
   Fax number /
   E-mail

2. Nature of the applicant organization Proprietary / partnership/Pvt. Ltd./Ltd. company along with certificate of registration).
3. Name and address of the parent company, if any.
4. Details of foreign collaboration, if any
5. Line of IT activity proposed I already undertaken (Enclose a brief project report/outline of business plan)
6. Projected turnover over the next three years in IT activities (Give domestic and export turnover separately).

Year	Export turnover	Domestic turnover	Total turnover
Year 1			
Year 2			
Year 3			

7. Details of performance for the last five years or since inception (for existing units).

Year	Investment made during the year	Employment generated during the year	Export turnover for the year	Domestic turnover for the year	Total turnover for the year

8. Details of projected employment creation for the next three years.

Category of staff	Year 1	Year 2	Year 3	Total
Managerial staff				
Technical staff				
Skilled labour				
Unskilled labour				
Clerical and other staff				
TOTAL				

9. Requirement of land
Location of the land (village, survey number)
Extent of land required (in acres/ sq yards)

- o For office,
- o For production units,

- o For development units,
- o For open space,
- o For other purposes (to be specified),
- o Total,
- o What is the built up area proposed (in sft)?

10. Power requirement

- **Power required in KVA/M. W.**
- Date from which required/connected already
- If connected the details of the service connection with date
- Development of load

  At commencement of unit

  o Over the next three years

11. Water requirement
    - Immediate requirement in KL
    - Requirement over next three years
12. Dates by which
    - o The construction of civil works starts
    - o The construction of civil works completes
    - o The commercial production commences

Any other relevant information

Declaration

We hereby declare that the particulars as given in the application are correct to the best of our knowledge and belief

Signature
Name
Designation

J. SATYANARAYANA
SECRETARY TO GOVERNMENT

ANNEXURE-II

MEMORANDUM OF UNDERSTANDING

This Memorandum of Understanding ("MOU") is entered into on this the......................day of..........................at Hyderabad;

BY AND BETWEEN

Government of Andhra Pradesh, through its Information Technology and Communications Department, (hereinafter referred to as "GoAP") on the First Part;

AND

............................., a company incorporated under the Companies Act, 1956 having its registered office at and its corporate office at (hereinafter referred to as") on the Second Part.

RECITALS

WHEREAS, GoAP has announced an Information Technology Incentives Policy through G.O.Ms.No. 114, Finance & Planning (Plg. IT&C) Department, dated May 25, 1999 ("IT Policy"), pursuant to which..........................has agreed to set up an IT facility in the State of Andhra Pradesh to undertake various activities (as described in Exhibit A attached hereto and hereinafter referred to as "Activities", and which Activities fall within the scope of the IT Policy) and for this purpose wishes to purchase/acquire certain land (more fully described in Schedule I attached hereto and hereinafter referred to as "Plot") under the terms of the IT Policy and on the terms and conditions contained herein; and

WHEREAS, GoAP has agreed to facilitate the establishment of the facility by and the parties hereto have agreed to set out the broad terms of their understanding as under.

NOW THIS MEMORANDUM OF UNDERSTANDING WITNESSETH AS FOLLOWS:

1. Basic Understanding

In consideration of the purchase price determined by APIIC if Plot in phased manner as per the schedule being paid by....from time to time GoAP has agreed to cause APIIC to sell and...agrees to purchase from APIIC the Plot subject to the various terms and conditions contained herein. The parties hereto further agree that...and/or its Affiliates shall use the Plot for the purpose of undertaking the Activities. It is further clarified that the Plot can be used by the sub-contractors or vendors of and/or its Affiliates, provided such sub-contractors or vendors are undertaking the Activities as a special project for.................... ....and/or its.. Affiliates. For the purpose of this MoU the term "Affiliate" means and includes any body corporate in which..................either directly or indirectly subscribes to not less than 26% of the share holding of such Affiliate.

2. Conditions Precedent

The completion of the transaction envisaged under this MoU is subject to the fulfillment of the following conditions precedent:

(a) Completion of satisfactory due diligence by....of the Plot and the Additional Property, (as defined in Clause 5 hereinafter) including, but not limited to, an environmental due diligence of the Plot and Additional Property, suitability of the Plot and the Additional Property for the purpose of undertaking the Activities in the manner satisfactory to....availability of adequate utilities and ownership title of the Plot and the Additional Property;

(b) Obtaining by.........................., of requisite corporate and regulatory approvals, (including approvals from the parent company) including approvals to install and operate the various communication facilities on the Plot and the Additional Property, and APIIC facilitating such assistance that......may reasonably require in order to obtain such approvals as may be necessary and required by ....to undertake the Activities;

(c) APIIC facilitating the provisions of adequate water supplies, telecom linkages, electricity load and other utilities as per the requirements indicated by.....on payment as per applicable norms in existence.

3. Consideration

The parties hereby agree that.........................will be entitled to the rebate in the cost of the Plot as per the norms enumerated in the IT Policy provided..................................eligible employees are employed by................................ undertakes that it and/or its Affiliates or its subcontractors or vendors working on a special project for.........................of its Affiliates, shall employ eligible [as per G.O.Ms.No. 114, Finance and Planning (Plg. IT&C) Dept. Dt. 25-05-1 999] employees (whether such employees are working on the Plot or Additional Property or otherwise within Andhra Pradesh) by the end of third year from the Completion Date. The parties understand that the GoAP on this understanding is providing the rebate on the cost of the Plot.

Further the parties agree that if by the end of three years from the Completion Date, the total number of eligible employees is less than.........................., then in such an event...................... shall refund the rebate pro-rata, on the value of the Plot indicated by APIIC on execution of this MoU, equivalent to the shortfall along with interest calculated on a daily product basis at 16% per annum with quarterly rests from the Completion Date to the date of payment, without there being any other liability, financial or otherwise, resulting from shortfall in employing eligible employees by the end of the third year.

Under this MoU, the Completion Date shall mean the date on which all the conditions, precedents stated in Clause 2 above are completed as per the requirements indicated by........, execution of definitive agreements by the parties, registration of the conveyance/sale deed for the Additional Property with the appropriate Sub-Registrar of Assurances and handing over the vacant and peaceful possession of the Plot and the Additional Property to.........

4. IT Policy

All terms of the IT Policy shall be applicable to the proposed Purchase of the Plot by.................

5. Further Purchase

The Parties hereto further agree that, GoAP will cause APIIC to sell, and shall purchase, property adjacent to the Plot (herein referred to as "Additional Property", and more fully described in Schedule II attached hereto), for a purchase price of Rs................., per meter as indicated by APIIC.

The Parties hereto agree that initially the purchase of the Additional Property shall be outside the purview of the IT Policy. If at any time within the period of five years from the Completion Date, the total number of.................................eligible employees (as defined in the IT Policy) is in excess of....................(as committed by ....), then any benefits that............. will be entitled to under the IT Policy, including any rebate, hall accrue to..............In such an event, APIIC shall pay to........... the rebate amount along with interest calculated at the rate of 11% per annum from the Completion Date to the date of payment.

6. Miscellaneous

(a) **Use of Premises:** For a period of three years from the Completion Date............not assign; transfer, or in any manner alienate the Plot or the Additional Property to any person without obtaining the prior written consent of APIIC, provided that, nothing contained herein shall be deemed to restrict the Affiliates or sub-contractors or vendors of................ from........................ utilizing the Plot or the Additional Property for the purpose of undertaking the Activities for the benefit of,............or its Affiliates.

(b) **Term:** This MoU shall remain in force for a period of three months from the date of execution, unless such term is extended by the mutual consent of the parties hereto.

(c) **Non-binding:** This Memorandum of Under-standing constitutes an expression of interest, and should not be in any manner construed to be a legally binding commitment for either party. Both parties understand that prior to proceeding to execute a definitive agreement......and APIIC are required to obtain certain corporate and regulatory approvals, and in the event such approvals are not obtained before expiry of the term of this Memorandum of Understanding, then the Memor-andum of Understanding would terminate without any liability to either party. On obtaining the requisite approvals the parties shall communicate the same to each other. However............., shall endeavour to obtain all necessary approvals/clearances within (90) days from the date of entering into the MoU.

IN WITNESS WHEREOF, the aforementioned parties have affixed their signatures and seal on the date, month and year first above written.

Government of Andhra Pradesh ....
Name: .... Name:.......................
Secretary, IT&C Department Designation:......................

Schedule I to the Memorandum of Understanding dated........................

DESCRIPTION OF THE PLOT

All of the freehold land located at APIIC Industrial Development Area, Survey No ....village.....................Mandal...................... ....District, Andhra Pradesh, ad-measuring about....................................acres, carved out...................... by APIIC, and acceptable to......................

Schedule II to the Memorandum of Understanding dated:.................................

DESCRIPTION OF ADDITIONAL PROPERTY

All of the freehold land located at APIIC Industrial Development Area, Survey No.......................village........................ Mandal................ District Andhra Pradesh and contiguous to the Plot and ad measuring about....................acres.

J. SATYANARAYANA
SECRETARY TO GOVERNMENT

FORWARDED BY ORDER

SECTION OFFICER

Annexure-III

Draft Bank Guarantee

Andhra Pradesh Industrial Infrastructure Corporation Limited

This performance bank Guarantee made this..................

day of..............................by..................having its Registered Office at.....................and branch in.......................... in favour of the Andhra Pradesh Industrial Infrastructure Corporation Limited, (APIIC) a Government Company incorporated under the Companies Act 1956 and having its Registered Office at Parishrama Bhavan, 6th Floor, Fateh Maidan Road, Hyderabad — 500 004, A.P.

(A) Whereas...a company incorporated under the Companies Act 1956 and having its corporate office at.. had purchased......(Conveyance Deed), on the terms and conditions contained therein in consideration of the rebate (as the term is defined in the Conveyance Deed) offered by the Government of A.P. through APIIC under the Information Technology Incentives Policy (IT Policy) issued by the Govt. of Andhra Pradesh vide its G.O. Ms. No. 114, Fin., & Plg., (Plg.IT&C) Dept., dt, 25.5.99.

(B) The rebate was provided by the Govt., of A.P. through APIIC on the condition that a minimum of............ eligible employees (as the term is defined in the Conve-yance Deed, land hereinafter................target eligible employees) by the third anniversary of the Conveyance Deed and the target eligible employees must have completed two years of continuous employment by the Fifth anniversary of the conveyance deed on the terms and conditions contained in the Conveyance Deed.

(C) Further under the Conveyance Deed, APIIC and........... have agreed that in the event...........fail, to fulfill the above conditions, in full or in part then in such event is to refund all, or as the case may be part of the rebate (calculated in terms of the formula laid out in section 3.3 of the Conveyance Deed and hereinafter "claim amount"); and

(D) In order to secure the performance of.............to pay the claim amount on the terms and conditions contained in the Conveyance Deed, the APIIC has............. required...................... to provide a Bank Guarantee and accordingly.........................has requested the Bank to provide a Guarantee and the Bank hereby guarantee the payment of the claim amount subject to the following terms and conditions.

NOW THIS BANK GUARANTEE WITNESSE AS FOLLOWS :

(1) All capitalized terms used herein and in Annexure hereto if not specifically defined shall have the same meaning assigned to them under the Conveyance Deed.

(2) The Bank hereby irrevocably guarantee and undertake to pay to APIIC, on written demand, in form and content Annexed hereto as Annexure (demand), and within fifteen business days of the receipt of such demand, all or portion of the claim amount which remains due and unpaid by........ Without demur, reservation, contest, recourse or protest. The demand raised by the APIIC must state the amount of claim amount that has become due from..........., but remains unpaid, the manner in which the refundable amount has been calcu-lated and a confirmation by an authorized officer of APIIC that APIIC has made a demand on........... and.........has not paid the claim amount in full.

(3) Notwithstanding anything contained herein above, the bank's maximum liability under this guarantee is strictly restricted to........(Indian Rupees only) plus interest there on at the rate 16% per annum, from the date of receipt of the demand till the date of payment to APIIC.

(4) The Bank's maximum liability under this guar-antee as stated in Article 3 above shall be automatically reduced by the amounts paid by......, and to the extent corresponding or proportionate to the land resumed by the Seller or surrendered by the Purchaser.

(5) This Guarantee will come into force on the date of execution of the Conveyance Deed and shall remain in force and valid for a period of five years from the date of this guarantee and shall be extendable further for a maximum period of six months at the sole option of APIIC.

(6) This unconditional and irrevocable Bank Guar-antee shall be available for invocation and pay-ment at the Bank counters in Hyderabad or Secunderabad. Any demand under this guarantee must be made in writing, and must be dispatched at the Bank's address at......whilst the guarantee remains in force as above.

On receipt of such demand, the guarantor shall pay, APIIC the amount of the demand within fifteen business days following the invocation of the guarantee by the APIIC in writing as aforesaid.

The courts located in the Twin Cities of Hyderabad and Secunderabad shall have jurisdiction over any dispute arising out of this guarantee.

In witness whereof the guarantee is executed by Shri/ Smt..........................and Shri/Smt.................on behalf of the Bank who as Principal Officers of the Bank are authorized and competent to execute such like guarantees including the present one.

J. SATYANARAYANA
SECRETARY TO GOVERNMENT

Annexure V

GOVERNMENT OF ANDHRA PRADESH

ABSTRACT

Information Technology—Promotion of telecommunication infrastructure—Laying of Optical Fibre cables along State properties—Guidelines issued

Finance & Planning (Plg IT&C) Department

G O Ms No.5

Dated 11-2-2000

Read the following:

Ministry of Surface Transport, Govt of India No RW/ NH12037/826/98 —KNT dated 17-8-99

ORDER

1. The Govt of AP has been making several efforts to promote IT in the State with the objectives of improving the state of economy, enhancing the quality of life of the citizens, provide good governance and ensure development with equity. Some of these efforts are attracting investments in IT sector, implementation of electronic governance projects, promoting IT education. Besides the ongoing efforts, the Government is

committed to encourage distance education through use of IT tools, IT-enabled Services for providing large-scale employment and also to take Internet to the villages at the earliest to spur the growth of e-commerce in rural areas also.

2. All the above efforts essentially need availability of a robust telecommunication infrastructure with adequate bandwidth across the length & breadth of the State. At present DOT is the predominant agency operating throughout the State. It is felt that the efforts of DOT will have to be supplemented to create enough bandwidth and make it available at affordable rates. Hence the Government has been contemplating to leverage private sector initiatives in providing widespread, high-speed , broadband communication infrastructure speedily.

3. The globally accepted method of creating broadband networks is through laying optical fibre as the backbone. The optical fibre is to be laid along roads like the National Highways, State Highways and other road network belonging to the R&B, Panchayat Raj, Municipal Administration & Urban Development and Forest Departments. The agencies intending to lay the optical fibre are required to take permission from the authorities in these departments. In the absence of general guidelines, the proposals are sent to higher authorities and this causes delay. Keeping this in view, the Government has decided to issue guidelines for issuing permissions to the agencies, especially telecom operators, desirous of implementing optical fibre projects in the State.

4. The Government of India has issued guidelines on the subject of permitting laying optical fibre cables along the National Highways in the reference read above. According to this policy, the permission is to be given free of any charge subject to, *inter alia*, the licensee producing a Bank Guarantee for an amount calculated at the rate of Rs. 25 per RM.

5. Keeping the above circumstances in view, the following guidelines are issued in the matter of according general permission to agencies desirous of laying optical fibre cable along roads belonging to the State in the R&B, Panchayat Raj, Municipal Administration & Urban Development and Forest Departments.

(a) Any agency which has license from the Department of Telecom as may be required from time to time, may apply to the Engineer-in-Chief, R&B, Principal Chief Conservator of Forests, Engineer-in-Chief, Panchayat Raj, and Engineer-in-Chief, Municipal Administration and Urban Development for issue of permission for using the right of way for laying optical fibre cables along the highways and roads belonging to the State.

(b) The agency shall specify the roads along which and the lengths for which permission is sought. The permission shall be accorded by the Engineer-in-Chief, R&B, Principal Chief Conservator of Forests, Engineer-in-Chief, Panchayat Raj, and Engineer-in-Chief, Muni-cipal Administration and Urban Development, as the case may be, within 2 weeks of application, subject to the applicant executing the agreement specified in sub-para (c) and providing the Bank Guarantee specified in clause (iv) of the agreement. Before giving such permission the requirement of widening of the roads should be kept in view.

(c) The agencies to which permission has been accorded under this order shall enter into an agreement with the Engineer-in-Chief, R &B, Principal Chief Conservator of Forests, Engineer-in-Chief, Panchayat Raj, and Engineer-in-Chief, Municipal Administration and Urban Development, as the case may be, as per the enclosed format.

(d) The agencies to which permission has been accorded under this order, shall not sell, lease or otherwise trade on the extra space available in the ducts laid by them, except after obtaining specific prior permission of the Government, subject to such terms and conditions as may be decided by the Government.

(e) The agency shall restore the road or the margin which has been dug, to its original quality at his cost and to the satisfaction of the Engineer-in-Chief, R & B, Principal Chief Conservator of Forests, Engineer-in-Chief, Panchayat Raj, and Engineer-in-Chief, Municipal Administration and Urban Development, as the case may be.

6. The departments of Roads and Buildings, Forests, Panchayat Raj and Rural Development and Municipal

Administration and Urban Development shall take necessary consequential action for ensuring the implementation of these orders forthwith.

(BY ORDER AND IN THE NAME OF THE GOVERNOR OF ANDHRA PRADESH)

VANANDARAU
CHIEF SECRETARY TO GOVERNMENT

To

The Engineer-in-Chief, R & B Dept.,
Principle Chief Conservator of Forests,
The Engineer-in-Chief, Panchayat Raj Dept.,
The Engineer-in-Chief, Municipal Admn., & Urban Development Dept.,

Copy to

The Secretary to Govt., T.R.&B. Dept.,
The Prl. Secretary to Govt., E.F.S & T., Dept.,
The Prl. Secretary to Govt., P.R. & R.D. Dept.,
The Prl. Secretary to Govt. M.A.& U.D., Dept.,

Forwarded by Order

Research Officer.

LICENCE FOR THE USE OF THE LAND OF R&B/ FOREST/PR/MA&UD DEPARTMENTS

Agreement to lay Optical Fibre Cable from_______to _______ Km of R&B/Forest/PR & R.D/MA&UD land in the state of AP.

This Agreement made this _____ day of______(Month) of _____ (year) between Governor of AP acting in his executive capacity through the Government of AP, (hereinafter referred to as GOVERNMENT OF AP) which expression shall unless excluded by or repugnant to the context, include his successors in office and assigns) of the one part, and M/s.________________ a company registered under the Companies Act 1956 and having its Registered Office at______________________________ (hereinafter called the Licensee) which expression shall unless excluded by or repugnant to the context, include his successor/ administrator assignees on the second part.

Whereas the Government of AP is responsible *inter-alia* for development and maintenance of Roads in AP and is also the owner of the land.

Whereas ____________ is a company wanting to lay Optical Fibre Cable in the State of AP.

WHEREAS the licensee has applied to the GoAP for permission to lay Optical Fibre Cable from Km........................ to Km.................................... of.. ....Road up to.....................and Km.......................to Km ....of............................Road from.................... to..................................

AND WHEREAS GoAP have agreed to grant such permission on the terms and conditions hereinafter mentioned.

Now this Agreement witnesseth that in consideration of the conditions hereinafter contained and on the part of the Licensee to be observed and performed, the GoAP hereby grants to the licensee permission to lay Optical Fibre Cable as per the approved drawing attached hereto subject to the following conditions, namely:—

(i) The cable shall ordinarily be laid at the edge of the Right-of-Way or at a minimum distance of 15 m from the center line of the nearest carriageway where the road land is wider.

(ii) The top of the casing/conduit pipe containing the cables shall be at least 1.2m below the surface of the road subject to being at least 0- .3 m below the drain inverts.

(iii) The licensee shall ensure making good the excavated trench for laying of cables by proper filling and compaction, so as to restore the land in the same condition as it was before digging the trench, clearing debris/loose earth produced due to execution of trenching at least 50 m away from the edge of the Right-of-way.

(iv) The licensee shall furnish a Bank Guarantee for the amount calculated at the rate of *Rs. 25* (Rupees twenty five only) per metre to the Engineer-in-Chief, R&B/ Principle Chief Conservator of Forests/Engineer-in-Chief, PR/Engineer-in-Chief, MA&UD, for a period of one year for ensuring making good the excavated trench for laying the cables by proper filling and compaction, clearing debris/loose earth produced due to execution of trenching at least 50m away from the edge of the Right-of-Way. No payment shall be payable by the GoAP to the licensee for clearing debris/loose earth. In case the work contemplated herein is not completed to the satisfaction of the Engineer-in-Chief, R&B/Principle Chief Conservator of Forests/ Engineer-in-Chief, PR/ Engineer-in-Chief, MA& UD within a period of eleven months from the date of issue of the Bank Guarantee, the licensee shall either furnish a fresh guarantee or extend the guarantee for a further period of one year. In case of the licensee failing to discharge the obligation of making good of the excavated trench, Engineer-in-Chief (R&B)/Principle Chief Conservator of Forests/ Engineer-in-Chief, PR/ Engineer-in-Chief, MA&UD shall have a right to make good the damages caused by excavation, at the cost of the Licensee and recover the amount by forfeiture of Bank Guarantee.

(v) The licensee/licensees shall make his own arrangement for crossing of cross drainage structure, rivers etc. In case, this is not feasible, the cables may be carried on the outside of the railings/parapets and supporters on brackets fixed to the outside of the bridge superstructure. The fixing and supporting arrangement with all details shall be got approved in advance from the Engineer-in-Chief (R&B)/Principle Chief Conservator of Forests/ Engineer-in-Chief, PR/ Engineer-in-Chief, MA&UD.

(vi) The licensee shall shift the cables within 90 days from the issue of the notice by the concerned Engineer-in-Chief (R&B)/Principle Chief Conservator of Forests/ Engineer-in-Chief, PR/Engineer-in-Chief, MA&UD to shift/relocate the cables in case it is so required for the purpose of improvement/widening of the road and restore the road land to its original condition at his own cost.

(vii) The licensee shall be responsible to ascertain from Engineer-in-Chief (R&B)/ Principle Chief Conservator of Forests/Engineer-in-Chief, PR/ Engineer-in-Chief, MA&UD /Chief General Manager, Telecommunications of the area regarding the location of other cables etc. He shall ensure the safety of already existing cables before commencement of the excavation. He shall be responsible for any damage to the existing cables of DOT or any other communication network and will have to get the same repaired or replaced at his cost. Engineer-in-Chief (R&B)/ Principle Chief Conservator of Forests/ Engineer-in-Chief, PR/ Engineer-in-Chief, MA&UD shall have a right to make good the damages caused by excavation at the cost of the licensee and recover the amount by forfeiture of Bank Guarantee.

(viii) If the licensee fails to comply the condition (vi) and (vii) above, to the satisfaction of the Engineer-in-Chief(R&B)/ Principle Chief Conservator of Forests/ Engineer-in-Chief, PR / Engineer-in-Chief, MA&UD, the same shall be got executed by the Engineer-in-Chief (R&B)/ Principle Chief Conservator of Forests/ Engineer-in-Chief PR/Engineer-in-Chief, MA&UD at the cost and risk of the licensee.

(ix) The licensee shall be responsible for safety and all other underground facilities such as electric line, pipes for water supply and gas, sewage lines etc. During trenching. The licensee shall also be responsible for safety of cross drainage structures. The licensee shall procure Insurance from reputed Insurance company against damages to these lines during trenching.

(x) As far as possible, the lincensees should avoid cutting of the road for crossing State Highway, and other State Roads and try to carry out the work by drilling a hole beneath the road pavement. In case any damage is caused to the road pavement in this process, the licensee/ licensees will be required to restore the road to the original condition at his cost. If due to unavoidable reasons the road needs to be cut for crossing or laying a cable, the lincensee shall deposit the restoration cost as assessed by Engineer-in-Chief (R&B)/ Principle Chief Conservator of Forests/Engineer-in-Chief, PR/ Engineer-in-Chief, MA&UD in charge prior to taking up of the work.

(xi) The licenesee shall inform Engineer-in-Chief (R&B)/ Principle Chief Conservator of Forests/ Engineer-in-Chief, PR/ Engineer-in-Chief, MA&UD at least 15 days in advance before digging trenches.

(xii) Each day the extent of digging the trenches should be

strictly regulated so that cables are laid and trenches filled up before the close of the work that day. Filling should be completed to the satisfaction of the Engineer-in-Chief (R&B)/ Principle Chief Conservator of Forests/ Engineer-in-Chief, PR/ Engineer-in-Chief, MA&UD.

(xiii) The licensee/licensees shall indemnify Engineer-in-Chief (R&B,/ Principle Chief Conservator of Forests/ Engineer-in-Chief, PR/ Engineer-in-Chief, MA&UD all damages and claims, if any, due to the digging of trenches for laying of the cables.

(xiv) This permission shall be for a period of 15 years or the period for which the licensee has been given the licence by the Department of Telecommunications whichever is less. The permission granted by the Agreement will automatically cease in case of premature termination of the licence granted to by the Department of Telecommunication. GoAP also have a right to terminate the permission and also to extend the period Agreement. In case the licensee wants shifting, repairs or alteration to optical fibre cable, he will have to furnish a fresh Bank Guarantee for the purpose mentioned in clause (iv) above.

(xv) That the licensee/licensees shall not without the prior permission in writing of the Engineer-in-Chief, R&B/ Principle Chief Conservator Forests/ Engineer-in-Chief, PR/ Engineer-in-Chief, MA&UD undertake any work of shifting, repairs or alterations to the said Optical Fibre Cables.

(xvi) That the licensee/licensees shall be liable for any loss or damage caused to the GoAP by drainage obstruction or any other like cause due to the said Optical Fibre Cables.

(xvii) The Licensee shall not sell, transfer, lease or otherwise dispose of the cables without the previous consent of the GoAP in writing.

(xviii) That the permission granted by this licence shall not in any way be deemed to convey to the Licensee any right to or any interest in State Highway land other than what is herein expressly granted.

(xix) That during the subsistence of this Licence, the Optical Fibre Cable located in State Highway land shall be deemed to have been constructed and continued only by the consent and permission of the GoAP so that the right of the licensee to the use thereof shall not become absolute and indefeasible by lapse of time.

(xx) That the licensee shall bear the stamp duty charged on this agreement.

(xxi) The Optical Fibre Cables shall not be brought into use by the licensee unless a completion certificate to the effect that the Optical Fibre Cable have been laid in accordance with the approved specifications and drawings and the trenches have been filled up to the satisfaction of Engineer-in-Chief, R&B/ Principle Chief Conservator of Forests/ Engineer-in-Chief, PR/ Engineer-in-Chief, MA&UD has been obtained from the concerned Engineer-in-Chief, R&B/Principle Chief Conservator of Forests/ Engineer-in-Chief, PR/ Engineer-in-Chief, MA&UD.

(xxii) Notwithstanding anything contained herein the licence may cancelled at any time by the GoAP for a breach of any condition of the licence and the licensee shall not be entitled to any compensation for any loss caused to it by such cancellation nor shall it be absolved from any liability already incurred.

(xxiii) The licensee/licensees shall have to provide a barricading, danger lighting and other necessary caution boards while executing the work.

(xxiv) If any traffic diversion works are found necessary during the working period such diversion shall be provided at the cost of licensee.

(xxv) After the termination or expiry of the agreement, the licensee shall remove the cable within 90 days and the site shall be brought back to original condition failing with the licensee will lose the right to remove the cable. However, before taking up the work of removal of cables the licensee shall furnish a Bank Guarantee to the Engineer-in-Chief, R&B/ Principle Chief Conservator of Forests /Engineer-in-Chief, PR/ Engineer-in-Chief, MA& UD for a period of one year for an amount assessed by Engineer-in-Chief, R&B/ Principle Chief Conservator of Forests/ Engineer-in-Chief, PR/ Engineer-in-Chief,

MA&UD for making good the excavated trench for laying cables by proper filling and compaction, clearing debris/ loose earth produced due to excavation of trenching at least 50m away from the edge of the Right-of-Way.

(xxvi) The Licensee to which permission has been accorded under this order, shall not sell, lease or otherwise trade on the extra space available in the ducts laid by them except after obtaining specific prior permission of GoAP, subject to such terms and conditions as may be decided by the Government.

(xxvii) The licensee has to abide by the directions of the concerned Engineer-in-Chief, R&B/ Principle Chief Conservator of Forests/ Engineer-in-Chief, PR/ Engineer in-Chief, MA&UD and no appeal/correspondence shall be entertained.

This Agreement has been made in duplicate each Agreement on a Stamp Paper. Each party of this Agreement has retained one stamped copy each.

WITNESS WHEREOF THE PARTIES HERETO HAVE HERUNTO SET THEIR RESPECTIVE HANDS THE DAY AND THE YEAR FIRST ABOVE WRITTEN.

SIGNED, SEALED AND DELIVERED BY Engineer-in-Chief/ R&B / PR/

M.A.& U.D

FOR AND ON BEHALF OF GOVERNOR OF Principal Chief Conservator of

AP IN THE PRESENCE OF Forests.

1.

2.

AND ON BEHALF OF LICENSEE MANAGING DIRECTOR

OR

NAME & ADDRESS OF TELECOM HIS AUTHORISED

LICENSEE HEREINUNTO AFFIXED REPRESENTATIVE

BY VIRTUE OF RESOLUTION OF THE

BOARD OF DIRECTORS PASSED

IN THE MEETING HELD ON

______________ IN PRESENCE OF:

1.1 GoAP's Vision of e-Government

Internet technology is **empowering** consumers to make personal choices on how they access and receive goods and services. This is leading to an increasing dependence on electronic business resulting in a realignment of virtually every sector and a variety of customer-centered relationships between service providers and customers. Government is no exception to these phenomena.

As public awareness and Internet usage increase, the demand for online Government interaction and simplified, standardized ways to access Government information and services becomes increasingly important. At the same time, the public must have confidence that their online communications with the Government are secure and their privacy protected. Therefore, to help its citizens gain one-stop access to Government information and services in a secure way, and to provide better, more efficient, transparent and responsive services, Government of Andhra Pradesh (GoAP) has embarked on a scheme of e-Government to *leverage* the tools of ICT (Information & Communication Technology) in serving its citizens.

The Government of Andhra Pradesh cherishes the vision of establishing a Simple, Moral, Accountable, Responsive and Transparent Government—<SMART> Government. e-Government is one of the vehicles that can be gainfully used in reaching the goal of SMART governance. GoAP's IT vision to leverage Information Technology (IT) is amply reflected in its IT vision statement:

The Vision

"Andhra Pradesh will leverage Information Technology to attain a position of leadership and excellence in the information age and to transform itself into a knowledge society" Vision 2020

1.2 Objectives of e-Government Initiatives

Recognizing the need for technology-enabled service delivery and, as a part of its e-Government strategy, GoAP has initiated an innovative broad based, enterprise-wide approach to service delivery.

The targeted benefits of GoAP's e-Government programme include the following:

Benefits to Citizen & Business

- Streamlined, standardized electronic information gathering and access.
- Electronic delivery of services to meet citizen expectations and requirements.
- Convenient, anytime, anywhere citizen services.
- Support for e-commerce initiatives (*e.g.*, online filing, payments etc.).
- Significant improvement in Government to Citizen (G2C), and Government to Business (G2B) interfaces.

Benefits to Government

- Increased employee productivity.
- Facilitation of information reuse across and within the departments of GoAP.
- Reduced system maintenance and training requirements by adopting standard systems and processes for GoAP.
- Cost-effectiveness in the operations of Government agencies.
- Improvement in Government-to-Government (G2G) interfaces.

1.3 Approach to e-Government

GoAP's strategy for implementing e-Government has been unfolding over the last few years. It has implemented e-Government projects in a few key departments, which yielded encouraging results. The following are some examples of these early initiatives:

- **CARD** — Computer-aided Administration of Registration Department.
    - o Demystification of procedures for registration of legal documents like sale deeds, mortgage deeds, gift deeds etc.
    - o Automation of processes at 239 sub-registrar offices.
    - o 2.8 million deeds registered digitally in 3 years after launch.
    - o 1.4 million title searches & 2.1 million property valuations done

- **MPHS** — Multi-Purpose Household Survey Project:
  - o 1125 field offices of revenue department computerized.
  - o Database of 75 mil. citizens & 25 mil. land records created.
- **C-TAS-** Computerized Treasury Accounting System:
  - o 233 district treasuries & 300 sub-treasuries computerized.
- **COMPACT** - Computerized Administration of Commercial Taxes:
  - o Computer-based system of registration of dealers & processing of their sales tax returns

Based on these initial successes, various other government departments have embarked on developing departmental applications.

1.4 The Essential Frameworks for e-Government

GoAP recognized the state's potential for employing Internet communications and Web technologies to improve government services and promote economic development. The desire to translate this potential into a reality, soon brought to fore a number of challenges, like the ones mentioned below:

- Fast-changing horizon of **technology,** making it difficult to evaluate options and arrive at appropriate cost-effective, scalable and inter-operable solutions.
- The need for huge **resources** to be invested at a fast pace to implement a large number of inter-related projects in a synchronized mode, to create the required impact.
- The compelling need to **prioritize** the e-Government applications, given that there are about 1500 services that can be improved through the use of ICT.
- The need to ensure that the e-Government projects are **implemented** in a way that the benefits to the citizens are provided in a cost-effective and sustained way.

GoAP has designed suitable frameworks to meet the above challenges. They are depicted below (figure 1).

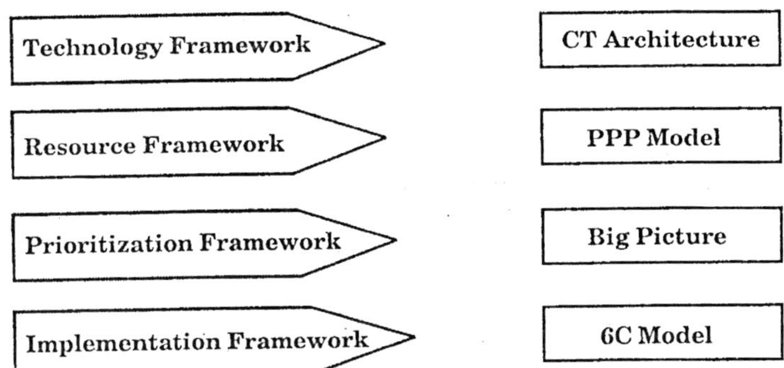

In this paper an attempt has been made to briefly describe the **Technology Framework,** also called as the **ICT Architecture** and the **Prioritization Framework,** also called as the **Big Picture.** Details of the other two frameworks namely, the **Resource Framework** or the **PPP Model** and the **Implementation Framework** or the **6C Model** can be found at the web-site www.ap-it.com.

2.1 The ICT Architecture for e-government

From its experience in implementing a few e-Government projects at the department/agency level, the GoAP realized that such individual projects implemented by the departments on a ***stand-alone*** basis would result in duplication of work, besides creating islands of excellence, which are not interoperable. Integration of these disparate systems at a later time would involve tedious *plumbing.* A standards-based approach was felt to be the need of the hour. In January 2001, GoAP developed a statewide IT architecture & technology standards, Security Policy and PKI Strategy with the consultancy services provided by **Pricewaterhouse Coopers,** over the preceding 5 months. Common business models/processes and shared technology infrastructure services were identified as key success areas during the exercise. Standards for various technology components were identified to enable re-usability and ensure inter operability and integration. An abstract of the IT Architecture envisioned by the GoAP is available at www.ap-it.com. These standards have been mandated, through a policy document (G O Ms 40 of IT&C Department dated. 14.08.2001), for compliance by all departments and developers implementing e-Government projects.

2.2 Key learning from the study on ICT Architecture

The study conducted by Government of Andhra Pradesh for building the ICT Architecture for e-Government, has thrown up a few key earnings that are useful to draw up the implemen-tation plans — logically the next step in this evolutionary process. Government of Andhra Pradesh has immensely benefited from these key learning, which helped in sharpening the under-standing of the vision for e-Government. Four such key learnings are described below:

2.2.1 Enterprise Approach

In order to implement and gain the advantages of e-government, a state must consider itself as one entity in which all parts work together for the common good by avoiding duplication of efforts, enabling sharing of technical assets, and exchanging information from its multitude of databases (while protecting privacy of records of the citizens). The **enterprise approach** for e-Government emphasizes the statewide perspec-tive (versus an agency view). The state must view itself differently from a technology perspective. It can no longer afford to be an agglomeration of separate and disjointed organizations, programmes, and assets.

This enterprise approach strategically plans and imple-ments the synchronization of multiple applications that run on a number of infrastructure components, necessary to deliver digital government services to the citizen.

Departments would need to work cooperatively, yet independently, to realize the vision of digital government. No department can successfully deliver digital government services alone. Mutual, interdependent application development and service delivery among state departments is necessary for citizens to experience online services through a single window.

In order to identify the core initiatives for e-Government, GoAP used this approach that treats the state as a single enter-prise. The single enterprise concept includes development of a set of **core policies, core applications and core ICT infra-structure** that span across departments. Given the charac-teristics of the fast-paced Internet application development process and rapid changes in technology, these three areas need to be developed in parallel. This concept of core initiatives developed more fully in a later exercise, has been described in sections 3.2 to 3.4.

2.2.2 Develop and follow Internet standards and guidelines. Standards and guidelines are fundamental to the development of a single, secure, enterprise-wide infrastructure to support the States's development of products and services for the web. They serve as a common framework and rule-set for the application development lifecycle. One of the strong recommendations that has been thrown up is the compelling need to develop all future applications, especially the citizen-facing applications, adopting Internet technology standards. Though obvious, prescription of this standard has made a fundamental difference in several projects.

2.2.3 Build once, use many times. Developing a single architecture and enterprise commerce infrastructure will allow the State to build the infrastructure once and leverage it across multiple new applications. The infrastructure must be able to support current applications, and be the foundation for future initiatives. In a like manner, the core applications should be designed generically, on the lines of a product, such that they can be used across all the departments or large groups of departments. This approach results in considerable saving in cost and effort in design, development, implementation, training and maintenance of applications. Typical examples are the core applications relating to Financial Information System, Human Resource Management System, e-Procurement etc.

2.2.4 Leverage new models for enterprise integration. As in the case of an enterprise infrastructure, whenever possible, the State should seek to employ the concept of leverage. An excellent example is the use of standard Middleware commercial off-the-shelf (COTS) packages for the integration of legacy applications within the Finance department and its associated departments such as Treasuries, Accountant Generals (AG's) office, etc., rather than developing applications from scratch. The use of COTS applications offers the opportunity to dramatically reducing development time and costs as well as reducing maintenance costs associated with upgrades over time.

3. Priontization Framework

3.1 The Rationale

Having developed the ICT Architecture and having realized the importance of the key learning that followed from it, the

Government of Andhra Pradesh seemed to be technologically equipped to build large applications that would enable it to realize its grand vision of e-Government. Very soon it was realized that the task of identifying the various applications and prioritizing them for implementation was formidable. In particular, the following challenges were confronted:

(a) Which are the applications that need to be taken up first, and which later?
(b) How to identify the applications & projects, which, when implemented would ensure that the global best practices in e-Government permeate the related government departments and agencies?
(c) What are the linkages, explicit & implicit, between the various applications?
(d) What are the supporting policies and components of infrastructure that need to be put in place?
(e) At what pace should the whole implementation proceed?

The Government of Andhra Pradesh felt that the answers to the above questions can be found only through an exhaustive ground level survey of the governance practices within its major departments and agencies on one hand and of the global best practices in those sectors on the other. This has led to engaging the consultancy services of PWC for a survey of 50 government departments with the development of an 'e-Government blue print' as a key deliverable.

The survey of the government departments proceeded along the following steps:

- Logical grouping of secretariat departments, based on comparable objectives/functions.
- High level assessment of key processes/support processes/services for each of the logically grouped departments.
- Mapping of Core Processes across the departments.
- Prioritization of services based on a critically and feasibility matrix for each group.
- Categorization of the services as those that need to be 'Targeted', Pursued, 'Permitted' and 'Kept On Hold' during the implementation of GoAP's e-Government Programme.

3.2 Objectives of the e-Government Roadmap Survey of 50 departments

Typically, e-Government initiatives are implemented with a view to achieve the end objectives in view. The 50 departments survey is being taken up to achieve the following objectives:

- Identification of services/applications that have e-Government opportunities within/across departments.
- Assessment of the opportunities to apply Public Private Partnership (PPP) Model which implementing the identified services/applications.
- Preparation of high level e-Government Roadmap/blue print for GoAP covering aspects such as IT policies, Technology model and the interdependencies of applications identified in different departments.

3.3 Definition of Core e-Government Initiatives

Moving forward GoAP has attempted to identify core initiatives, which provide maximum benefits to its stakeholders (citizens, businesses, employees) and also form the backbone for future e-government initiatives. An initiative could be a policy, an infrastructure or an application.

Some of the key characteristics that have been considered by GoAP in the identification of Core Initiatives are as follows:

- Usability by large no. of departments.
- Statewide geographical coverage.
- Impacts key stakeholders.
  1. Citizens (Urban and rural locations).
  2. Business (Organizations/institutions/vendors who deal with government);
  3. Employees (serving and retired).
- Any other key variable that is critical for the realization of State's vision.

3.4 Framework for Prioritization of Core e-Government Initiatives

- The framework used for prioritization of Core Initiatives is shown below:

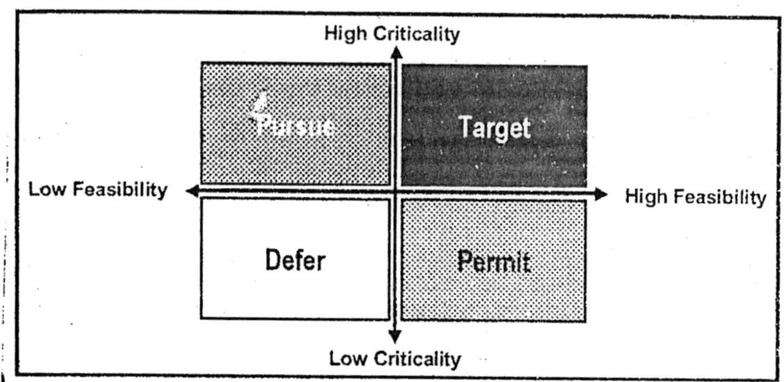

Figure 4: Core Initiatives Prioritization Framework

3.5 Core e-Government Initiatives of GoAP

Based on the application of the above framework and criteria, GoAP has identified the Core Initiatives, and classified them according to interdependent components. These initiatives provide GoAP an opportunity to improve its efficiency in providing its services in a cost effective manner. These are shown in Table 2 below.

Table 2: Core Applications Projects

Initiatives	Description	Status as of April. 2002
1	2	3
1. OLTP — Online Transaction Process System, focus on Citizen data management system Integrated land management system Geographical Information System	* Provides a single window to citizens to access the services across multiple departments * Archives horizontal and vertical integration of departments at Mandal (lowest administrative unit), District and State levels.	* 2 pilots under implementation in Bhongir & Shadnagar mandals involving 10 departments * Expected to be launched in August, 2002
2. E-seva (electronic services to citizens acting as a single window)	* Rolling out E-seva across the state * Already implemented across the state capital of Hyderabad	* 18 service centers operational in Twin cities * 12000 citizens served a day * RFP for extension to 50 other towns

1	2	3
	* 100% potential for PPP model	to be used in April, 2002
3. Single window for businesses	* Provide single window to business to access the services across multiple departments * 100% potential for PPP model	To be planned
4. Social Benefits Management system	* Monitoring and tracking various welfare schemes * Better targeting of beneficiaries.	RFP to be issue in April, 2002
5. Complaints redressal —Help Desk and Call Centre	Centralized complaints receipts, distribution and tracking	To be planned along with data center
6. Integrated Financial Information System	* Integration of application in Finance department and its associated departments * Use of middleware product	Project to be awarded in April, 2002
7. E-Procurement	* Applying e-government concepts and technologies to the area of purchasing to reduce prices of goods and services * 100% potential for PPP model * COTs solution preferred * E-procurement to be handled by a govt-led private exchange (govt. >15% stake)	* Project to be awarded in April, 2002 * Pilot in 4 departments, (APSRTC, APTS, APHMHIDC, CoT) to be implemented by July, 2002 * Rollout to 10 more departments by December, 2002
8. Human resource management system	* centralised payroll and G2E portal * Self-service zone for 1 million government employees.	RFP to be issued in April, 2002
9. Generic Office Management system (smartgov)	* Workflow automation + KM in AP Secretariat.	* Project to be launched in a phased manner

1	2	3
	* A bundle of 483 applications across 30 departments of Secretariat.	during May - August, 2002 * To be productized and implemented in HoDs, District Offices etc.
10. Government Portal	Common gateway for all state services, application, and information	* Aponline gov. in launched on 27th March, 2002 * To be fully developed over next 12 months.
11. Secure intranet	* Communication infrastructure to connect all the locations of government offices. * Connectivity available from Hyderabad to District offices.	To be planned
12. Data center	* One central facility where the application and database servers are located * To be implemented under a PPP model * The focal point for hosting all major applications and data of government departments.	RFP to be issued by April, 2002
13. Kiosks in rural areas	* Access points for rural location * Implementation under PPP model	Being planned
14. Public Key Infrastructure	* Secure transactions over internet * Digital signature * Implementation under PPP model	RFP being floated in April, 2002
15. Identity cards for citizens	Unique identification number (SSID) for citizens based on MPHS data	To be planned
16. Data warehousing	* To analyze the huge historic data generated in the computerized departments &	* Project implemented jointly by GOI & Govt. of A.P. * Did not yield desired result

1	2	3
	agencies.	* RFP to be issued in May 2002 for implementing the project on fresh lines.
17. IT organization	* To manage the IT infrastructure	
18. Architecture	* A compilation of open technology standards * A set of best practices in deployment of ICT, with spl. reference to government. * Already developed & published on the Internet@www.ap-it,com in February, 2002 * Standards have been mandated through Government order for compliance by all departments/developers * The Architecture developed is being updated with last technology developments * Model to be improved incorporating role for NGOs	
19. Security policy	Already developed	
20. PPP for e-government	* Policy for funding e-Government initiatives * ------through G.O. Ms. No. 40 dtd. 14.8.2001	
21. Change management policy	* Framework to manage the organisational change due to e-Government	To be planned
22. Privacy policy	* How to safe guard the information and provide confidence to stakeholders	To be planned

Andhra Pradesh's vision of e-Government—The Big Picture:—Government of Andhra Pradesh conducted a research on various aspects of e-Government over the last few years through implementation of a few projects and through external

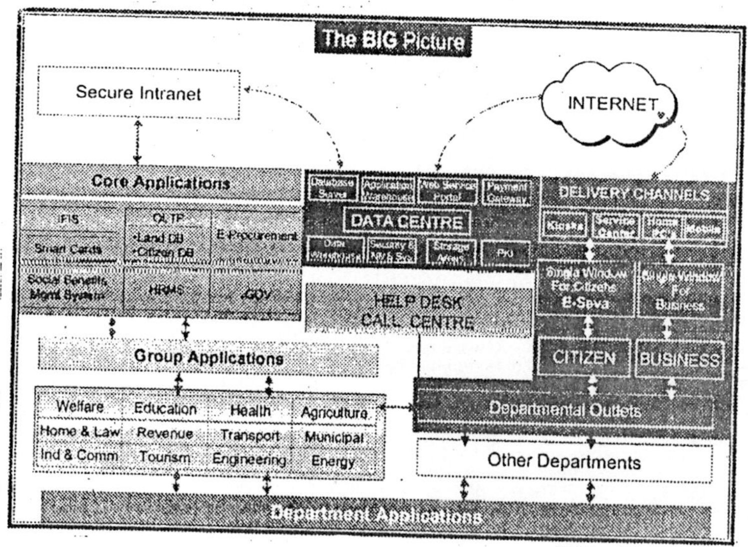

Fig.

The 'Big Picture' has sharpened the understanding of Government of A.P of the key components of e-Government, their inter-se priority, interdependencies and linkages. The Big Picture' is not static but is being constantly reviewed and fine-tuned

consultancies. The concepts and models developed in the process have been described in the foregoing portion of this paper. It was felt appropriate to draw **'The Big Picture'** by visually representing all the components of e-Government (other than the policies). The following picture emerged as a result of this effort.

It is the earnest wish of Govt. of A.P to convert the 'Big Picture' into a ground reality substantially by the middle of 2003.

Information Technology Policy: Assam

INTRODUCTION

Information Technology (IT) occupies a key position in our modern age and is one of the fastest growing sectors in the world economy. Applications of IT have become pervasive, covering all spheres of life. Government of Assam has recognized this fact and has formulated the policy below keeping in mind all facets of IT.

OBJECTIVES OF THE POLICY

The basic objectives of the Information Technology policy of Assam shall be:

To accord primacy for the growth of I.T industry for the purpose of socio-economic development of the State.

To accelerate the use of Information Technology industry at the governmental level with the view to provide better services to the citizens of the state.

To improve productivity and efficiency of the Government services to the citizens of the state.

To serve as an important tool to enhance employability as well absorb a major portion of the educated employed in the state.

To enable the state reach an eminent position in the Information Technology sector.

- To encourage and accelerate the growth of both the domestic and the export oriented I.T units in the state and make the state an attractive destination for I.T investment within India and abroad.
- To encourage and accelerate the use of Information Technology in schools, colleges and educational institutions in the state to enable the youth to acquire necessary skills and knowledge in this sector making them highly employable.
- To set up training institutes in the private sector and the joint sector in order to prepare skilled manpower within the existing system.

— To organize Manpower Development Training in the field of Computer Applications for the successful implementation of the Information Technology Policy of Assam.
— To develop appropriate networks between various departments and different spatially spread out administrative hierarchies through well designed database management systems.
— To encourage the spread of IT in the private sector.

1. SALIENT FEATURES OF THE POLICY

The salient features for the Information Technology Policy of Assam shall be:

3.1 Information Technology Policy for the Government Administration:

3.1.1 The Industry & Commerce Department would function as nodal department, for implementation of the IT Policy, which would co-ordinate with all the other departments of the government of Assam in order to ensure that the detailed objectives and goals of the IT Policy are achieved.

3.1.2 The Government shall endeavour to have connectivity among all its offices within 2004 so that communication can flow through e-mail/ video conferencing etc., to enhance productivity. The Government shall endeavour to provide video conferencing & e-mail facilities in all district headquarters to enable communication with the State Secretariat.

3.1.3 The Government shall endeavour to improve the process of governance so that citizens could file their documents required by the Government electronically. Web applications would be developed in the local language of the state.

3.1.4 The Government shall endeavour to put in place training programme to enable all government employees to use Information Technology to enhance productivity.

3.1.5 The Government shall make a special budget allocation of at least 2-3 % of the plan fund allocated to the Government departments every year to complete its computerisation programmes in each Department. An I.T sub-plan would be formulated department-wise and closely monitored.

3.1.6 The Government shall improve infrastructure such as laying of communication cables for interconnecting the departments, setting up of data transfer exchanges, routers etc., and ensure reliable power supply, transport system etc., to improve the quality of work.

3.1.7 The Government shall encourage the use of Information Technology in all educational institutions by way of giving special grants every year to enable them to put up the necessary infrastructure. Connectivity between the various educational institutions would also be established by 2004.

3.1.8 The Government shall with the help of the industry start training programmes for teachers to help them use information technology in the teaching process.

3.1.9 The Government shall endeavour to teach the school level children the use of computers and to impart training through computers. All college students in the state of Assam would be encouraged to undertake three months course in the use of Information Technology and in working on computers by 2004.

3.2.0 The Government shall endeavour to increase the number of college students specialising in Information Technology to meet the needs of the Information Technology industry to cater to both the export and the domestic market. The syllabi for specialisation in computer education would be standardised and recognised to make it more relevant. The education department would monitor the placements on offer and make suitable changes in the design of courses according to the needs of the jobs.

3.2.1 The Government shall strengthen the Assam Electronic Development Corporation Ltd (AEDC Ltd). AEDC will play the role of facilitator and assist various govt. Departments in selection of appropriate Hardware, Software and training programmes in accordance with their needs.

3.2.2 For specialised training in emerging areas of Computer and Communication Technology, the Government shall consider sponsoring employees of various Government departments, undertakings, autonomous organisations and other non-governmental organisations to institutions situated within or outside the state. All efforts would be made to set up an autonomous IIIT at Guwahati with assistance from Private sector and Union Government.

3.3. Information Technology Policy for the Industry.

3.3.1 Government shall set-up a Software Technology Park (STP) at Guwahati in the first phase with comprehensive infrastructural facilities which would include adequate power, water and telecommunication facilities. Adequate residential areas shall also be developed in and around the STP to enable easy accessibility to the professionals working in the STP units.

3.3.2 Government shall encourage the private sector to establish STPs in the State of Assam.

3.3.3 Government shall permit establishment of the IT industries in residential areas.

3.3.4 The Government shall endeavour to set up an electronic sub-urban town in an appropriate location having fully developed integrated infrastructural facilities. This Electronic City shall be solely for the use of the Information Technology Industry and allied services, The state government will encourage private sector participation in development of such infrastructure.

3.3.5 The Government shall co-ordinate and liaison with the Software Technology Park of India (STPI), the nodal agency for development for the software industry and organisations such as Videsh Sanchar Nigam (VSNL), Department of Electronics, Department of Telecommunication, National Informatic Centre, and other such organisations of Government of India to expand communication links in the state of Assam. These agencies shall be encouraged to set up gateways and earth stations and Government shall try to provide land / building / space and other facilities whenever needed on priority basis.

3.3.6 In order to ensure that the Information Technology industries in the state are in a position to meet international quality certification like ISO 9000 etc., and Software Engineering Institute (SEI) certification which are insisted upon by International companies, efforts would be made to establish such an organisation or its branch at Guwahati, which shall be authorised to issue such certifications as may be necessary.

3.3.7 For development of 100% Export Oriented Units (EOU) in Assam, Government of India would be requested to designate an Officer at Guwahati to grant necessary clearances and approvals under 100% Export Oriented Scheme.

3.3.8 Information Technology industries in the State would be assisted with the development of telecommunication network in the state for which Government and its agencies would constantly liase and co-ordinate with Department of Telecommunication and draw up time bound action plans for up-gradation and strengthening of telecommunication net works. As a short-term measure, development agencies of the Government of Assam *viz.* Assam Industrial Development Corporation Ltd., Assam Small Industries Development Corporation Ltd., Assam Electronic Development Corporation Ltd. & Assam Industrial Infrastructural Development Corporation Ltd. shall make block bookings for telecommunication connections in potential areas and locations. This would ensure that entrepreneurs who come forward to set-up Information Technology Industry can be sanctioned telecommunication facilities immediately on application.

3.3.9 Government shall endeavour to arrange financial assistance to the Information Technology industries to be established and set-up in the state. Government will initiate dialogue with the Banks and Financial Institutions to evolve a suitable procedure for obtaining finance for the units on a priority basis. The state Govt. would create a corpus of funds as venture capital fund with AIDC to provide assistance to the IT sector.

4. Definitions and Eligibility

Information Technology includes Information Technology and telecommunications.

Information Technology industry includes IT hardware and software industries; IT software industry includes IT software, IT services and IT enabled services, but excludes training institutions in this field.

Information Technology infrastructure means the physical infrastructure built by the Central Government, State Government, a firm, a builder and sold to an IT industry for its own use or the infrastructure built by an IT industry for its own use.

New unit means an IT unit which has commenced commercial production on or after the date on which the policy has been notified.

Existing unit means an IT unit, which is or was in

commercial operation at any time prior to the date on which the policy has been notified.

100% Export Oriented Unit means an IT unit, which undertakes to export its entire value added goods subject to relaxation as permitted by the Government of India from time to time.

Fixed Capital means and includes cost of land & its development, building including operational space, godown, laboratory, plant & Machinery & its installation cost, pre-operative expenses capitalised, Electrical and such other equipment which are directly related to operational activity.

Expansion of an IT unit means additional fixed capital investment exceeding at least 25% of the capital investment of the existing unit. For the purpose of calculation, gross value of all the capital investment made on land, building and plant and machinery of the existing unit will be taken into consideration. Expansion shall also imply an increase of at least 25% in the existing installed capacity as well as increase in an additional employment by least 10%.

Modernisation means separately identifiable investment made by an industrial unit involving new/improved technology having definite advantages in reduction of cost of production provided the additional investment in fixed assets should not be less than 25% of the gross fixed capital.

4.1 Eligibility

All industries defined as IT industries shall be eligible for the incentives enumerated.

The units undergoing expansion / modernisation shall be eligible for incentives for the increased capacity created after expansion / modernisation of the existing unit.

4.2 INCENTIVES FOR PROMOTION OF INVESTMENT IN IT SECTOR:

Incentives shall be available to the new units as well as to the existing units undergoing expansion/modernisation. The package of incentives shall be as follows:

4.2.1 Sales Tax Exemptions

All new units and existing units undergoing substantial

expansion / up-gradation / diversification shall be granted sales tax exemption on sale of finished products, value added products and purchase of capital goods and raw materials for the following period. However, sales tax exemption for purchase of capital goods will be given only if such goods are purchased locally:

1. New units—10 years
2. Existing units — 10 years
(undergoing expansion/up-gradation / diversification)

(A separate notification will be issued by the Finance (Taxation) Department in this regard)

However, the sales tax exemption will be reviewed by the Industries and Commerce Department after 5 years to decide their continuation or otherwise.

4.2.2 Power Subsidy

Power subsidy shall be available for a period of 5 years from the date of going into commercial production. The amount of subsidy shall be 50% subject to a ceiling of Rs. 5.00 lakh per year.

4.2.3 Subsidy on Generating set

The subsidy on captive generating set including non-conventional energy generation set shall be 50% of the cost of the generating set subject to a ceiling of Rs.10.00 lakh per industrial unit.

4.2.4 State Capital Investment Subsidy

State Capital Investment Subsidy of 30% on the capital investment on land, building, plant & machinery etc., subject to a ceiling of Rs.10.00 lakh shall be provided to an IT unit under the policy. For 100% EOU and for units run by women S.C. and ST. Entrepreneurs the ceiling of subsidy shall be Rs.15.00 lakh.

4.2.5 Subsidy on Infrastructure:

50% subsidy on shed rent payable to STPI shall be available for a period of three years from the date of going into commercial operation subject to a ceiling of Rs. 2 lakh per annum.

4.2.7 Subsidy on Hot line/Lease line connectivity:

30% subsidy on Hot line/Lease line connectivity paid to

STPI or VSNL subject to a ceiling of Rs. 5.00 lakh per annum shall be available to the units for a period of three years from the date of commercial operation.

4.2.8 Manpower Development subsidy:

Subsidy on Manpower development shall be provided in respect of training/technical upgradation/Skill upgradation of local persons in a recognised training organisation/institution subject to the following ceiling:

Investment in fixed capital	Total ceiling
Up to Rs. 20.00 lakh	Rs. 1.50 lakh
Rs. 20.00 lakh to Rs. 25.00 lakh	Rs. 2.00 lakh
Rs. 25.00 lakh to Rs. 50.00 lakh	Rs. 3.00 lakh
Rs. 50.00 lakh to Rs. 100.00 lakh	Rs. 5.00 lakh
Above Rs. 100.00 lakh and above crore	Rs. 10.00 lakh

The above amount shall be available for a period of five years from the date of commercial operation of the unit only.

4.2.9 Subsidy on Quality Certification:

50% of the cost for getting ISO: 9000, Software Engineering Institute (SEI) certification and Quality Assurance Institute (QAI) certification shall be subsidised subject to a ceiling of Rs. 2.00 lakh.

4.3 For mega projects the government would consider special incentives on a case by case basis in addition to the benefits already provided. A mega project may be defined as one having an investment of Rs.100 crore and more.

5. Special incentives for IT Enabled Industries

In addition to the benefits provided to IT Industries the following benefits shall be provided for IT enabled services.

5.1 Power subsidy shall be available for a period of 5 years, from the date of going into commercial production. The amount of subsidy shall be 60% subject to a ceiling of Rs.10.00 lakh per year.

5.2 The subsidy on captive generating set including non-conventional energy generation set shall be 60% of the cost of the generating set subject to a ceiling of Rs.15.00 lakh per industrial unit.

5.3 State Capital Investment Subsidy of 40% on the capital investment on land, building, plant & machinery etc., subject to a ceiling of Rs.15.00 lakh shall be provided to an IT unit under the policy.

5.4 60% subsidy on shed rent payable to STPI shall be available for a period of three years from the date of going into commercial operation subject to a ceiling of Rs. 5 lakh per annum.

5.5 40% subsidy on Hot line / Lease line connectivity paid to STPI or VSNL subject to a ceiling of Rs.10.00 lakh per annum shall be available to the units for a period of three years from the date of commercial operation.

The eligibility criteria specifically for the IT enabled sector are as follows :

(a) The unit should provide employment for minimum 100 local persons.

(b) Employment should be provided for a minimum period of three years.

(c) A minimum wage of atleast Rs. 4500 per month per employee shall be provided by the unit.

6. The Government would take all necessary steps to exempt the IT Industry from the relevant provisions of the following regulations -

(a) Factories Act, 1948

(b Employment Exchange (compulsory notification of vacancies) Act, 1959

(c) Payment of Wages Act, 1936

(d) Minimum Wages Act, 1948

(e) Contract Labour (Regulation & abolition) Act, 1970

(f) Workmen Compensation Act, 1923

(g) Shops and Establishment Act, 1971

(h) Employees State Insurance Act, 1948

(i) Zoning Regulations under the Guwahati Metropolitan Authority Act, 1985

(Notification for zoning *vide* No.TCP.79/83/56, dtd. 25.9.1986 published in Gazette on 24.12.1986).

7. Implementing Agency:

The Industries and Commerce Dept. Would be the nodal agency for implementation of Information Technology Policy of

Assam on behalf of the State Government. The Policy shall come into effect from the date of notification of this policy till such time, the Government may consider it fit and proper. The Government also reserves the right to make any amendments in the policy.

8. Eligibility Certificate:

8.1 Eligibility Certificate is a certificate, which shall be issued by the Udyog Sahayak Cell to be constituted at the Assam Electronic Development Corporation Ltd. For the purpose of implementation of this policy.

8.2 No right or claim for any incentives under the policy shall be deemed to have been conferred by the policy merely by virtue of the fact that the unit on its part has fulfilled the conditions of the scheme.

8.3 The incentives under the scheme cannot be claimed unless the FINAL Eligibility Certificate has been issued under the policy by the implementing agency and the unit has complied with stipulations / conditions of the Eligibility Certificate.

8.4 The decision of the implementing agency, subject to such direction as Government may issue from time to time in this regard shall be final and binding.

9. Procedures for application:

Separate guidelines for issuance of Eligibility Certificate & submission of claims for incentives would be issued.

10. Priority for disbursement:

The disbursement of the incentives by the implementing agency shall be in accordance with the chronological order of approved claims. Priority shall however be given to 100% Export Oriented Units.

11. Interpretation:

The decision of the Industries & Commerce Department, Government of Assam, as regards to interpretation of this policy resolution/incentive scheme shall be final. The State Government reserves the right to increase or decrease the incentives or frame new guidelines, amend any provision(s) including withdrawal of any of the incentives/subsidies provided in this policy.

12. Implementation and Monitoring of the Policy:

12.1 Information Technology Cell (ITC):

In order to provide various information and facilities to the IT industry and to ensure proper delivery of all services a separate Cell known as Information Technology Cell (ITC) shall be created at the Assam Electronics Development Corporation Ltd. (a Government of Assam undertaking). The primary objective of the ITC shall be to provide adequate information to the entrepreneurs, identification of projects and its implementation and also to keep in touch with similar organisational institutions on the line of IT within and out side the state.

12.2 Functions of ITC:

All administrative Departments shall refer all issues related to implementation of the Information Technology Policy to the ITC and keep the ITC apprised of all actions taken in this regard. ITC will perform the following functions:

(i) Ensure adequate publicity of the Information Technology Policy of Assam, 2000 as well as render all assistance to the entrepreneurs to avail the benefit of the incentives.

(ii) Identification of prospective entrepreneurs, building up a data bank to guide and motivate the entrepreneurs and also to prepare viable project profiles in different categories of investment.

(iii) Enlistment of applications and issuance of eligibility certificate under the policy.

(iv) Co-ordinating with the connected agencies / administrative departments for implementation of the IT Policy.

(v) Proper and effective implementation of all incentives and issuance of sanctions thereof.

(vi) To refer all relevant issues to the Government or to the Committees framed thereunder for any matter connected with implementation of the policy.

(vii) To take up any other matter entrusted by the Government from time to time.

12.3 Procedures for issuing eligibility certificate:

The application for issuance of eligibility certificate shall be submitted to the Assam Electronic Development Corporation Ltd., directly for issuance of Eligibility Certificate. The Government shall issue a separate notification on constitution of a committee entrusted with the powers of approval on the proposals.

12.4 Information Technology Task Force:

An Information Technology Task Force of the State (ITTFS) shall be constituted under the Chairmanship of the Chief Minister to review the implementation of the Policy as per references given below:

1.	The Chief Minister of Assam	Chairman
2.	The Minister of Industries & Commerce, Assam	Vice-Chairman
3.	The Chief Secretary of Assam	Member
4.	The Commissioner & Secretary/Secretary to the Govt. of Assam, Industries & Commerce Department	Member "
5.	The Commissioner & Secretary/Secretary to the Govt. of Assam, Education Department	"
6.	The Commissioner & Secretary/Secretary to the Govt. of Assam, Finance Department	"
7.	The Commissioner & Secretary/Secretary to the Govt. of Assam, Science & Technology Department	"
8.	The Commissioner & Secretary/Secretary to the Govt. of Assam, Planning & Development Department.	"
9.	Four representatives from the IT industry to be nominated by the Government	"
10.	The Director IIT Guwahati	"
11.	The Chief General Manager, DOT, Assam Circle	"
12.	The Director, STP, Guwahati	"
13.	The Director of Industries & Commerce, Assam	"
14.	The Managing Director, AIDC Ltd.	"
15.	The General Manger, SIDBI	"
16.	The Chairman NEDFI	"
17.	The Managing Director, AEDC Ltd.	Member

Chairman/Vice-Chairman may co-opt at least five expert Secretary(s) as members of the committee.

Function of the Committee:

1. To review the implementation of Information Technology Policy of Assam, 2000 and to make suggestions for improvement in this regard to the concerned departments from time to time.
2. To advise the State Government for constitution of any sub-committees or any study team for effective implementation of the policy for the State.

3. To examine the problems faced during the implementation of the policy and suggest remedial measures to solve such problems.
4. To discuss inter developmental co-ordination problems to suggest remedial measures.
5. To review and monitor development of infrastructure for IT Industry.
6. The Committee shall meet as and when necessary but not less than thrice in a year with the approval of the Chairman.

12.5 Inter-Departmental Information Technology Committee:

To co-ordinate inter departmental activities to propagate development of Information Technology in the State and to monitor the development in the sectors like education, Industry etc. An Inter Departmental Information Technology Committee (IDITC) shall be constituted under the Chairmanship of the Chief Secretary as below:

1.	The Chief Secretary, Govt. of Assam	Chairman
2.	The Commissioner & Secretary/Secretary to the Govt. of Assam, Industries & Commerce Department	Member Secretary
3.	The Commissioner & secretary/Secretary to the Govt. of Assam, Finance Department.	Member
4.	The Commissioner & Secretary/Secretary to the Govt. of Assam, Planning & Development Department.	Member
5.	The Commissioner & Secretary/Secretary to the Govt. of Assam, Education Department	Member
6.	The Commissioner & Secretary/Secretary to the Govt. of Assam, Revenue Department	Member
7.	The Commissioner & Secretary/Secretary to the Govt. of Assam, Science & Technology Department	Member
8.	The Managing Director, AIDC Ltd.	Member
9.	The Managing Director, AEDC Ltd.	Member
10.	The Director of Industries & Commerce.	Member

Chairman may co-opt at least two expert(s) as members for the committee.

Function of the Committee will be as follows:

1. To review the implementation of Information Technology Policy of Assam, 2000 and to make suggestions to the

Information Technology Task Force from time to time.

2. To monitor the implementation of the various objectives of the policy and to suggest growth of IT industries in the State.
3. To examine the problems faced during the implementation of the policy and suggest remedial measures.
4. To look into the matters of different Government departments in relation to IT.
5. The Committee shall meet once in quarter in a year with the approval of the Chairman.

I.T. Policy of UT Chandigarh

1.0 Introduction

Information Technology is an important and extremely effective tool through which development and progress can take place with the co-operation of all strata of society including government and the public. Chandigarh Administration is committed to providing a responsive and effective administration for the welfare of the public keeping in view the national objectives. Chandigarh Administration recognises the need to harness the growing power of I.T. for the betterment of the life of the residents of the Union Territory of Chandigarh.

2.0 The I.T. Vision of Chandigarh Administration

The vision of Chandigarh Administration is to create a knowledge-based society through extensive use of Information Technology. Chandigarh Administration envisages a scenario wherein every citizen shall be able to access the benefits of Information technology by the year 2005. The residents of this UT are enlightened enough to realise the significance of the IT revolution and it is expected that they shall wholeheartedly participate in this movement. The ultimate goal is to use IT as a medium for effective interaction between the Administration and the public so that exchange of information and access to government departments is speedy and easy, leading to a better quality of life.

3.0 The I.T. Mission of Chandigarh Administration

- To provide **public service** for the residents through e-governance which is efficient, speedy and cost effective.

- To promote **Industrial development** through Information Technology. Creation of IT Infrastructure would be given emphasis so that Industry can utilise this infrastructure for modern isolation to increase productivity.
- To reduce unemployment by generating more jobs in Information Technology. The requirement of trained I.T. Professionals is far in excess of the availability and therefore Institutions would be created to bridge this gap.
- To increase **exports** in the I.T. field by creating a platform for excellence in software development by utilising the services of software professionals.
- To make Chandigarh an ideal **I.T. destination.**

4.0 Chandigarh — An ideal I.T. destination

Chandigarh provides an ideal stage for the growth of the IT culture and optimum utilisation of the benefits of the IT. revolution. The following features make Chandigarh a potential IT leader:

4.1 **A planned city like no other** — Chandigarh is one of the successes of modern architectural planning and its planned infrastructure provides the ideal foundation for the growth of the I.T. Industry.

4.2 **A micropolitan city** — A city where the quality of life is excellent, and the disadvantages of large metropolitan cities are not present.

4.2.1 The farthest point from anywhere in Chandigarh is only 9 kms.

4.2.2 A Pollution free environment exists.

4.3 **Geographical Advantage** — The city is very close to the national capital and is well connected with the rest of the country. Excellent road, rail and air links exist.

4.4 **The Institutional edge** — The educational environment of the city is highly conducive to the growth of the IT Industry. A University, Engineering College, Medical Colleges, Polytechnics and Major Computer Institutes already exist. Computer education is being introduced in schools.

5.0 Advisory Committee on I.T. applications

This committee shall be set up in order to ensure optimum use of the IT. potential of UT Chandigarh. The purpose of the Advisory Committee is to provide a vision and direction to the I.T. Implementation Committee so that the aims and objectives of the IIT policy can be achieved. The details of the committee are given at Annexure A.

6.0 Salient features of the I.T. Policy

- I.T. Infrastructure.
- Development of I.T. Industry and Business.
- e-Governance.
- Human Resource Development—Training.

6.1 I. T. Infrastructure

The creation of a suitable base in the field of IT infrastructure is essential before further progress can be made. Chandigarh Administration shall endeavour to create infrastructure which shall provide an ideal platform for the growth of the IT sector.

6.1.1 **Wired City** — Chandigarh shall be developed as a 'Wired City". The Administration shall create a connectivity Backbone Network within the city of Chandigarh. Internet access and establishment of a Wide Area Network (WAN) for the entire UT including all government/corporate offices and private institutions and individuals, shall be given priority. A Local Area Network (LAN) would be set up in all important government offices.

6.1.2 **Software Development Units**—Setting up of Software **Development** units in the UT in large numbers. A single window scheme shall be started to consider requests for public/private sector Software Development Units on priority basis.

6.1.3 **Information centres/Kiosks**—Use of intelligent Network Service for dissemination of public information. Kiosks (Information Centres) shall be set up for providing information and facilitating public services, throughout the UT. These shall be connected through Internet.

6.1.4 **ISPs/Gateway**—Promotion of Internet Service Providers (ISPs) operations including provision of real time connectivity to International gateways. DOT shall be requested to lease the spare capacity of the existing fibre optic network for data transmission to ISPs.

6.1.5 **Internet through cable**—Establishment of Internet Access through the Cable T.V. Network shall be done throughout the UT so as to provide speedy connectivity to all the residents of the UT.

6.1.6 **Multimedia**—To promote further the use of multimedia services including Fax/e-mail and Internet. The aim shall be to reach out to the maximum number of residents who shall benefit from the I.T. revolution.

6.1.7 **Rural Areas**—Internet penetration in rural areas shall be increased and efforts shall be made to educate the rural population about the benefits of Information Technology. Various departments like Agriculture and Health shall be urged to enlighten the people of rural areas about the benefits of IT.

6.2 **Development of I.T. Industry and Business**

The following incentives and facilities shall be provided for the purpose of encouraging companies to come forward for setting up IT. units in the UT.

6.2.1 i. **T. Towers** — Construction of IT Towers shall be undertaken for the software industry. Plug and play facilities shall be provided, with real time connectivity. These IT Towers shall provide the ideal platform for software units to be set up in large numbers in Chandigarh.

6.2.2 **Exemption from Inspections**—IT services companies shall be exempted from inspections under the Factories Act and the Shops & Establishments Act.

6.2.3 **Depreciation norms**—These shall be as per approved Govt. of India Policy.

6.2.4 **Loaning by Financial Institutions**—Loans for Capital Investment and working capital requirement would be given as per GOI policy by the Delhi Financial Corporation (DFC). Priority shall be given to IT services for provision of financial aid. A number of attractive schemes shall be introduced for the I T industry

6.2.5 **Investment and Venture capital** — Financial Institutions and Banks shall be allowed to invest in the IT sector in the form of equity. A fund has already been set up by the

Delhi Financial Corporation (DFC) to provide venture capital for the IT sector.

6.2.6 **Single Window Clearance** — Single Window Clearance shall be provided for all IT companies interested in setting up units in Union Territory of Chandigarh.

6.2.7 **Annual Awards** — Annual awards of excellence shall be given by the Chandigarh Administration for outstanding performers in IT. These awards shall be given in the fields of software exports, training and e-commerce.

6.3 e-Governance

A Committee for implementation of the IT policy in Administration shall be set up in order to make optimum use of the power of IT. ({ HYPERLINK "http://chandigarh.nic.in/" "Annexure 'B' " }). The Committee shall ensure that e-governance provides the ideal environment for the welfare of the public by facilitating easy access to government offices through networking. A Task Force shall be set up in each department for this purpose ({ HYPERLINK "http://chandigarh.nic.in)" "Annexure 'C' " }).

The Action Plan for the implementation of the IT policy and e-governance in UT Chandigarh is at (HYPERLINK "http:/ chandigarh.nic.in!' " "Annexure 'D' " }.

6.3.1 **Departmental Plans**—Each government department and agency in U.T. Administration shall prepare a five year IT plan which shall broadly define the goal of the department in specific sectors using IT.

6.3.1.1 **Excise and Taxation Department**—The implementation of the taxation system prevailing in the UT shall be modified in accordance with the increasing usage of IT. Online connectivity shall enable simplified procedures for levying of commercial taxes. This shall eliminate delays and bottlenecks in the taxation procedures. A database of registered dealers shall be maintained. Issuance of licences (ST No. & CST No.) shall be computerised and STy registers (Both CHA and CST) shall be automatically updated. Automatic generation of notices, defaulters and pending payments shall be possible.

6.3.1.2 **Education Department** — All colleges and schools shall be fully computerised and all students shall be encouraged to be IT. literate. The Education department shall be connected online with all educational institutions including Medical and Engineering colleges. A data bank of students who are IT. literate shall be maintained and a tie-up with industry for employment shall be ensured. More courses will be introduced in all institutions to produce IT Professionals.

6.3.1.3 **Municipal Corporation**—The residents of Chandigarh shall benefit from the introduction of the I.T. culture in the Municipal Corporation of Chandigarh. All services provided by the Corporation shall be computerised and residents shall be able to access the various departments of the corporation online from the kiosks, which shall be set up throughout the UT. Public grievances shall be given priority and shall be resolved speedily by the use of computers and interconnectivity. Mapping of the whole area of the UT shall be done and co-ordination between the various departments shall be ensured to prevent repeated inconvenience to the public as and when digging or construction activities are carried out.

6.3.1.4 **Estate Office** — For the benefit of the residents of Chandigarh, the Estate office shall provide information to all residents *via* terminals, which shall be set up throughout the UT. Procedures shall be simplified through the use of computers and interconnectivity. Various forms and instructions shall be available online to the general public. All the files of the Estate office shall be computerised and information from them as per requirement shall be made available to the public, while keeping in view the necessity for keeping certain documents confidential.

6.3.1.5 **Driving Licences and Registration** — All driving licences and Registration certificates shall be computerised and procedures for issuance of new licences and registration certificates and also for their renewal shall be made convenient for the public through online connectivity. Delays shall be totally eliminated and an effort shall be made to provide these documents the same day as the application is made. Smart Cards shall be introduced for registration certificates and driving licences.

6.3.1.6 **Treasury** — The government treasury shall be computerised and connected online with the UT secretariat and other important offices. All bills and other documents shall be computerised and manual processes shall be minimised. Necessary security checks shall be carried out and a foolproof system shall be introduced.

6.3.1.7 **Police** — Officers and officials of the Chandigarh Police shall be made IT literate. Connectivity between all the police stations and the police headquarters shall be ensured and these offices shall be connected with those of the district magistrate and also the sub divisional magistrate. The UT secretariat and the Police Headquarters shall also be connected online for speedy communication and exchange of information for ensuring greater efficiency in policing.

6.3.1.8 **Other Applications** — Computerisation of Ration cards Arms licences, and Births and Deaths certificates shall also be done. Other departments shall be taken up in a phased manner.

6.3.2 **Web site** — The Chandigarh Administration already has its own **web site ({ HYPERLINK "http://chandigarh.nic.in"** }). Comprehensive information about Chandigarh and its various aspects, including the IT. policy of Union Territory Chandigarh, shall be available on the web site. Interactive web sites shall be developed for all major departments of the Administration.

6.3.3 **Budget**—At least 1% of the Plan Budget of the Administration shall be earmarked for IT applications in the Administration every year. The investment would include expenditure on IT Hardware, software, IT. services and I.T. Training.

6.3.4 **Provisions** — The re-appropriation of each Department's IT budget will be done by its Administrative Secretary. The IT budget sub-head shall be within the delegated powers of the HOD, subject to the condition that not more than 65% of the IT budget shall be spent on hardware and peripherals.

6.3.5 **Accessibility**—U.T. Administration will establish a central repository of data elements in government and make it accessible as per Govt. of India policy.

6.3.6 **New Appointments** - U.T. Administration would give preference in appointment to IT literate persons for employment to all public sector and government posts.

6.3.7 **LAN/WAN**—The UT Secretariat and other government offices shall be intra-connected and interconnected to increase efficiency. In a time bound programme personal computers and mobile E-mail/Fax communication will be provided to senior government officers. UT Secretariat will be linked with all departments at other locations in Chandigarh using FO link.

6.3.8 **Government Notifications**—All government circulars, instructions, notifications, tenders shall be published on web site of Chandigarh Administration.

6.3.9 **File Management**—An automated, transparent file movement system shall be introduced at various levels of each department/PS U.

6.3.10 **Awards**—Awards shall be given to the departments/PSUs, which carry out outstanding work in the IT. field.

6.4 Human Resource Development (Training)

For creating a conducive IT environment, Human Resource Development shall have to be given great emphasis. The success of any new technology revolves around the success of this activity. To develop the required manpower in terms of expertise and number the following shall be pursued.

6.4.1 **Infrastructure**—All educational institutions will have computer laboratories and access to Internet. An IT course module shall be made a compulsory component of all degrees/ diploma courses in educational institutions. Courses will be designed to meet current requirement in I.T. industry. I.T. training will be made compulsory for all the students as part of their course in the ITIs/Polytechnics.

6.4.2 **I.T. College**—The demand for IT professionals is growing tremendously in the region. The setting up of an IT College, with advanced centres for IT, shall be given priority. B Tech. (Information Technology) courses shall be started. Professionals from I.T. industry will also be engaged as faculty to provide practical exposure to the students. Regular visits to I.T. industries in the region will also be arranged to provide practical training. Special courses on Project Management, Software Technology, and Software Marketing, shall be offered by the I.T. College. The courses will be redesigned and restructured regularly to train the students in the latest technologies.

6.4.3 **I.T. in Schools**—An IT course module shall also be made available in schools. The infrastructure created in schools shall be used as a training centre for the public after school hours by the institute, in return for free training to a proportionate number of students from weaker sections. A centralised library with educational CD-ROMs shall be set up, from where the schools can obtain CDs. Schools in rural areas shall have multimedia labs where regular demonstrations in English, Hindi and Punjabi language shall be given, to spread the IT culture

6.4.4 **Digital Library** — The U.T. digital library project will be launched. Efforts shall be made to make available the database of Central State Library and other major libraries — Punjab University, Punjab Engineering College, etc. This shall also be made available on the Net.

6.4.5 **Training for Government Employees**—I.T. training shall be made mandatory for all government employees. Courses with different skills shall be conducted for officials at different levels of different departments. Two or three officials from each department shall be identified and trained for in-house Systems Administration. These officials shall be nominated for short-term courses organised by reputed I.T. training institutes at departmental expenses. A few important areas of training at different levels shall include:

- Management Information Systems
- Office Automation
- Project Management
- Technology Trends
- Intranet & Internet
- Networking Tools
- Web Technology

Annexure 'A'

Advisory Committee for I.T. Application in U.T. Chandigarh

The Committee proposed below will meet at least quarterly.

1.	Advisor to Administrator	Chairperson
2.	Finance Secretary & Secretary IT.	Vice Chairperson
3.	Home Secretary	Member
4.	Commissioner Chandigarh Municipal Corporation	Member
5.	Deputy Commissioner	Member
6.	Joint Secretary Finance, Director Public Instruction (C)	Member
7.	Managing Director, CITCO	Member
8.	Inspector General of Police	Member
9.	Chief Engineer, UT.	Member

10.	Principal General Manager Telecom	Member
11.	Director Regional Computer Centre	Member
12.	Additional Director STPI	Member
13.	Director	Member
14.	Director Health	Member
15.	Director Technical Education	Member
16.	State Informatics Officer, National Informatics Centre	Member
17.	Additional Director I.T.	Member, Convenor

Annexure 'B'

I.T. Implementation Committee for U.T. Chandigah

The IT. Implementation Committee will monitor the progress of the departmental Task Forces, to implement the decisions/guidelines of the Advisory Committee. The purpose of this Committee shall be to carry forward the vision and direction of the Advisory Committee and get it implemented through the Task Forces. It will also co-ordinate the working of the Task Forces, so that they supplement each other.

The Committee proposed below shall meet after every two months:

1.	Finance Secretary & Secretary I.T.	Chairman
2.	Commissioner, Chandigarh Municipal Corporation	Member
3.	Deputy Commissioner	Member
4.	Senior Superintendent of Police (HQ)	Member
5.	Chief Engineer	Member
6.	Sub Divisional Magistrate (South)	Member
7.	Director Public Instruction (Schools)	Member
8.	Assistant Estate Officer	Member
9.	Director I.T.	Member
10.	State Informatics Officer, National Informatics Centre	Member
11.	Under Secretary I.T.	Member
12.	Deputy Excise & Taxation Commissioner	Member
13.	Additional Director I.T.	Member, Convenor

Annexure 'C'
I.T. Task Force

There will be a Task Force in each department, which shall be responsible for the implementation of the I.T. policy in that department. The Task Force shall meet at least once a month and shall monitor the progress of the department's I.T. plan. Each Task Force shall submit periodic reports to the I.T. Implementation Committee.

The Task Force shall consist of the following—

1. Head of Department (HOD) Chairman
2. Nodal Officer
3. Representative of NIC
4. Representative of I.T. Department

Annexure 'D'
ACTION PLAN

Implementation of Information Technology and e-governance in Union Territory Chandigarh for Chandigarh Administration

SYSTEM ANALYSIS

1. Identify the functionality of various U.T. departments in respect of public interaction and internal documentation and records.
2. Identify the existing functional modes in each department.
3. Identify the interface levels of the department with public or other departments.
4. Identify the existing manpower in respect of their I.T. skill level.
5. Identify the required skill levels for proper public interface.
6. Identify the training modules required for smooth interfaces and gradual change over to e-governance.
7. Identify the training schedules/schemes creating awareness among the staff to minimise hesitation and resistance.

SYSTEM DESIGN

1. Design basic network services to be provided in the City.
2. Design the departmental infrastructure.
3. Design the public interfaces.
4. Interested organisations for setting up such facility to be identified.

IMPLEMENTATION PLAN

1. Select priority services to be made functional through e-governance.
2. Select priority area to be networked.
3. Select priority department.
4. Implement the plan.
5. Check bottlenecks.
6. Review Feedback.
7. Make an efficient functional e-governance model.
8. Implement the model throughout the UT.

E-Governance Policy of Himachal Pradesh

1. Each Government Department of Himachal Pradesh shall prepare a Five Year IT Plan by March 2001. This plan shall address the extent of computerisation of its core activities, with special reference to its Citizen Interface, need for hardware and software resources, manpower requirement and training of employees.
2. National Informatics Centre (NIC) has prepared a comprehensive e-Governance proposal for networking the State Secretariat Offices in the State capital, District Collectorates, District level offices, etc. This proposal would be implemented as a joint venture between the State Government and NIC, Ministry of Information Technology, Government of India.
3. The entire Secretariat workplace would be connected with a high bandwidth optic fibre. Internet facility would be provided to all the users of the rank of Deputy Secretary and above.
4. All Districts/Departments would have video conferencing facilities and E-mail facilities with the Chief Minister as well as Chief Secretary's office to allow a quick and efficient channel of communication.

5. Tele-CM: A special project is being launched through which the Chief Minister would be able to use convergence technology to be able to have mobile video conferencing with any part of the state.
6. The existing training centres for Government employees, at the State and District headquarters, would be further strengthened for imparting appropriate training in IT.
7. Knowledge of word processing would be compulsory for the category of steno-typists after 2001. For the employees already in service, suitable training modules would be prepared and training imparted accordingly. The passing of the test in computer proficiency of a specified level would be made mandatory, for some selective cadres to begin with, for confirmation and promotion. In the Annual Confidential Reports (ACRs) of government employees for whom computer knowledge is prescribed as a pre-requisite at the entry stage, a column shall be introduced regarding contribution to 'IT utilization' in the department/organization.
8. All major IT projects have adopted English as the medium. However, for administration to be effective and for the benefits of computerisation to reach the common man, it is desirable to adopt Hindi as the medium. The Government will appoint a committee headed by Secretary (IT) to promote the local language initiative.
9. The creation of data warehouses, having local content, would be encouraged in each District. These centers would provide government information to citizens through information kiosks.
10. The Government shall endeavour to computerise the process of governance, so that the citizens could file the documents required by the Government, electronically. Priority areas with maximum citizen interface will be taken up for e-Governance. These include:
    - Rural Services such as land records, acquisition of land and registration of deeds.
    - Police services such as FIR registration.
    - Social services such as family pension, old age pension, etc.
    - Registration of licenses, ration cards, birth certificate,

Death certificate, Caste/Tribe certificate, Driving license, etc.

- o Public Information/Utility such as employment exchange registration, employment opportunities, examination results, hospitals / beds availability, road transport time tables, Government notifications, Government schemes, etc.
- o Agriculture/Horticulture sector—providing the information about Mandi rates in respect of identified commodities in important Mandis.
- o Electronic Filing of tax returns, state excise duty, house tax, property tax, road tax, etc.

Computerization:

1. Computerization projects of Revenue earning departments and agencies having high level of public contact shall be fully operationalized by the year 2002.
2. The Tax Departments of the Government would be fully computerized during the next three years. The various offices of the tax departments would be interconnected to allow flow of information. The staff of the tax departments would be trained in the use of information technology to increase tax collections, reduce delays and improve productivity. All assesses would be allowed the facility of filing their returns electronically. All assesses would be allowed the facility of paying their tax through electronic transfer of funds.
3. All departments shall be encouraged to establish websites. These will be linked under an overall umbrella of State Government website. Departments, where databases are already established shall be asked to upgrade the same to provide dynamic information and use their sites as platforms for Citizen: Government interface.
4. **Electronic Kiosks:** The Government would encourage setting up of internet kiosks on the lines of public telephone booths not only to serve the information needs of the citizens but also to provide employment to a large number of educated youth.
5. In the long run, citizens must have unique identification

card—the citizen ID. It would require a statutory enactment as well as amendments in many other laws to integrate the citizen database. Necessary statutory and non-statutory systems shall be established for registration of Himachal Pradesh citizens and issue them a multi-purpose card, on basis of which a citizen can receive a number of services, such as birth and death certificates, caste certificates, driving license, passport, ration card, personal income tax, property registration, electoral roll etc.

6. **Cyberlaws:** Himachal Pradesh is committed to ensuring that the overall local regime is in consonance with the requirements of transactions and interactions in the electronic medium. The State Government shall examine all the state level legislations and statutes so as to ensure the necessary harmonization, with the above objective in mind. The overall objective is to provide a transparent, simple and enforceable set of laws, which shall facilitate e-business and all other IT enabled activities
7. As recommended in the IT Action Plan of Central Government, the State Government shall establish framework contracts with the leading and reputed IT Services vendors so as to avail a wide range of IT consultancy, specialist services and IT products at lower cost and with a shortened procurement cycle. To minimize the technological obsolescence factor and to avoid the large upfront expenditure and expenses on maintenance, procurement of computer hardware can also be done through leasing.
8. The Government shall take initiative to establish an Inter-State IT exchange panel. Regular seminars and conferences shall be conducted where interaction with the officers of other States as well as private sector will take place.

IT Policy of Delhi

I. Citizen interface

1. Government of Delhi will use IT not merely to automate its existing procedures but also to reinvent government processes

and to redefine the role of bureaucracy. This would enable the government to make its functioning citizen-centric, transparent and efficient.

Nine Departments to go "on-line"

The government has identified nine major public dealing departments that will go 'on-line' by the year 2002. These departments are revenue, transport, sales tax, excise, education, social welfare, co-operatives, health and labour. Of these sales tax, excise and transport will go on-line by June 2001. The government will provide assistance for computerisation of Local and Autonomous Bodies such as MCD, NDMC, DVB, DJB etc. working under it.

Govt. transaction through Internet

In order to this, the government will set up the legal machinery to implement cyber law provisions regarding recognition of digital signature and electronic records and their use in government. By December 2003, it shall enable the citizens to conduct most of their transactions with the government through the Internet. Some examples of these transactions are: obtaining driving licenses, registration of vehicles, registration with employment exchanges, registration of births and deaths, obtaining ration cards, payment of various bills, lodging of various complaints and their redressal, delivery of pensions, tendering, filing of tax returns and applying for admissions. To ensure that this process is monitored periodically some important milestones have been fixed.

Heads of Departments and the OSDs

The heads of department shall be responsible for the preparation and implementation of their respective departmental action plans. An Officer on Special Duty will assist each head of department in this task. He will also act as the nodal officer in the department for implementing IT policy. The heads of departments shall allocate 3% of their departments' budget for implementation of this policy.

Employee Support

In addition, a detailed plan for employee training shall be implemented. The Civil Service Training Institute shall design new modules for IT courses for imparting computer training and education to produce knowledge workers in the government. The annual confidential reports of the employees shall reflect the employee performance in implementation of this policy. The possibility of relaxing the scheme for loan to employees for purchase of computers and peripherals shall be explored. For all new employees appropriate level of computer literacy shall be made an essential requirement in the recruitment rules.

Information through Internet

Milestone One: *December 2000*

By the end of December 2000, the citizens will be able to access information relating to transactions with the government through the Internet. Some examples of such information are: downloading of non-priced forms, information about eligibility, rules, documents required to be submitted along with various application forms, formats of affidavits, and information relating to tenders. The filing of complaints of suggestions through the Internet will also be made possible.

Simultaneously, the government will also put on the internet information that ought to be in public domain. This will enable the citizens to play the role of a watchdog and to ensure transparency. Some examples of this type of information are: land owned by the government and the gaon sabha, details relating to the civil works and payments made for them, mandi market prices, availability of hospital beds, citizens' charters, cause list of various revenue courts, names of licensees under different provisions of law and the terms and conditions thereof.

Right to Information Act

Later this information set will be further expanded and their placement in public domain will be made legally enforceable through the Right to Information Act.

Citizen Service Points

Milestone Two: June 2001

By this date some transactions with the government will be carried using telephones, stored-value credit or debit cards. This will be achieved through the intermediation of the banks. Paying bills for government services is one example. IT will make travel to the government offices unnecessary. The citizen will be able to transact business with a few major public-dealing departments from one place. These points — Citizen Service Points (CSPs)—will be electronically linked to these departments. These Points will be set up in private sector that will recover its initial cost of setting up these Points by charging the citizens a transaction fee.

Suwidha Points

Besides these CSPs, the government will set up Suwidha Points in each department to enable the citizens to interact at only a single point called the Suwidha or single user-friendly window for handling applications which have to be submitted by a certain date. At these Suwidha Points the applications will be accepted and acknowledged and the citizens will be given a date by which they may expect a response from the department. The government proposes to allot these Suwidha Points to senior citizens who will be allowed to charge handling costs.

Self-Certification exemption for IT Industry

By this date the department will explore the possibility of introducing self-certification/exemption for IT software industry under various Acts/Regulations mentioned in para D (a) (viii) above.

Use of Smart E-cards

Milestone Three: December 2001

The third milestone will be reached when citizens will be able to use electronic cards for accessing services offered by different departments. The government will consider issuing multi-purpose cards to citizens that would serve the purpose of being a ration card, an identity card, a driving license etc. The citizens will be required to register their personal details only once. To begin with, ration cards and a single electronic card in selected areas on an experimental basis will replace driving licenses by June 2001.

Race to the Finishing Line

Similar milestones will be identified for the between December 2001 to March 2003 in detailed departmental plans in such a manner that the goal of transacting business over the internet is achieved.

IMPROVING INTERNAL EFFICIENCY

II. A more efficient government

IT will also be deployed to improve government's internal efficiency. This will be done in two main areas: in internal communication and in data handling.

Use of E-mail, Bulletin Boards and Video Conferencing

Internal communication will be improved by increasing use of e-mail, bulletin boards and video conferencing in the government. Routine circulars, meeting notices, and minutes will be communicated through e-mail. Video-conferencing will be used to decide urgent matters in consultation with senior officers without calling them over from their offices. This will make them accessible to the people even while being in a position to confer with other officers in matters which are urgent and cannot wait for a formal meeting to be convened.

Data Handling

Data handling comprises data capture, data sharing, data storage, and data retrieval, data processing and data presentation. Some examples of the projects which lend themselves to data handling are Executive Information Systems for the departmental heads, computerisation of land records and hospital OPDs, ICT based delivery of education in formal, informal and non-formal sectors of education, data capture on violation of laws/rules using remote cameras or other recorders with online data updation and generation of reports in such areas as traffic violation and pollution monitoring. These projects with their target dates of completion shall be detailed in departmental plans of action. The expected progress at the milestones identified earlier *i.e.* December 2000, June 2001 and December 2001 are stated below :

Routine Communications

Milestone One: December 2000

By December 2000, all routine communication between CM's Office and departments and among departments themselves shall be done through e-mail and bulletin boards. A beginning in the use of video conferencing will be made by that date.

Networking Departments

Milestone Two: June 2001

The next milestone will be reached in June 2001. By this date all the departments shall be internally networked and projects of all departments will be under implementation.

Land Records Computerisation

Milestone Three: December 2001

By December 2001 some important projects would have been completed. These include networking of different departments, the departmental Executive Information Systems and the Land Record Computerisation.

Task Force

III. Implementation enabling mechanism

A mechanism to ensure that these milestones are reached is necessary. This is specially so because at the time of implementation many complex technical, legal, financial and institutional problems will arise. Some of these will be related to the need for process change and culture change. The government will, therefore, constitute a Task Force headed by the Chief Secretary to implement this policy. It will lay down uniform guidelines for the departments to follow so that common issues are not handled differently by different departments. A technical committee comprising representatives from IT industry and academia will assist the task force. The Task Force's first main responsibility will be to ensure that all the major public departments prepare their respective plans to implement this policy.

Incubation Centre

c. Creating an atmosphere conducive for the growth of IT Industry & IT Infrastructure

The state government will set up an "Incubation Centre" that will guide entrepreneurs to make business plans, advise on mergers and acquisitions and network with venture capital companies including the Venture Capital Fund Company to be created by the government of Delhi. The Centre will undertake financing of small IT companies.

Zero Sales Tax on IT Software and Hardware

The government is in favour of zero sales tax on the transactions of the following IT related hardware and software:

- Sale and leasing of computers and its accessories.
- Inter-state sales of computers, parts, accessories and computer consumables.
- CD-ROMS, optical disc media or magnetic media containing text, data, or multimedia.

However in keeping with the ruling of a uniform sales tax in all states, the government shall fix the sales tax on hardware and software not above the agreed Uniform Floor Rate (UFR). The state government would however lobby for zero sales tax on all IT products along with other states and central government.

IT Industries in residential localities

The state government shall strongly recommend to the Govt. of India to permit software and service units to function in residential areas subject to such reasonable restrictions as may be imposed by the government in public interest.

IT Software & service industry entitle to Industry status

All IT software and service industries including Services and Training Institutions in IT will be entitled to "Industry" status. Such units shall be eligible for all concessions and incentives applicable to Industries. For the purpose of this clause, accredited Training Institutions will also be eligible to claim industry status subject to certain norms which will enable them to obtain Term Loans and Bank Finance at industry rates.

Exemption from Routine inspection for IT industry and facility for self-certification

- IT Software and IT services companies, being constituents of the knowledge industry, shall be exempted from routine inspection by inspectors like those for Factory, Boiler, Labour, Pollution, Environment Industry in line with the approved policy of Government of India. Moreover the State Government agrees in principle to self- certification/exemption as far as possible for the IT software Industry from the provisions of the following Acts/Regulations:

- Factories Act;
- Employment Exchange (Compulsory Notification of Vacancies) Act;
- Payment of Wages Act;
- Minimum of Wages Act;
- Contract Labour (Regulation and Abolition) Act;
- Workmen Compensation Act;
- Shops and Establishments Act; and
- Employees State Insurance Act.

Permission for three shift operation

General permission is accorded, subject to such orders issued by the Police Commissioner of Delhi as may be necessary from time to time in public interest to run a three-shift operation to the IT software and Services industry.

ROW Clearance

The government shall assist in getting speedy clearance for Right of Way and use of infrastructure of utilities like DVB.

Protection of IPR

The government shall set up a regulatory framework to implement cyber laws. The intellectual property rights of creator of content and software shall be protected through vigorous enforcement of relevant copyright laws.

IT Parks

The government will establish modern IT parks in collaboration with private sector. The park will have high speed telecom facility and plug and play built up modules for minimising gestation period of new projects. The first such park will be established by the year 2002.

International Gateway

The government will encourage private companies to set

up international gateway for providing high-speed Internet connectivity.

Campaign for e-Commerce

A massive campaign will be launched to encourage e-commerce and computerisation in the local industries. It shall attempt to increase e-commerce activities by at least three times in the next two years. A suitable framework to encourage and support electronic money transfer, electronic benefited transfers (EBT cards) and electronic tagging like bar coding will be established.

IT for Industries

The government will initiate an **"IT for industries"** project. Under this project, advice will be given to the local industries to adopt use of IT or to diversify into IT activities.

IT Enabled Services

IT enabled services like Medical Transcription, Call Centres, Data Processing, Back-Office Operations, GIS, Revenue Accounting etc. are considered as niche areas for the state. A special scheme will be announced to help local industries to diversify into IT enabled services. The benefits of the scheme would also be applicable for companies setting up IT enabled services in the State.

Seminars and Workshops

The government will encourage conduct of seminars/ workshops to disseminate information of IT to local industries and thus work towards increase in usage of IT in local industries.

Establishment of regional hub

With an extremely widespread telecommunication system, the state of Delhi can take lead in establishing and serving a regional hub for Internet, e-commerce and digital services traffic.

State Level Awards

State level awards will be given to IT companies with outstanding performance in exports and in domestic segments.

GOVERNMENT OF HARYANA
INFORMATION TECHNOLOGY POLICY 2000

Preamble

Information Technology (IT) would have a prominent and progressive role in the new millennium as the single most important enabler for improving efficiency and effectiveness in organisations. The State Government recognises the role of IT as an effective tool in catalysing economic activity, in efficient governance and in developing human resource.

This policy seeks a deep impact initiative by the State Government in encouraging replacement of traditional delivery system of public services by IT driven system of governance that works better, costs less and is capable of serving the citizens' needs with ease. A high degree of public satisfaction through transparent and efficient functioning of public domain activities would be at the focus of IT initiative. Application of sunrise technologies in transition to a knowledge based society, providing equal opportunity to all in reaping the benefits of development, harnessing vast potential of human endeavour and enriching quality of life shall provide the long term underpinning of socio-economic transformation of the State.

This policy further seeks to facilitate private domain initiative in transition of Haryana by providing critical infrastructure, systems framework and enabling environment.

IT Vision

To transform Haryana into an IT driven economy

Objectives

The IT Vision is sought to be realised by achieving the following objectives:

1. Upgrading the standard and quality of administration, particularly in social and public services sector through a process of modernisation and rationalisation of the administrative set up,
2. Providing public centred, efficient and cost-effective Government,
3. Extensive percolation of IT literacy and education in the State,
4. Promoting investments in IT industry,

5. Encouraging private sector initiative in IT related infrastructure and services,
6. Increasing the share of IT in State Gross Domestic Product,
7. Generating IT related employment opportunities, and
8. Enhancing earning capacity of the residents thereby ensuring a better quality of life.

IT Policy and Public Domain

Re-engineering of administrative processes

The State shall undertake intensive re-engineering and administrative reforms, redefining its role, and recasting the structure and functioning of its administrative Departments to facilitate adaptation to IT. This exercise shall be carried by removal of redundancies, resource optimisation and rationalisation of rules and procedures to bring about transparency in working and enhancing efficiency and productivity.

IT application in transaction automation and creation of information databanks will be mandatory for all Departments, Boards and Corporation to achieve accountability and efficiency in administration. This process will be completed by the year 2003.

As a part of administrative re-engineering, integration of projects across various Departments to provide a single point of contact to citizens for electronic delivery of services would be put in place.

IT Budget

Each Department, Board and Corporation shall earmark 5% of its budget for IT applications. This budget shall be spent for complete transition to e-Governance by the year 2005. Individual organisation specific IT plans will be finalised by 31.3.2001. The allocated budget shall be spent on procurement of hardware, systems software, establishing IT centres, networking, web technology, development of applications software, training and technical consultancy, etc. This initiative will be supervised by Hartron and NIC.

IT Initiative Fund for e-Governance

An IT initiative fund for e-Governance shall be established with contributions from profit making State PSUS, co-operative institutions and other public sector organisations. The initiative fund shall be utilised for developing replicable and reusable models of e-Governance, IT innovations in administration re-engineering, IT supported resource optimization, decision support systems, MIS, intranets and other applicable enabling technologies. The fund shall have an initial Corpus of Rs. 10 Crores and shall be administered by a Governing Body headed by the Principal Secretary to the Chief Minister. An Executive Committee of the Governing Body headed by Secretary, EIT shall be constituted for appropriations from this fund.

State-wide Area Network

The State shall establish backbone network **Haryana State Wide Area Network (HARNET)** for voice, data and video transmission and dissemination. The network shall be utilised for inter department connectivity, multi-user and multi-service facilities, video conferencing, file transfer facility, e-mail, on-line application processing, query and response. HARNET shall enable better communication, information sharing, allowing people to work together more effectively resulting in cohesive administration. Phased implementation of HARNET will cover strengthening the existing intranets at State Secretariat, Haryana Bhawan and 19 Districts Head Quarters with existing NIC/DOT infrastructure. The second phase shall extend HARNET to all Government Departments, State Secretariat, Districts, Sub-Divisions, Tehsils, Sub-Tehsils and Block Head Quarters. Hartron shall implement this extended HARNET in association with private sector. Where DOT is not in a position to provide suitable links, such connectivity shall be achieved through private initiative.

The State Government Departments shall establish departmental intranets and local area networks which will lay the foundation of Centralised Data Repository of public domain information for 'Anytime-Anywhere" usage.

Flagship/Proof-of-concept Applications

Flagship applications will be developed as proof-of-concept applications for building confidence in other Departments, Boards and Corporations. These applications shall be finalised by the Steering Committee.

SMART Cards

SMART Card based citizens ID with multi-functions that enable citizens to interact with services, make payments, act as a Voter ID, obtain ration card, passport, driving licence and vehicle registration etc. shall be introduced in association with the private sector by the year 2003.

Use of Hindi

The State Government shall promote use of Hindi in Information Technology to increase the outreach to the common man. For this purpose specific initiative will be taken for use of Devnagari in Computers and developing Web Applications.

Government Tendering/Procurement Process

Electronic procurement and settlement system with supporting databases and transparent decision making shall replace the existing system by the year 2002.

MIS for Different Levels

An efficient and effective department specific IT based Decision Support System/Management Information System shall be evolved concurrently with the process of re-engineering in the State Government. Abstract on all developmental parameters, revenue collections, crime rate, key agricultural inputs, condition of irrigation facilities, status of power generation and distribution, social infrastructure etc. will be integrated in this system. Wherever citizen interface is involved, Web enabled applications will be developed. Online Analytical Processing (OLAP) would be developed for planning and decision making. This initiative shall be supported by the Secretariat for Information Technology. The process shall be completed by the year 2003.

Standardisation of IT Infrastructure, data and applications

It shall be mandatory for all Departments, Boards and Corporations to procure hardware, software, networking equipment etc. according to specifications and standardisation laid down by Hartron which shall be the sole agency of the State Government to procure software and equipment. General use application software like payroll, personnel information system, inventory management system, budget expenditure control, grievance handling and office automation systems etc. shall in future be developed by Government Departments, Boards and Corporations on the technical advice of Hartron.

Standardisation of data shall also be carried out by organisations to the feasible extent.

These steps shall enable integration of resources into the State Intranet, creation of **Central Data Warehouses** and predictable architecture ensuring the manageability, portability and inter-operability of systems. These efforts shall culminate into public domain information availability on centralised servers reducing future costs of IT applications.

Use of GIS Technology

GIS shall be extensively used in integrating, analysing and visualising different types of data for spatial planning, environmental protection, utility management, traffic regulation etc. Digitised maps of Haryana already available with NIC-HSU will be utilised for providing GIS based services. Augmentation of digitised base maps shall be made as and when required.

Development of Portal Website

A Portal website of the State would be set up by Hartron by interconnecting website of every department and organisation who in turn shall develop their own websites. The portal site developed by Hartron shall be updated dynamically. All Government tenders, employment news, public domain information and notices issued by Government for general public shall be published on this website.

IT Literacy in Government

The Government shall implement an IT Literacy Plan (ITLP) for its employees to achieve 100% IT literacy in the Government by 2002. IT literacy will have a minimum level of defined proficiency which will include word processing, e-mail, data entry and access etc. Suitable incentive/disincentives shall be designed to achieve desired level of proficiency.

Each department shall create an **IT Cell** to be headed by **Chief Information Technology Officer (CITO)** who shall co-ordinate and supervise implementation of e-Governance. The CITO will be a qualified computer professional. Where suitable officer is available within the department, his level of skills will be enhanced through requisite training. The Departments shall undertake review of existing manpower and replace adequate number of posts with IT personnel without any additions to overall establishment budget. Senior and Middle level functionaries in the departments shall be trained in relevant IT applications and management techniques apart from achieving minimum defined proficiency level.

This initiative will be supported by Hartron and NIC. All manual/electronic typewriters shall be phased out, use of e-mail, internet and computers in general shall be maximised.

e-Citizen Interface

Digitisation of Public Domain Information

All public domain information like official gazette notifications, acts, rules, regulations, circulars, policies and programme documents would be digitised and made available for electronic access on Web. This process shall be completed by the year 2002.

Public Information and Facilitation Counters (PIFCs) in Government offices shall be set up so that public domain information is available without any harassment. These PIFOs shall also function as e-mail access into **grievance suggestion databases.**

Delivery of Public Domain IT Services

The State Government proposes to establish electronic delivery of services in the public domain in its Departments, Boards and Corporations using state-of-art technology. Such delivery of services shall be permitted on transaction fee basis to be charged from the users. Flexibility to individual departments to fix transaction fee shall be permitted. Quality assurance for such delivery shall follow well laid out norms.

IT and Private Domain

Electronic Commerce

The development of electronic market places is transforming the structure of global economy. B2B and B2C applications, e-Banking require a number of legal issues to be addressed. The State Government will give due emphasis on e-Commerce and will endeavour to develop **International Electronic Commerce Hub** in Gurgaon. This hub will be set up in joint venture with VSNL/private sector. The State Government will remove hurdles to EC growth and development and will expedite it through joint venture pilot projects in association with the private sector. Legal frame work required for speedy implementation shall be expedited.

Promotion of IT-enabled Services or Remote Services

The State Government shall promote establishment of units for providing IT-enabled Services or Remote Services as these have vast employment generation potential. Technical know-how, marketing support and financial assistance will be provided by State Government Organisations for setting up such units.

Promotion of IT Industry

The State Government recognised the need to give fillip to investments by the private sector in IT Industry. The role of the State Government shall be to facilitate such investment by creating investor friendly environment, escort services, speedy clearances and reliable infrastructure. The IT industry has already been recognised as the major thrust area under the Industrial Policy, 1999. A special package of incentives, which provide opportunity for competitive growth under this IT Policy has been specifically worked out for the IT Industry.

IT Infrastructure

Communication Backbone

The State Govt. shall encourage establishment of backbone networks by the private sector with potential of covering the last mile. Such networks using optical fibre and other reliable media including satellite communication and wireless communication technologies will create adequate bandwidth for meeting mass connectivity needs and will facilitate IT-enabled services. The State Government shall formulate policy on right of way (ROW) and shall facilitate backbone networks.

The State Government shall also promote private initiative in creating dedicated networks for use by research institutions, libraries, educational institutions, universities etc. having outreach to other centres of learning within the country and abroad.

Service Delivery Points (SDPs)

The SDPs shall be encouraged in the private sector for citizens to access services. This will include **Information Kiosks, Public Tele Info Centres (PTICs), Interactive Voice Response Systems (IVRS)** for interaction with databases.

Internet Community Centres

The State Government will promote setting up of Internet Community Centres by private sector to provide Internet facilities through out the State and upto last mile linkage.

Hi-tech Habitate/ITT Complexes/private Software Technology Parks (STP)

The State Government will set up Hi-tech Habitat/ITT Complexes at Gurgaon, Panchkula and other candidate sites in the State. In addition, the State Government will promote setting up of private STPs by liberalising the Government procedures and policies. Special encouragement shall be given to setting up of IT incubators.

Cyber City

For nucleating the IT concept and germination of medium and large software companies, a world class Cyber City shall be set up at a suitable location in the State. The self-contained 'Intelligent City' shall be planned with high quality infrastru-cture, attractive surroundings, high-speed communication access, uninterrupted power, clean and hygienic living spaces, institutional areas, hotels and entertainment facilities etc. This city shall be planned using the best international talent on highly futuristic concept and design. The project shall be implemented in joint sector with HUDA/Hartron/HSIDC in association with international/private partners as lead entrepreneur. Full autonomy and liberal administrative guidelines would be framed to enable setting up of ventures on the fast track in the Cyber City. This city shall be set up initially over an area of around 2000 acres of land.

IT Based Human Resource Development

Human resource development shall occupy highest priority with the State Government. The HRD upgradation will be with the twin objectives of providing necessary manpower to the IT sector for its growth and to improve the employability of the residents in IT:

1. IT literacy in Government schools and colleges shall occupy high priority. Enhancement of IT literacy shall be carried out jointly by Hartron and Education Department in association with the private sector. The phased plan for IT literacy shall be implemented by the year 2003. The basic courses shall be so designed as to provide ready employment opportunities in low end IT enabled services.
2. IT module in engineering and non-engineering degree and diploma courses shall be introduced.
3. The Government shall encourage setting up internet clubs for students in all educational institutions.
4. The output of students in IT in technical institutions shall be tripled in the next three years to meet the growing market demand.
5. **Promotion of Distance Education**—In order to enable access to Centres of Learning 'Anywhere, Anytime', initiative will be taken for promotion of distance educa-tion using electronic classrooms. Universities, other educational institutions, vocational training and technical education centres will be encouraged to create infrastructure throughout the State to achieve this objective. Private sector contribution and other feasible sources of investment including local initiative shall also be encouraged.
6. **Networking of Centres of Learning**—The State Government shall promote networking of all the universities and other centres of research and learning. The HARNET shall be made freely available for this initiative.
7. For making the e-citizen interface successful, citi-zens will be trained in information retrieval and transmission.

Indian Institute of Information Technology (IIIT)

The State Govt. has approached the Government of India for setting up of Indian Institute of Information Technology in the State. The Government is committed to providing necessary support like adequate land and other infrastructure for setting up IIIT in the Government sector.

The State Govt. shall also encourage setting up of Advanced Institutes of Information Technology and specialized schools of Information Technology by private promoters as Centres of excellence in IT. Such Institutes shall be developed for providing high-end education in Information Technology, research and development and shall be ultimately developed as deemed Universities.

The Government shall also encourage setting up of Institutes in the private sector for development of IT professionals and for up gradation of skills of high-end IT professionals answering the needs of IT industry.

Certification/accreditation to IT professional shall be granted by the Secretariat for Information Technology (**SIT**) in association with private sector. A separate academic wing shall be established in **SIT** for this purpose.

Institutional Frame Work

The IT developments in the State shall be governed on the philosophy of maximum facilitation and minimum interference by creation of investor friendly environment. The State Government shall set up a separate **Secretariat for Information Technology (SIT)** which shall monitor the implementation of IT initiative and take necessary steps to remove hurdles in successful implementation of the IT Policy. The Secretariat shall be headed by Secretary, Electronics and Information Technology and will report to the Chief Minister.

A State Level Steering Committee—IT PRISM (P=Planning; R=Reengineering; I=Implementation; S=Steering and M=Monitoring) headed by the Chief Secretary shall oversee computerisation and application of IT in public domain. This committee shall be assisted by a **Technical Committee** headed by the Secretary, Electronics & Information Technology. The constitution, role and functions of these Committees are given at **Annexure-1.**

A Facilitation Committee of State Government officials and IT Industry shall be set up under the Chairmanship of Principal Secretary to the Chief Minister to coordinate and facilitate private investments in IT. The constitution of this committee is given at **Annexure-1.**

Package of Incentives for IT Industries

1. **Preferential allotment of land for IT industry:** The State Government shall give preferential treatment for allotment of land to the IT industries on an ongoing basis in all industrial areas developed by State agencies.
2. **Continuous—uninterrupted power supply for IT industry:** The State Government shall endeavour to provide continuous and uninterrupted power supply for IT industries and shall exempt them from scheduled power cuts. Encouragement to captive power generation in IT Parks/IT locations shall be given.
3. **Facilities on Generator Sets:** Captive power generation sets installed by the Information Technology Industry will be eligible for total exemption from payment of electricity duty without any time limit.
4. **Liberal change of existing industry to IT:** The State Government shall permit setting up of IT Software units/IT Parks in urban areas and change of existing industry to IT/IT Parks.
5. **Change of land use:** No charges for change of land use [CLU] shall be levied for the IT industry/IT Parks for 3 years *i.e.*, up to 31.03.2003. Permission for sale/leasing/subleasing in constructed buildings and open spaces shall be permitted for optimum utilisation of infrastructure. Licences for setting up STPs shall be given liberally and on easy payment terms.
6. **Floor Area Regulation (FAR):** Relaxation in FAR shall be permitted up to 100% for IT units and in all IT Parks.
7. **Clearances and Support:** Escort services and Single Desk Clearance for obtaining

easy clearances and approval of various Government Departments shall be facilitated for the IT industries. On-line Clearance & Support Network (OCSN) will be established linking all the related Departments/ organizations. The Secretariat for IT shall coordinate approvals and facilitation.

8. **Registration and Stamp Duty:**
Rebate on registration and transfer of property charges and exemption from stamp duty on a tapering scale shall be given for sale/lease of built-up space to the IT Industry establishing facilities in private STPs/Government STPs/ IT Parks as under:
   (i) For facilities established and sold/leased before 1.6.2001, 90% rebate.
   (ii) For facilities established and sold/leased before 1.6.2002, 75% rebate.
   (iii) For facilities established and sold/leased before 1.6.2003, 60% rebate.
   (iv) For facilities established and sold/leased before 1.6.2004, 45% rebate.

   The rebate would be applicable on the combined levy of registration fee, stamp duty and transfer of property duty and no total exemption of stamp duty would be extended. This concession would be available only for the first transaction, when the first sale by the infrastructure company is made to an IT industry.

9. **Sales Tax Concession:**
Sales Tax Concession to new units and for expansion/ diversification will remain same as already provided for in the Industrial Policy, 1999 and as given at Annexure '3'.

10. **Applicable rate of Sales Tax:**
IT Software Industry will be totally exempted from payment of sales tax. The applicable rate of sales tax on computers and computer peripherals shall be reduced to 0.25%.

* **Definitions: Definitions of IT Industry, Software, Computers and Computer peripherals for the purpose of sales tax concession and applicable rate of sales tax as mentioned at points 9 and 10**

are given at Annexure '2'.

11. **IT as priority sector for lending:**
    IT Software and IT Services shall be considered as a priority sector by of the State Level Financial Institutions for lending assistance.

12. **Exemption from Pollution Control:**
    IT Software industry shall be exempted from the purview of NOC and consent regime of the Haryana State Pollution Control Board, except in respect of power generation sets of more than 10 KVA Capacity.

13. **Self-certification/exemption from various Acts:**
    Self-certification/exemption for the IT Software Industry shall be permitted as far as possible regarding requirement of the Factories Act, Employment Exchange (Notification of Vacancies Act), Payment of Wages Act, Minimum Wages Act, Contract Labour (Regulation and Abolition) Act, Workmen Compensation Act, Haryana Shops and Establishments Act ; and Employees State Insurance Act.

14. **Awards of excellence:**
    The State will declare awards of excellence for outstanding performance in exports/domestic segment/ employment generation.

15. **Strengthening telecom and communication infrastructure:**
    The State shall pursue with DOT for establishing reliable, adequate and efficient telecom and communication infrastructure including Internet Nodes in all districts of Haryana.

16. **Special Incentives for Mega Projects:**
    Customized package of special incentives will be permitted for prestigious projects having an investment of Rs. 30 crores and above. A High Powered Committee under the chairmanship of Chief Minister will be constituted to decide the package in individual cases.

ANNEXURE-1

State Level Steering Committee - IT PRISM

Constitution

The constitution of the committee shall be as follows:

1. Chief Secretary — Chairman
2. Principal Secretary to Chief Minister
3. Secretary, Finance,
   Secretary, Planning,
   Secretary, Commercial Taxation,
   Secretary, Education,
   Secretary, Revenue,
   Secretary, Administrative Reforms,
   Secretary, Health,
   Secretary, Food & Supply,
   Secretary, Local Bodies,
   Secretary, Transport,
   Secretary, Power,
   Secretary, Panchayat & Rural Development,
   Secretary, Electronics & IT,
   Secretary, Technical Education
   Secretary, Agriculture,
   Secretary, Cooperation.
4. Director General, NIC or his nominee.
5. Three experts in IT to be nominated by the State Government.
6. MD, Hartron/Director, EIT—Member Secretary
7. Any other Secretary/HoD to whom specific agenda applies.

Role and functions

1. To set the priorities of sectors to be taken up for Computerization.
2. To review the progress of implementation IT Action Plan of various Government Departments, Boards and Corporations.
3. To approve budget and sanction posts & expenditure for IT. The approval by this committee shall be deemed to be final & no further reference to AD/FD will be required.

4. To devise the ways and means for the promotion of IT Education in Haryana.

Technical Committee

Constitution

1. Secretary, E & IT—Chairman
2. MD, Hartron—Member Secretary
3. SIO, NIC, Haryana State Unit—Member
4. Three IT Experts to be nominated by the State Government.

Role and Functions

1. Standardization of hardware, software and databases.
2. Evaluation of Technologies for IT including LAN/ WAN.
3. Establishing framework contracts.
4. Fixing up norms for hardware and software purchase.
5. To approve the course curricula for all types of computer courses.
6. To assist the Steering Committee.

Facilitation Committee

Constitution

1. Principal Secretary to Chief Minister—Chairman
2. Secretary, Power
3. Secretary, Labour
4. Secretary, Excise & Taxation
5. Secretary, Local Bodies
6. Secretary, Industries
7. Secretary, Electronics & Information Technology
8. Secretary, Town & Country Planning
9. MD, HSIDC
10. MD, HFC
11. Chief Administrator, HUDA
12. Director, Industries
13. Labour Commissioner
14. MD, Hartron—Member Secretary

Six representatives from industries associations.

ANNEXURE -2

Categories of Industries included in the scope/ definition of Information Technology Industry

(A) **Computing** devices including:

Desktop

Personal Computer

Servers

Work-station

Nodes

Terminals

Network P.C.

Home P.C.

Lap-top Computers

Note Book Computers

Palm top Computer/PDA

(B) **Network Controller** Cards/Memories including:

Network Interface Card (NIC)

Adaptor — Ethernet / PCI / EISA / Combo / PCMICA

SIMMs — Memory

DIMMs - Memory

Central Processing Unit (CPU)

Controller — SCSI / Array

Processors — Processor / Processor Power Module/ Upgrade C) Storage Units including:

Hard Disk Drjves/Hard Drives

RAID Devices & their Controllers

Floppy Disk Drives

C.D. ROM Drives

Tape Drives — DLT Drives/DAT

Optical Disk Drives

Other Digital Storage Devices

(D) **Others:**

Key Board

Monitor

Mouse

Multi-media Kits

(E) **Printers and Output Devices including:**

Dot matrix

Laserket

Inkjet
Deskjet
LED Printers
Line Printers
Plotters
Pass-book Printers

(F) **Networking products including:**
Hubs
Routers
Switches
Concentrators
Trans-receivers

(G) **Software including:**
Application Software
Operating system
Middleware/Firmware

(H) **Power supplies to Computer Systems including:**
Switch mode power supplies
Uninterrupted Power supplies

(I) **Networking / Cabling & related accessories (related to IT Industry)**
Fibre Cable
Copper Cable
Cables
Connectors, Terminal Blocks
Jack panels, patch cord
Mounting cord/wiring blocks
Surface mount boxes

(J) **Consumables including:**
C.D. ROM/Compact Disk
Floppy Disk
Tapes DAT/DLT
Ribbons
Toners
Inkjet Cartridges
Inks for Output devices

(K) **Electronic Components:**
Printed Circuit Board/populated PCB
Printed Circuit Board/PCB
Transistors

Integrated Circuits/ICs
Diodes/Thyristor/LED
Resistors
Capacitors
Switches/(On/Off, Push button, Rocker, etc.)
Plugs/sockets/relays
Magnetic heads, Print heads
Connectors
Microphones/Speakers
Fuses

(L) **Telecommunication Equipment including:**
Telephones
Videophones
Fascimile machines/Fax cards
Tele-Printers/Telex machine
PABX/EPABX/RAX/MAX — Telephone Exchange
Multiplexers/Muxes
Modems
Telephone answering machines
Telecommunication Switching Apparatus
Antena & Mast
Wireless datacom equipment
Receiving equipment like Pagers, Mobile/Cellular Phones, etc.
VSATs
Video Conferencing Equipment

* Including Set Top Boxes for both Video and Digital Signalling.

ANNEXURE-3

Sales Tax Concessions

The benefit of sales tax concessions would be available to new units on graded scale or on fixed slab scale at the option of the eligible unit.

For the purpose of granting sales tax concession incentive, the State shall be divided in 3 categories:

Category 'A' Areas within the municipal limits of Gurgaon Town, Gurgaon Block of Gurgaon district (except

Manesar), the municipal limits of Faridabad Municipal Complex, Faridabad and Ballabgarh Blocks of Faridabad district.

Category 'B' Controlled areas of Kundli, Bahadurgarh and Panipat towns, IMT Manesar and Panchkula urban estate.

Category 'C' Rest of the State except those mentioned above.

The maximum limit of sales tax concession to new units in SSI units and L&M units and the maximum period of exemption for which the benefit would be available is as under: -

CATEGORY	EXTENT OF CONCESSION		TIME LIMIT	SCALE OF CONCESSION
	SMALL SCALE	MEDIUM/LAROE SCALE		
A	125% of fixed capital investment	100% of fixed capital investment	9 years.	50% exemption from 1st year to 9th year
B	125% of fixed capital investment	100% of fixed capital investment	10 years	1st year 80% 2nd year 60% 3rd year 60% 4th year 50% 5th year 50% 6th year 50% 7th year 50% 8th year 40% 9th year 40% 10th year 20%
C	150% of fixed capital investment	125% of fixed capital investment	11 years	1st year 80% 2nd year 60% 3rd year 60% 4th year 50% 5th year 50% 6th year 50% 7th year 50% 8th year 50% 9th year 30% 10th year 30% 11th year 20%

Note 1: The benefit of sales tax concession will not be admissible to units falling in the negative list. (Annexure II)

Note 2: All new industrial units in category 'B' and 'C' after availing the benefit of sales tax exemption shall continue their production atleast for the next five years not below the level of average production in preceding five years.

Note 3: New industrial units falling in category 'B' and category 'C' can opt for the scale of concession on fixed slab scale as applicable to units in category 'A'. In case of this option the condition in Note 2 above shall not apply.

Note 4: The eligible units will be allowed to collect applicable sales tax and retain the permissible benefit as State subsidy.

Note 5: The investment in land and building shall not exceed the investment made in plant and machinery for the purpose of calculating fixed capital investment.

Note 6: The maximum extent of concession to agro based units shall be 250% of fixed capital investment and for information technology/software/electronics will be 300% of fixed capital investment.

Note 7: The existing industrial units availing sales tax exemption/deferment under previous policies would have the option to avail tax incentives as per this policy for the balance entitlement/period.

Sales Tax Concessions on Expansion/Diversification

Industrial units under going expansion/diversification would be given the benefit of sales tax exemption as per the above scale only on the investment in plant & machinery. The benefit will be restricted to the 50% fixed slab scale and will be given for five years.

5

Information Technology Industry Policy Document

Preamble

1.1 This IT Industry Policy document endeavours to delineate a strategy for harnessing the opportunities and the resources offered by Information Technology for the comprehensive social and economic development of the State. This strategy has been conceived keeping in view the fact that Information Technology constitutes the primary Instrument for facilitating Kerala's emergence as a leading knowledge society in the region.

1.2 This blueprint for IT development has been formu-lated in the context of emerging developmental trends and imperatives that are relevant to the growth strategy of the State.

The growth of Kerala in coming years will be increasingly driven by the knowledge and service-based sectors, where ease of information transactions will be a key determinant of success. Recent trends in the convergence of technologies have thrown up new opportunities and new services for the State, such as IT enabled services, e-commerce and multimedia.

- Kerala has a large traditional agricultural and industrial sector; and the infusion of IT into these domains would be essential for its survival and growth in the face of imminent international competition.
- IT has opened out new channels for service delivery in areas such as e-Governance, education, e-health and information

dissemination. IT can serve as the platform for widening the reach of the advances made by the State in domains like health, education and participative local governance.

1.3 Kerala offers fertile ground for the effective utilization of these new technologies; on account of its densely networked communities which possess high awareness and literacy levels, its superior telecom connectivity, and its propensity for quick technology absorption.

1.4 IT offers exciting possibilities for radically enlarging and improving human resource skills. Kerala's core competence is its near universal literacy and awareness levels, and this can be transformed into economically rewarding and employable skills by deploying the tools offered by JT.

1.5 The primary impetus for growth in IT has to come from private enterprise and community energies. The IT policy accordingly envisages the role of Government as being primarily that of a facilitator for creating an enabling environment where the energies of the private sector and of civil society can be most effectively deployed. The objective of the Government is to put in place a package of policy measures and incentives, which will make Kerala one of the most attractive investment destinations in IT.

1.6 The CII sponsored independent study of 18 Indian States 'How the States are Doing' placed Kerala at #3 in terms of overall composite score, #1 in Health and Education, #1 in Law & Order, #8 in Labour; #5 in investment attractiveness, and #13 in Invest-ment. These are not IT sector specific. A comparative statement of all parameters is attached as per Annexure III. Through the measures enunciated in this policy document the Kerala Government seeks to improve its relative position on both labour and investment into the top 3 ranks amongst States in the country, making it #1 in overall composite score amongst all States.

2. **The Policy initiatives delineated in this document comprise a three pronged strategy aimed at:**

- Creating an appropriate pro-business, pro-enterprise, legal, regulator)' and commercial framework to facilitate the rapid growth of the IT industry in the State
- Establishing Kerala as a global centre for excellence in Human Resources, through the creation of a large pool of

diverse, multi-skilled, technically competent manpower in the State; and

- Establishing an internationally competitive business infrastructure and environment for the IT industry in the State, on par with the best facilities and practices worldwide.

3. **In line with this broad strategy, the Government have set the following immediate objectives for the promotion of the IT industry in the State—**

1. To establish Kerala as a leading IT destination in the country within the next five years.
2. To provide a nurturing and enabling environment conducive to the vigorous growth of the local IT industry in the State.
3. To significantly enhance direct and indirect employment creation in the IT sector.
4. To attain a minimum growth level of 100% every year in IT.
5. To significantly accelerate the levels of investment inflows including foreign capital into the hardware, software and ITES sectors.
6. To aggressively promote the State as the destination of choice for emerging IT business opportunities including IT Enabled Services, new media products and E-services. To establish ITES as the definitive core competence of the State.
7. To develop Kochi as an international media and ICT hub.
8. To consolidate and expand the Technopark, Trivandrum as a leading software and HR Centre in the region.
9. To provide the physical and institutional environment for the growth of SOHO and decentralized IT businesses.

4. Financial Incentives for the IT industry:

4.1The Govt. has formulated a comprehensive and unique package of incentives for the IT products, software and ITES industry in the State, which seeks to reward value creation, employment generation and enterprise excellence. The scheme called the Kerala IT Industry Incentive Schemes is enclosed as Annexure.

5. IT Infrastructure

5.1 *The Govt. Parks Initiative:*

1. The city of Kochi will be promoted as an ICT hub where facilities offered will match the best available worldwide. A hi-tech park will be developed here, comprising an area of 200 acres. An IT Corridor connecting the new international airport at Nedumbassery with the city will also be established as part of the larger proposed Special Economic Zone continuum. These facilities shall be developed through Joint Venture partnerships with the private sector and shall endeavour to provide an international business infrastructure and environment at Kochi. Kochi has all the necessary enablers in place in including virtually unlimited bandwidth on tap from the VSNL gateway, concentration of quality, technical and non-technical human resources, a cosmopolitan social infrastructure and environment, and excellent air connections. These advantages shall be leveraged to make the city amongst the most preferred IT investment destinations of India.

2. The Technopark, Trivandrum with about I million sq. ft of built up area, has established itself as one of the leading IT parks in the country. The campus is now home to several SEI-CMM companies and centres of HR excellence. The IIITM-K, which commenced functioning last year and which offers high-end training in emerging technologies is expected to move over to an independent campus shortly. In the second phase of expansion of the park, it is proposed to develop 26 acres with the participation of the private sector.

3. The total space availability for IT industry shall be augmented by a minimum of 750,000 sq. ft annually for the next two years. Thereafter, for the next three years a minimum of 1.5 million sq. ft space capacity shall be created annually. These additional capacities will be created through 100% private sector investments as well as Joint Venture projects between the Govt. and the private sector.

4. The IT Department shall shortly initiate, with the help of leading consultants, the exercise of preparing Master Plans for each of the designated IT parks/zones. These Master Plans

shall delineate the blueprint for park development and framework for facilitating private sector participation.

5. The Govt. shall endeavour to maintain uniform, international quality standards for park infrastructure and services across all State promoted and managed IT parks. A professional Parks' Management team will be set up under the Kerala IT Department for ensuring this.

6. The built-up space for IT industry shall be classified under a new category "IT Industry" under the Kerala Building Rules with applicable FAR of 5. This classification shall apply only for newly built-up space that shall be used predominantly (at least 80% of carpet area) for IT software industry for a minimum period of 5 years from the date of first occupation/ commissioning.

7. The Govt. shall proactively encourage and facilitate the development of ancillary social infrastructure in a planned manner including hotels, restaurants, entertainment multiplexs, hospitals, schools, colleges etc. within and appurtenant to the IT parks.

5.2 Private Parks Scheme:

1. To accelerate the process of private sector led IT infrastructure development, the Govt. shall, in association with reputed global IT parks' developers/ consultants, announce a minimum set of standards to qualify as 'Parks' Standard' certified IT park. Compliance shall be assessed, on formal request, at the pre-construction/design stage and thereafter on project completion. 'The State IT Parks' Management team shall serve as the nodal agency for compliance assessment and administration of the 'Private IT Parks Scheme'.
2. All 'Parks' Standard' compliant IT parks shall be entitled to the FAR classification as applicable to IT industry under Kerala Building Rules. For other compliant IT parks that are either entirely for IT hardware industry or for both IT hardware and IT software industry companies, classified under 'Industrial' category' of the Kerala Building Rules, additional FAR of 50% shall be permitted (over

currently applicable FAR of 1.5).

3. The Kerala State Electricity Board, the Kerala Water Authority, and the Office of the Chief Town Planning Authority shall each designate a Nodal Officer who shall facilitate the process of inspection, application processing and application closure, for their respective responsi-bility areas. Response standards shall be announced by these agencies for the fast track clearance process.
4. A certified private IT park shall be governed by the same set of industry enabling regulations that are applicable for the State promoted IT parks.
5. A private park that qualifies for certification under this scheme shall be promoted by the State Govt. as an integral part of the State's IT Infrastructure, provided the promoter of the park so desires.
6. The scope of the 'Private IT Parks' scheme shall be restricted to projects that seek to provide a minimum of 50,000 sq. ft per project either through creation of fresh built up space or through conversion of existing space for use by IT industry. Projects less than the 50,000 sq.ft qualifying stipulation shall still have the benefit of FAR provided tinder point 1 provided they are otherwise compliant with the Parks' standard.

5.3 Leveraging Submarine Cable Landing at Kochi for Industry.

Kochi has the unique connectivity advantage of being the landing point of two major international submarine cables linking to US, Europe and the far East. All IT Parks partially or fully promoted by the State Govt. shall be connected by OFC to the Kochi gateway. Data communication bandwidth, a strategic input for the IT sector, shall be thus made available to IT industry through the SII with assured quality of service across the State.

6. State Information Infrastructure (SII)

The State Information Infrastructure, which is to be set up within the coming two years shall endeavour to provide robust and seamless connectivity' to industry across the state.

(a) Present Status

Kerala enjoys the highest telephone density in the country today. 100% of the 982 telephone exchanges in the State are digital, covering all 14 district headquarters, all 63 taluk headquarters, and all 1468 panchayats/villages. The BSNL telephone exchange is collocated with the panchayat headquarters in a majority of the panchayats, and the balance is within a maximum of 3 km from the nearest telephone exchange. 945 of the 982 exchanges are networked through optic fibre cable (OFC), and the balance 37 shall also be connected on the OFC backbone within 3 months. 266 exchanges currently support ISDN service. Further, another 100 digital telephone exchanges shall be commissioned by BSNL across Kerala this financial year.

VSNL has made substantial investments in its Kochi gateway where two submarine cables—SEA-ME-WE-3 and FLAG land. Kochi is one among two locations nationwide which has submarine cables landing. With 10 GBPS bandwidth supported, it currently handles about 70% of the nation's data communication traffic. Sourcing bandwidth from VSNL at Kochi and Thiruvananthapuram provides significant savings *vis a vis* most other locations in the country.

Subsequent to the 'Rights of Way' policy announced in 2001, a number of telecom companies have come forward to establish OF based data/voice networks in the State.

(h) Purpose of the SII

The Govt. has identified target beneficiaries of IT led development as (i) citizens/ individuals (ii) industry (iii) academic institutions and (iv) the different bodies of Government. For the benefits of IT to be exploited in full measure, but at minimal cost, the Government recognizes the need for a communication infrastructure backbone—the State Information Infrastruc-ture—that spreads across the State and reaches out to all targeted beneficiaries. Further, there is the critical need to entire that a minimum grade/ quality of service is available from the SII so that the target beneficiaries can in turn plan software applica-tions and hardware deployment based on the availability and quality of the SII.

The industry shall benefit from direct Optic Fibre Cable Connectivity into the Kochi gateway from most towns within the State, and that at a significant cost advantage. This would drive IT enabled services that are bandwidth intensive and which require reliable, failsafe operations including Business Process Out sourcing operations, Multimedia call centres, and Multimedia Content Development/Processing centres. Schools and colleges within the State as well as the Panchayats can today look forward to an era of seamless connectivity for commu-nication within their communities as well as the world at large. Finally and most importantly, the SII would enable the ushering in of a new era of transparent, efficient, citizen-responsive governance from the Kerala government.

Quality of Service (QOS) Definition for Data Communication Services

Service providers within the State shall be urged to maintain and transparently share quality of service data with their consumers. This minimum grade of service shall apply irrespective of the location within the State. This step is expected to ensure uniform quality of internet access and community level intra-networking across the State. Further, this shall prepare the State for an era when 'voice over internet protocol' (VoIP) communication shall be permitted in India. Appropriate mechanism shall be established to measure, report, analyse and provide feedback to service providers to maintain/improve network performance. The QOS requirement shall be reviewed with concerned service providers and consumers, on an annual basis to reflect changes in network capabilities as well as consumer requirements.

7. Ancillary and Support Infrastructure

7.1 Power

IT industry units are entitled to tariff under HD I industry and LT IV industry depending on the supply of and connected load to the IT industry. This classification shall be maintained even in the case of IT software industry units brought under the purview of the Kerala Shops and Commercial Establishments Act 1960.

7.2 Roads

The Govt shall ensure that access roads from the nearest city or airport to designated IT Parks/zones shall be of the highest quality and designed/upgraded to minimize travel time. This is recognized as a basic need of industry. Such activity shall be encouraged on a build-operate-transfer basis with the private sector.

8. Thrust Areas in IT

8.1 IT Enabled Services

1. The Govt. shall endeavour to promote Kerala as a favoured ITES destination in this part of the world and to aggressively market ITES as the State's core competence. The focus domains in this sector shall be Business Process Outsourcing (BPO), Customer Interaction Centers, Multimedia Content Creation and E-services. Kerala already has the basic enablers in place to make this vision a reality—best in class communi-cation infrastructure to support bandwidth intensive ITES operations, a large pool of English speaking personnel, low cost of operations and low employee attrition. The Govt. is also putting in place a regulatory framework, which would address the specialized employment requirements of the industry.
2. To leverage the natural advantages the State has in this sector, focused training inputs shall be delivered throughout the State to create a large pool of trained manpower for Business Process Outsourcing Centres, voice and non-voice based ITES centers, including voice/web/email based call centers, Geographical Information Systems, and Animation/Content Creation. The content shall be created with the help of experts from the ITES industry and delivered using innovative methods.
3. English is the universal language of business. Kerala Govt. realizes that its front runner advantage in universal coverage and reach in the State's education network can be leveraged to ensure frontline status in

the use of English for enhanced employability of its people. To improve the communication skills of the local populace in English, Colleges and Universities in the State shall be encouraged to upgrade the quality of English language courses to accepted international standards. Further, the Govt. shall also encourage the introduction of Japanese, French and German language courses in a phased manner in Colleges so that a pool of manpower trained in these languages is available within the State.

4. Kerala shall host an annual International Business Process Out sourcing Conclave each year. This event, the first of its kind in India, shall be the lead and definitise event for the Indian and regional BPO industry.

8.2 Supply Chain management Operations

The Govt. recognizes it as an imperative to attract global IT Products companies to Kerala. Kochi offers several natural advantages to become a choice location for Supply Chain Management Operations (SCM). Kochi has an all-weather port, an international airport well connected into the Far East through Singapore and into Western Europe/ USA through the West Asian countries. Further, Kochi is home to one of four Special Economic Zones of the country that provides a flexible, fast track environment for running predominantly export oriented SCM operations. Special incentives have been announced for such SCM units The IT products companies based at designated IT parks in the State have enjoyed harmonious labour relations over the last several years in addition to high productivity levels. The new labour regulatory framework shall lay the foundation for such operations to proliferate. The Govt. commits itself to playing a strong enabling role in this regard.

8.3 Establishment of a Global HR Centre in Kerala

In view of Kerala's peaceful, salubrious and cost competitive setting, the State is a natural location of in-house training facilities for IT companies. The State Govt. shall focus on this comparative advantage by promoting the Technopark as an attractive global HR centre. As a part of this endeavour, the Govt. shall encourage leading IT Corporates to set up their HRD centres in Kerala.

9. Performance Excellence Initiative

The State Govt. will promote international bench marking of the IT industry in the State by fostering a Performance Excellence Initiative for improving organizational excellence and business maturity. A Performance Excellence advisory group shall be constituted for prescribing short and medium term course and to devise operational guidelines as well as training inputs for the IT industry.

Performance Excellence calibration shall be undertaken and a system of awards and incentives shall be put in place.

10. Synergy with the Tourism Industry

IT and Tourism have been defined as Kerala's focus areas and both these sectors can benefit from mutual synergy. IT has a significant role to play in enhancing service levels, particularly in the high end tourism segment that Kerala dominates. The Tourism and IT Department shall develop a comprehensive plan for improving efficiencies, reducing costs and for creating customer delight in the tourism industry through the use of IT. Local IT industry shall be encouraged to develop/offer the necessary IT products and services. The State Information Infrastructure shall be made available to the tourism industry to serve the industry's communication needs. Special tourism packages shall be evolved to bring in leisure travellers from the IT industry into the State thus benefiting both the sectors.

11. Promotional Initiatives

The Govt. shall launch concerted promotional efforts to establish the State as a favoured investment locale within the country and abroad. These efforts shall comprise overseas business promotion, focusing on global IT centers as well as targeted individual efforts aimed at attracting large IT companies into the State.

11.1 Business Promotion Cell for IT Industry

The Kerala IT Department has set up a Business Promotion Cell for IT (IT-BPC), which shall:

- Direct enquiries from within Govt. as well as from industry elsewhere in India/abroad to IT units in the State, and
- Appropriately represent/promote IT units at the leading industry tradeshows/seminar that the IT-BPC participates in. This shall include provision of space at important exhibitions/tradeshows. IT units must register with the IT Department to participate in this programme.
- The ongoing interface mechanism between the IT-BPC and IT industry shall be transparent and open. The services of the IT-BPC shall be provided free of cost to It units until 31.12.2002. Thereafter, a nominal fee may be charged to cover the expenses of operation. Kerala based IT units have to register with the IT Department to participate in this programme.

11.2 Customer Facilitation Cell for IT Industry

The Kerala IT Department shall set up a Customer Facilitation Cell for KIT (IT-CFC) to facilitate the initial entry phase of business into the State. The services of the Cell shall include facilitation of single window clearance, including STPI registration and other statutory registrations; expedited import clearance, advising on company formation/setting up procedures; and other facilitation as may be necessary.

11.3 Incubation facilities

A Business cum Technology Incubation Fund shall be set up to assist young start up entrepreneurs. This Fund shall provide services including appropriate business and technical advice, and infrastructure and shall work in close co-ordination with the Kerala Venture Fund and the IIITM-K.

12. HRD for the IT Industry

12.1 Kerala's distinctive edge lies in the quality and adaptability of its human resource base. The high quality of manpower available in Kerala can be a lever not only for attracting high value IT investments into the State, but also for widening and disseminating the IT base into small towns and outlying areas spanning the entire State. The State's endeavour shall be to convert Kerala as a leading off sure center for provision of IT services worldwide.

12.2 *The policy measures delineated in this document seek* to *address the following two broad objectives:*

(a) To provide adequately trained manpower to meet the requirements of the IT industry; and

(b) To upgrade the productivity, skill and knowledge levels of the populace by equipping them with the appropriate level of IT literacy.

1. The Government has set up the IIITM-K as a centre of excellence in IT education, for imparting training in high-end and emerging technologies. The Institute will be leveraged as a key resource center for upgrading the quality of technical education in the State.
2. The State Govt. will promote the establishment of an International Business School in Cochin within the next three years. This school is envisaged as being a predominantly industry driven and industry led enterprise and shall focus on offering business education relating to the management of information. This institute will produce high calibre managers who will be equipped to run the information oriented enterprises of the entire knowledge society.
3. The State Govt. has recently embarked on a major policy initiative of liberalizing the professional and higher educational sector of the State. The Government has multiplied manifold the number of technical seats in the IT sector (including Engineering and MCA). With the liberalization of the technical education sector in Kerala, the number of seats available is expected to be increase four fold in the next five years.
4. Basic IT skills have become a *sine qua non* for exploring any branch of knowledge. Hence, a fundamental IT module will be incorporated as an

essential component of the curriculum for all degree courses in the State, including the Arts and Humanities courses.

5. The relevance of the course content and training imparted in the ITIs and Polytechnics shall be reviewed and appropriated changes made in the course design and curriculum to ensure compatibility with requirements of the local industry.
6. The State Govt. shall promote the deployment of a state-wide educational grid to cover all colleges and institutions of higher learning which will facilitate the creation of subject specific e-learning communities centring around designated institutions as resource centres for various subjects. The objective of the grid shall be to formulate dynamic partnership between existing institution of higher education and centres of excellence for upgrading the quality of course content and teaching. IIITM-K shall prepare the basic blue print for the educational grid and shall function as the nucleus of the grid.
7. The Govt. shall also promote the establishment of a Media Information and Resource Centre for Education under the IIITM-K as a nodal agency for the creation of educational content in relevant disciplines.
8. The Govt. shall form an Expert Committee with experts drawn from academia, IT industry to review the content of IT in the higher education curriculum in the State on an initial basis, particularly for non-Computer Science Engineering and Electronic Engineering students and for Science, Arts and Commerce streams.
9. Supplementary training programmes in IT shall be introduced in professional and non-professional colleges with support from nationally accepted training agencies such as the NCST and other repeated training institutes.
10. The Govt. shall undertake career aptitude assessment programmes in co-operation with private

organizations with proven expertise in the area to help develop cost-effective programmes that provide appropriately trained human resources for the IT industry. The whole assessment process shall be monitored by a group of eminent experts from industry, academia to ensure that the objectives are substantially met, without compromise in quality.

11. The Govt. shall formulate minimum guidelines for IT training institutions in the State.

13. Industrial Relations & Labour laws

In an area like IT, where the nature of the labour inputs are highly flexible and mobile and where there is an intense competition between States and regions for attracting inward investment, the Govt. recognizes the need to ensure a regulatory environment and an employment regime that will be a positive inducement for investment:

(a) The Govt. shall declare by notification that IT Software industry units are deemed 'establishment' under the purview of the Kerala Shops and Commercial Establishments Act, 1960.

(b) Further, the Govt. shall exempt these units from the profession of the Kerala Shops and Commercial Establishments Act, 1960 in respect of the following:

(i) Working hours stipulation under Section 6 of the Act. This shall enable 'Flexitime' operation.

(ii) Employment of female employees between 7PM and 6 AM, under Section 20 of the Act, subject to (a) Special arrangements being made for protection of female employees tiring these hours, (b) female employees should be employed jointly or in a minimum group of 10 female emplo)'ees, (c) arrangement of a rest room should be made separately for the female employees. (d) the IT software industry unit shall employ a minimum of 50 persons (including female employees) between these hours.

(iii) 'Spread Over', under Section 9 of the Act.

(iv) 'Opening and closing hours', under Section 10 of the Act.

(v) 'Closing of establishment and grant of weekly holidays', under Section 11 of the Act.

(vi) Further, by virtue of the IT Software industry being deemed an 'establishment' under the Kerala Shops and Commercial Establishments Act, 1960, there shall be no restriction on a three shift operation.

(c) Loading and Unloading Work for the IT Industry

The Govt. shall through necessary enactment regulate the presence and activity of headload workers on the premises of the IT industry establishments, as well as state promoted IT Parks in general, to ensure smooth, undisturbed functioning of the IT industry.

(d) Self certification

The Govt. shall permit self-certification, to the extent possible, of IT industry in respect to the following Acts/ Regulations:

(i) Payment of Wages Act

(ii) Minimum Wages Act

(iii) Contract Labour (Regulation & Abolition) Act

(iv) Workmen's Compensation Act

(v). Employees State Insurance Act

(vi) Employment Exchanges Compulsory Notification of Vacancies Act

(vii) Kerala Shops and Commercial Establishments Act

(viii) Payment of Gratuity' Act

(ix) Kerala Casual, Temporary, Badli Workers' (Wages) Act.

(e) Public Utility Services

The Govt. shall declare the IT Industry as a 'Public Utility Service' under the Industrial Disputes Act, 1947.

(f) Part-time Working

The Govt. recognises the need for the IT industry to deal with fluettiating demand for services, cost effectively. The Govt.

shall put in place special provisions for part-time employment for IT industry.

(g) Tele-Commuting

The Govt. shall put in place special provisions to encourage tele-commuting in order to ensure greater efficiency in functioning of It Software industry.

14. Accelerating PC and Internet access and usage penetration :—

1. Kerala with its unique social fabric, socio-economic development, penetration levels of the press, audio-visual media, telephone, mobile telephony, and with the best information infrastructure in the country represents fertile ground for the use of IT products and services by the population at large, and for the introduction of viable services targeted at and involving the citizen, the community, panchayats, and Government bodies.
2. The ability to generate Malayalam language content at a decentralised level by the individual for the immediate and extended community, with resultant content being managed centrally, can possibly evolve into a viable business model. The Government eminent shall encourage private sector initiative to attempt a Proof of Concept of this or similar models that encourages creation and use of Malayalam language content.
3. An Expert Advisory Group with leading experts from the Internet and Competitor industries has been formed under the aegis of the IT Department to recommend the enabling steps to accelerate the process of PC and Internet penetration in the State.

15. Role of Open or Free Software

The Government wishes to encourage the judicious use of open source/free software that complements/supplements proprietary software, to reduce the total cost of ownership of IT applications/solutions without compromising on the immediate and medium term value provided by the application. The Government welcomes research into the use of open/free software in the context of education, governance, and for general use at home, to make IT truly a part of the daily lives of the people of the State. The Government also encourages projects such as the Simputer that is low cost, based on open software and attuned to the needs of the common man.

16. Software Piracy, IPR, Data Protection, Patents

The IT Department shall centrally make available resources that will simplify the process of applying for patents in India and the U.S. This will be backed by an expert committee on IPR/Patents (not restricted to IT) that will advise and guide the serious inventor through the process of patent application.

The Government shall provide orientation programmes to its law enforcement agencies to understand the intricacies of the laws under the IT Act 2000 to curb software piracy.

17. Role of Industry Associations

The Government shall work closely with industry associations including NASSCOMM, MAIT, CII and GTECH (Group of Technopark Companies that represents Kerala IT industry) and others to ensure a coordinated and smooth industry-Government interface on all matters of common concern, for the vibrant development of the IT industry in the State.

18. Accessibility

Kerala has traditionally been at the forefront of enlightened social initiatives. The Government shall examine the means by which access to and use of information and services by indivi-duals with disabilities shall be made comparable to that available to individuals without disabilities. IT is a significant enabler of accessibility. An Expert Committee with members from organizations representing the disabled, from industry, and from the relevant departments of the State Government shall be constituted within 3 months under the chairmanship of the Minister for IT & Social Welfare to chart out the steps to be taken in this regard. The report by this committee shall be submitted not later than 6 months from the effective date of this policy.

The Government is aware that rapid change and transformation is the essence of this sector, and acknowledge the need for a dynamically evolving policy that caters to the changing I.T. environment. Hence this policy document is envisaged as an evolving blueprint, that sets out an indicative roadmap. The Government will endeavour to improve upon the components of this policy on the basis of suggestions from stakeholders as well as the changing requirements of the sector.

6

Kerala It Industry Incentive Scheme

Preamble

The Kerala Government recognises the potential of the IT industry to transform the economy of the State. The Government also realises the need to accelerate the growth of this industry by offering an incentive package that is simple to participate in, and that which rewards excellence in operations, marketing, human resources development, and process quality.

The incentive scheme seeks to achieve the following objectives:

1. Attract new IT companies to set up operations in the State as well as incentives the existing IT companies in the State.
2. Reward employment creation in the State.
3. Reward value addition by the IT industry in the State.
4. Reward acquisition of world-class quality/process certification by companies within the State.
5. Incentive the entry of India's top software exporters into the State.
6. Incentives the early setting up of a medium to large scale (in terms of employment and value) IT investment in the State.
7. Incentives premier electronics/hardware companies to set up assembly/supply chain management operations in the State.

Title

This scheme shall be known as Kerala Information Technology Industry Incentive Scheme, 2001-2003, hereafter referred to as 'incentive scheme'.

Operative Period

The incentive scheme shall become operative with effect from 1st of December 2001 and shall remain in force for a period of four years. However, a review of the incentive scheme shall be carried out after two years, and based on the needs of the IT sector and the experience of the Kerala Government the incentive scheme shall be amended, if necessary.

Area of Operation

The incentive scheme is operative for units operating and functioning in the State of Kerala.

Effective Date

1st December 2001.

Incentives

The incentives currently available to IT (hardware and software) industry companies that set up operations within the State after the effective date shall be modified as under.

IT INDUSTRY EMPLOYMENT PROMOTION SCHEME

Companies that set up operation after the effective date of this incentive scheme:

1. Standard Investment Subsidy (SIS) on Fixed Capital Investment (FCI) for software, hardware and ITES operations- 20% subject to a ceiling of Rs. 25 Lakhs.
2. Companies that employ minimum 50 employees in software (excluding ITES) or 25 employees in hardware industry, or 100 employees in ITES for a minimum of 12 months during the first 24 months of operation shall be entitled to an additional 7.5% investment subsidy over the Standard Investment Subsidy (SIS). The Net subsidy shall be 27.5% of total FCI. *i.e* the total incentive amount payable, including that paid earlier, shall be subject to a ceiling of Rs. 27.5 lakhs.

3. Companies that employ minimum 100 employees in software (excluding ITES) or 50 employees in hardware industry, or minimum 200 employees in ITES industry for a minimum of 12 months during the first 24 months of operation shall be entitled to an additional investment subsidy over that applicable for preceding slab (50/25/100 employees). The net subsidy shall be 30% of total FCI and the total incentive amount payable, including that paid earlier, shall be subject to a ceiling of Rs. 30 lakhs.
4. Companies that employ minimum 250 employees in software (excluding ITES) or 125 employees in hardware industry, or minimum 500 employees in ITES industry) for a minimum of 12 months during the first 24 months of operation shall be entitled to an additional 10% investment subsidy over that applicable for preceding slab (100/50/200 employees). The net subsidy shall be 40% of total FCI. The total incentive amount payable, including that paid earlier, shall be subject to a ceiling of Rs. 40 lakhs.

The companies may apply for the standard incentive on commencement of operations. Further incentives may be applied for on sustaining the employment criterion for each slab for minimum period of 12 months.

Existing Companies

Existing 'eligible IT companies' that set up operation before the effective date and have availed the 20% standard incentive in the past, and that which expand operations shall be entitled to the above incentives, provided they sustain the specified levels of employment for a minimum period of 12 continuous months.

Existing 'eligible IT companies' that set up operation before the effective date and have not availed of the 20% standard incentive in the past, may choose to participate in the newly announced 'IT Industry Employment Promotion' scheme.

Early Bird Scheme

IT Industry companies that set up operations in Kerala before 30th June, 2002 that fulfil the following conditions:

1. Employs minimum 250 permanent headcounts.

2. Employment level to be maintained for a minimum period of 12 months within a 36-month period.
3. The employee count includes all permanent employees. Temporary, part-time and contract employees employed by the IT industry in its primary business shall be converted to 'full equivalents' and included.

shall be entitled to the following incentives:

1. A flat one time incentive payment of Rs. 50 lakhs.
2. This incentive is over and above the incentives claimable by the company under any other scheme announced elsewhere under this policy.
3. This incentive shall be payable immediately once the conditions of the 'early bird' incentive scheme is fulfilled.

CMM Level V or COPC Certification

With the intention of encouraging Kerala based companies to obtain quality certification and thereby raise the maturity level of the IT industry in the State, a special one time incentive of Rs. 5 lakhs from the Kerala Government shall be provided to:

(i) An IT Software unit that has been certified at CMM Level 5 of the Capability Maturity Model of the Software Engineering Institute, Carnegie Mellon University; OR

(ii) An ITES unit that has been certified as compliant with COPC-2000 standard of the Customer Operations Performance Centre; OR

(iii) An ITES unit that has been certified for at least the e-SCM Level 3 capability of the services Capability Model of the ISRI, a division of the Carnegie Mellon University.

This incentive is restricted to companies with their registered office in Kerala.

Incentives for Kerala Based IT Industry in Government Purchases

IT Software Industry Units

An IT software unit that has its registered office in Kerala and employs a minimum of 30% of its total workforce in its Kerala operations, and otherwise compliant with the tender requirements, shall be entitled to 7.5% price preference on IT Software solutions required by Kerala Government/PSUs/ Government Bodies. Other conditions remaining the same, they shall be given higher preference.

IT Product Industry Units

An IT Product unit that has its registered office in Kerala and employs a minimum of 30% of its total workforce in its Kerala operations, that is either excise paying or ISO certified, and otherwise compliant with tender requirements, shall be entitled to 10% price preference on IT Products that is required by Kerala Government/PSUs/Government Bodies. Other conditions remaining the same, they shall be given higher preference. This shall apply to eligible existing IT Product units as well as new IT Product units that engage in electronics/ computer hardware assembly/supply chain management operations in the State.

Special investment promotion package

The Government shall offer special, customised incentive packages to any company that seeks to employ minimum 500 employees for a minimum period of 12 months in the first 36 months of operation. To attract investment in the computer hardware and computer peripheral sector, special incentives shall also be offered to any global, national level player to set up their supply chain management operations in Kerala subject to a minimum scale of operations of Rs. 100 Crore. turnover p.a from their Kerala operations.

Such special incentive packages shall be developed and proposed to the potential investor by a special Committee set up for this purpose within the Government. The Government realises that time is of the essence in all such interactions with investors from the IT industry and shall expeditiously process all serious applications, and a firm response shall be forthcoming to the investor no later than 4 weeks from receipt of proposal with full details.

INCENTIVES FOR KINFRA—IT PARKS

Kerala Industrial Infrastructure Development Corporation (KINFRA), a statutory body of Government of Kerala has developed several industry specific parks. KINFRA has developed two IT parks *i.e.* KINFRA Information Technology & Electronics Park (KITEL) at Kakkanad, Cochin and Malappuram, Calicut. The task of improving infrastructure would be given the highest priority by KINFRA. The plans for infrastructure development will take into account the resource endowment and growth potential of each area. Special emphasis will be given to the development of thrust sectors, which have been identified keeping in view their infrastructure requirements, growth potential and the capacity to generate employment.

KINFRA proposes the following incentives to attract investors in the KINFRA IT park and also its Joint Ventures (JV):

1. Incentives for infrastructure developers in KINFRA Parks for development of IT infrastructure—

(a) The Government of Kerala shall give all statutory clearance under various statutes pertaining to state.

(b) Exemption from stamp duty', registration fee and the transfer duty of land for infrastructure developer. Also the same exemption should be extended to stamp duty and the registration fee for loan agreements, credit deeds, mortgages and hypothecation deeds executed b)' the infrastructure developer in favour of banks or financial institutions.

(c) Concession offered to KINFRA sponsored IT parks will be made available to Infrastructure developers in Kinfra IT parks.

(d) The infrastructure developer in KINFRA IT park will be eligible for single window clearance as per the Kerala Industrial Single Window Clearance Boards and Industrial Township Area Development Act, 1999.

2. Special Incentives for Units in KINFRA IT Parks

(a) Exemption from Stamp duty' and registration fees for the units inside the park upon executing lease/sale agreement with KINFRA for lease/sale of land and built up space.

(b) Exemption from entry tax for goods like machines equipments, capital goods and construction materials procured for implementation of infrastructure projects.

(c) Rebate in the cost of land allotted to an IT industry in KINFRA IT park at Rs. 20,000 (Rupees twenty thousand only) per job created subject to the following conditions:

(i) The rebate shall be applicable only in respect of land allotted by KINFRA with prospective effect.

(ii) The rebate shall be restricted to Rs.20,000/-(Rupees

Twenty thousand only) per job created or the cost of the bare land (excluding development charges/cost) whichever is less subject to a ceiling computed (a 0.30 acres for every 100 jobs created

(d) As an investment promotion drive, first five acres of land in each KINFRA IT parks will be offered at 25 % discount.

(e) 50% discount will be given in service charges for the first ten pioneer units for an initial period of three years.

3. FAR shall be made at the level of 5

Notes

In all cases, the number of employees in the software unit shall not exceed [no. of computer workstations × 1.33 × no.of shifts normally run by the software unit.] As such, only permanent, full time, employees of the IT units shall be included for the purpose of the calculation. However, parttime employees and other consultant/temporary] staff shall be converted to man-year equivalents assuming 52 weeks of 48 hours per man-year. On-going contractual employment shall not be included in the employees calculation.

The minimum salary (based on standard cost to company calculations) to be paid for software development personnel must be Rs. 7500 p.m, while for other categories has to be Rs. 4500 p.m for inclusion of employees in the calculation for employment level related incentive schemes.

A company can claim incentives only once for each employment slab that it qualifies for, *i.e.* multiple applications within a given slab are not permitted.

The Government shall priorities and to the extent possible ensure prompt disbursal of all incentive claims to the IT industry.

The Kerala IT Mission shall be the nodal agency for receipt and processing of incentive applications from the IT industry. It shall appoint a reputed Chartered Accountancy firm to professionally administer the incentive scheme.

Definitions

(a) 'IT' includes IT and Telecommunications.

(b) 'IT industry' includes IT hardware and software industries; IT software industry includes IT software,

IT service and IT enabled service. However, it excludes IT training institutions that provide training to the public at large.

(c) 'IT infrastructure' refers to the physical infrastructure built by a firm or build up and sold to an IT industry for its own use; or infrastructure built by an IT industry for its own use.

(d) IT Software' is defined as any representation of instruction, data, sound, image including source code, object code recorded in a machine, readable form and capable of being manipulated or providing interactivity to use by means of automatic data processing machine falling under head 'IT' Products'. IT Software includes Operating System, Application Software, Middleware and Firmware.

(e) 'IT Service' is defined as any service which results from the use of an IT software over a s)'stem of IT products for realizing value addition.

(f) 'IT Enabled Service' is defined as any product or service that is provided or delivered using the resources of Information and Communication Technology.

(g) 'IT Products' is defined as computer, digital-data communication and digital data broadcasting products as notified by the Ministry of Finance, Government of India or Central Board of Excise & Customs.

Appendix I-A gives the list of IT industry heads

(h) The 'Eligible New Information 'Technology Unit' is defined as a new unit in IT industry set up after the effective date. It should also fulfill the following criteria:
   1. The new project should have registered with the STPI/ DOE under the EHTP scheme or the Kerala IT Mission.
   2. The new project should have a separate identifiable capital investment means that, it should not have any linkage with an existing manufacturing/IT industry unit.

(i) Eligible IT Unit

The 'Eligible IT Unit' is defined as an existing IT Unit which registers itself as an IT Industry with the STPI/ DOE under EHTP scheme or the designated State agency as the case may be, after the effective date although it commenced production before the effective date.

In case of any ambiguity in implementing/interpreting this policy clarifications issue from time to time by the Department of IT shall prevail.

(j) *Fixed Capital Investment*

The eligible Fixed Capital Investment includes—

(1) *Investment made in land*

The actual cost of the land including the legal charges incurred for acquisition of land needed for the project. A plot of land acquired under lease agreement, except from 'Technopark/KINFRA/approved private IT Parks on 25 years lease basis, shall not be considered as Fixed Capital investment.

(2) *New building*

New building means building required for the IT industry including that for production/ development, administration, canteen, and in-house training for staff and would include the cost incurred on purchase of old building or repairing cost.

(3) *Machinery*

This includes Plant & Machinery needed to set up 'Eligible New IT Unit'. This also includes 'IT Product' and 'IT Software'.

Further includes

IT Product and IT Software installed at the residence of the employees of the eligible new unit, subject to the limit of 5% of the eligible total Fixed Capital Investment. The cost of electrification, transportation, erection and installation will be capitalized under the head—plant and machinery. The investment made in acquiring air-conditioning plant/machine.

Transport facilities like bus/buses invested in for the conveyance of the workers to the work premises and back. Plant for non-conventional source of energy. Material handling equipment. Plant for purification of water. Plant for pollution control measures. Testing facilities.

The investment made in related furniture upto 10% of eligible Fixed Capital Investment.

(k) *Timing of Acquisition of Assets*

The eligible fixed assets acquired and bought up to eighteen months from the date of commencement of commercial production will be eligible as 'Eligible fixed capital investment'. No assets acquired, created and/or bought after the operative period of the scheme shall be considered eligible.

Assets acquired under hire purchase scheme or instalment system/lease scheme would be considered eligible, exclusive of cost of interest.

(l) *Ineligible Investment*

The following investment shall not be considered eligible for inclusion as fixed capital investments:

(1) Working Capital
(2) Commissioning fee
(3) Goodwill fees
(4) Royalty
(5) Preliminary and Pre-operative expenses
(6) Second-hand equipment purchased or reinstalled/ shifted
(7) Capitalized Interest
(8) Any other investment which is not expressly narrated as eligible
(9) Technical know-how fee

(m) The phrase 'company' is used interchangeably with the phrase 'unit'

(n) Floor area in sq. ft. for the purposes of the incentive scheme shall be at carpet area basis.

Appendix I-A

CATEGORIES OF INDUSTRIES INCLUDED IN THE SCOPE OF INFORMATION TECHNOLOGY INDUSTRY

A. Computing devices including

- Desktop Personal Computer ◆ Servers ◆ Work-station ◆ Nodes Terminals ◆ Network PC
- Home PC ◆ Laptop Computers ◆ Note book Competitors
- Central Processing Unit (CPU) ◆ Palm top Computers/ PDA.

B. Network controller cards/Memory/Processors including

- 'Network interface card (NIC) ◆ Adaptor-ethernet/PCI/ ElSA/combo/PCMCIA
- ◆ SIMMs-Memory ◆ DIMMs-Memory ◆ Controller-SCSI/ Array ◆ Processors-Processor/Processor Power Module/ Upgrade

C. Storage Units including

- ◆ Hard Disk Drives/Hard Drives ◆ RAID Devices & their Controllers ◆ Floppy Disk Drives ◆ C.D. ROM Drives ◆ Tape Drives - DLT Drives/DAT ◆ Optical Disk Drives ◆ Other Digital Storage Devices.

D. Printers & Output Devices including

- ◆ Dot—matrix ◆ Laser jet ◆ Ink jet ◆ Desk jet ◆ LED printers ◆ Line printers ◆ Plotters ◆ Pass book Printers

E. Net working Products including

- ◆ Hubs ◆ Routers ◆ Switches ◆ Concentrators ◆ Trans-receivers

F. Software including

- ◆ Application Software' ◆ Operating System ◆ Middle Ware/Firm Ware

G. Power Supplies to Computer Systems including

- ◆ Switch Mode Power Supplies ◆ Uninterrupted Power Supplies.

H. Net working/Cabling & related Accessories

(related to I.T.Industry)

- ◆ Fibre Cable ◆ Copper Cable ◆ Cables ◆ Connectors, Terminal Blocks ◆ Jack Panels, Patch Cord.
- ◆ Mounting Cord, Patch Panels ◆ Back Boards, Wiring Blocks ◆ Surface Mount Boxes

I. Electronic Components

- ◆ Printed circuit Board Assembly/populated PCB ·Printed Circuit Board/PCB ◆ Transistors.

- Integrated Circuits/Ics ◆ Diodes/Thyristor/LED 'Registers 'Capacitors ▪ Switches(On/Off, Push- button, Rocker etc.)
- Plugs/Sockets/Relays ◆ Magnetic Heads, Print Heads ◆ Connectors ▪ Microphones/Speakers Fuses

J. Tele-communication Equipment including

- Telephones ◆ Videophones ◆ Facsimile Machines/Fax cards ◆ Tele-Printers/Telex machines ◆ PABX/EPABX/ RAX/MAX -Telephone exchange ◆ Multiplexers/Muxes 'Modems ◆ Telephone Answering Machines ◆ Tele-Communication Switching Apparattis ◆ Antenna & Mast 'Wireless data communication Equipment ◆ Receiving Equipment like pagers, Mobile/Cellular Phones etc. ◆ VSATs ◆ 'Video Conferencing Equipment including Set Top Boxes for both Video and Digital Signalling.

K. Consumables including

- C DROM/Compact Disk' ◆ Floppy Disk ◆ Tapes DAT/DLT ◆ Ribbons ◆ Toners ◆ Ink jet cartridges ' Inks for out put devices.

L. Others

- Key Board ◆ Monitor ◆ Mouse ◆ Multi Media Kits ◆ Access Card ◆ Electronics Purse' Electronics Wallet ◆ Universal Pre-Payment card ◆ Smart card etc.

GOVERNMEN'T OF KERALA

Abstract

Information 'Technology. Department — New I.T Industry Policy and Incentive Policy — approved — orders issued

INFORMATION TECHNOLOGY DEPARTMENT

G.O.(MS) 25/ 2001/ITD Dated, Thiruvananthapuram 1-12-2001

ORDER

Government are pleased to approve the new IT Industry Policy along with the Incentive Policy as outlined in the appendix.

The policy shall come into force w.e.f. the date of this order.

By Order of the Governor

Aruna Sundararajan
Secretary to Government.

To

The Chief Secretary/Additional Chief Secretary
All Principal Secretaries/Secretaries/Special Secretaries to Government.
The Accountant General, Kerala (A&E) /Audit (This is issued with the concurrence of the Finance Department)
The Director, Kerala Information Technology Services Society.
'The Chief Executive Officer, Technopark, Thiruvananthapuram.
Managing Director, KELTRON, Vellayambalam, Thiruvananthapuram.
Managing Director, Kerala State Industrial Development Corporation, Thiruvananthapuram.
Managing Director, KINFRA, Vellayambalam, Thiruvananthapuram.
General Administration (SC) Department (vide proceedings No.574 dt 30-1 11-2001 of Council of Ministers)
The Finance Department (*vide* U.O No.92391 A-Expenditure B3/01/Fin dt.27-1-2001).
Copy to:
Principal Secretary to Chief Minister.
Private Secretary to M (Industries and Social Welfare).
C.A to Secretary (Information Technology).
CA to Additional Secretary (Information Technology).
Stock File/Office Copy.

Forwarded /By Order

Section Officer

7

Case Studies

e-choupal

e-Choupal provides one of the finest examples of private initiative in the governance field. 'e-Choupal' leverage Information Technology to virtually cluster all the value chain participants, delivering the same benefits as vertical integration does in mature agricultural economies of the west. Developed by one of the biggest conglomerates of India ITC these choupals makes use of the physical transmission capabilities of current intermediaries — aggregation, logistics, counter-party risk and bridge financing. In this manner a farmer is averted from the risk of intermediately and can expect to fetch the right price for his produce.

Real-time information and customized knowledge provided by 'e-choupal' enhance the ability of farmers to take decisions and align their farm output with market demand and secure quality & productivity.

The aggregation of the demand for farm inputs from individual farmers gives them access to high quality inputs from established and reputed manufacturers at fair prices. As a direct marketing channel, virtually linked to the 'mandi' system for price discovery, 'e-Choupal' eliminates wasteful intermediation and multiple handling. Thereby it significantly reduces transaction costs.

The farmers benefit through enhanced farm productivity and higher farm gate prices, ITC benefits from the lower net cost of procurement (despite offering better prices to the farmer) having eliminated costs in the supply chain that do not add value. It designed a hardware solution that includes a desktop computer with power backup through batteries charged with solar panels. ITC also convinced 175 local telephone exchanges to upgrade their equipment to support data transmissions, initially at ITC's expense.

To overcome limited bandwidth, they cached static content locally so that only dynamic content needed to be streamed. And to overcome illiteracy, ITC made the transactional capabilities of the site available to farmers through the registered sanchalaks.

All information based on the farmers' needs was gathered and the content rewritten in some cases by the farmers themselves for user-friendliness. Soil testing services offered at the sanchalak's office also provided ITC with a valuable database. Rather than leaving the middle-men completely out of the loop, a role was created for some of them in the logistics operations with the title of 'choupal samyojak'. An Internet kiosk was set up in the house choupal sanchalak. The site provides farmers with real-time information on the latest weather report, prices in various 'mandis', global prices and the best farming practices.

The farmer saves Rs. 250 per tonne on soya bean since he no longer has to pay for bagging, transporting, loading and unloading, plus wastage and wrong weighting at the 'mandis'.

The system also acts as an e-commerce portal for the company. A farmer cannot only sell his produce but can also purchase items for household use. For instance, it has tied up with Monsanto and Madhya Pradesh's Seeds Corporation for seeds and BASF for fertilizers. ITC charges a 10 per cent commission on the percentage of sales accrued in the choupals, one half of which is passed on to the 'choupal' sanchalak who executes the sale.

ITC plans to extend its e-choupal network to one lakh villages in the country, covering one-sixth of the population of rural India. Beginning with six e-choupals in June 2000, the company has so far set up 1,200 choupals in 6,000 villages.

GUJARAT STATE WIDE AREA NETWORK (GSWAN)

Gujarat State's E-Governance vehicle with a State-of-the-Art Converged Network

INTRODUCTION

People wants a Government which meets their needs at affordable cost, improve the quality of lives, which is available when they need it, and which delivers results to them. Physical separation between citizens and Government must not pose any limitation to the effective Governance. Information Technology is a key enabler to the process of **smart e-governance**, offering **access and delivery** of services to the expectations of people.

Horizontal and Vertical integration within the organization is essential for effective and efficient information exchange. This is to be followed by authorizing public access to administration at various points in this Horizontal and Vertical information corridor. Standardizing, and transforming all citizens' centric Government's applications into electronic form for interactive public use is the last step in e-governances process.

Government of Gujarat, with a focal emphasis on the "open standard **access (both inter intra and extra organization) converged network,** has succeeded in creating required infrastructures, unparallel any where in the country.

Today GSWAN achieves distinction in the category of state owned ICT infrastructure for (a) Voice, Video and Data —all services on IP, (b) 25 Districts and all 225 Talukas connected and functional, (c) About *560* offices in the network capable of handling high volume, high speed data and video conference (d) One of the robust campus area network at Secretariat (SCAN) connected with GSWAN enabling even Taluka level access for all officers at secretariat and *vice versa*, (d) Satellite interconnect with GSWAN Hub has made all services of the network omni present in the state/country through portable VSAT terminal which was put into services in June 2002.

Gujarat State Wide Area Network (GSWAN), a unique state-of-the-art, e-governance project commissioned by the Gujarat state, is discussed in this paper.

GSWAN & GUJARAT STATE

The State of Gujarat, with an area of 196000 sq. Kms,

occupies the northern extremity of the western seaboard from between 20.6 and 24.42 degrees north latitude and 68.10 and 74.28 degrees east longitude, with 1600 km long Arabian sea-coastline.

State of Gujarat is divided into 25 Districts with 225 Talukas, with marked administrative boundaries. Number of Talukas under a District varies from 8 -12. Gandhinagar is the capital city from where the state is administered through various departments, and other offices. Each department is headed by Secretary to the Government. For political guidance to every department there are Ministers, Ministers of state and Deputy Ministers which constitute the cabinet. The cabinet, in turn is responsible to the legislative assembly, for all its action to ensure well administered, progressive and benevolent state machinery for well being of its population.

GoG had decided to create state-of-the-art , Gujarat State Wide Area Network (GSWAN) to—

- establish a reliable horizontal and vertical communication corridor for within the state administration to make government more productive and compatible for electronic transactions;
- achieve e-governance commitment and bring governance closer to public;
- strengthen disaster management capacity;

Project report was prepared for state wide area network after undertaking a detailed feasibility study. Inclusion of various offices and their location, traffic load and its characteristics, security, LAN/WAN protocols, topology, bandwidth requirements and utilization, allocation of bandwidth ETC.., were some of the components considered while designing the project document. Various climatic zones, coastal areas and identified disaster prone areas were also taken into consideration while finalizing the project specifications.

Connectivity (bandwidth) needs were defined on the basis of traffic estimated between various network nodes. The project specifications included — bandwidth requirements, dialup connections. VSAT links (to impart mobility feature to WAN and to cover inaccessible location when required). Number of subscribers and the growth pattern were analyzed for arriving at various resources requirements on time scale. Assessment of

Internet bandwidth , email service, web hosting resources, DBM resources etc.. Was done keeping e-governance objectives into consideration. Web sites have been found very effective media for mass communication , specifically information dissemination to whole world at a any point of time. This was considered that each department shall have their web site for dissemination of information to the public and *vice-versa*. Wide Area Network resources design included intra, extra and inter networking requirements.

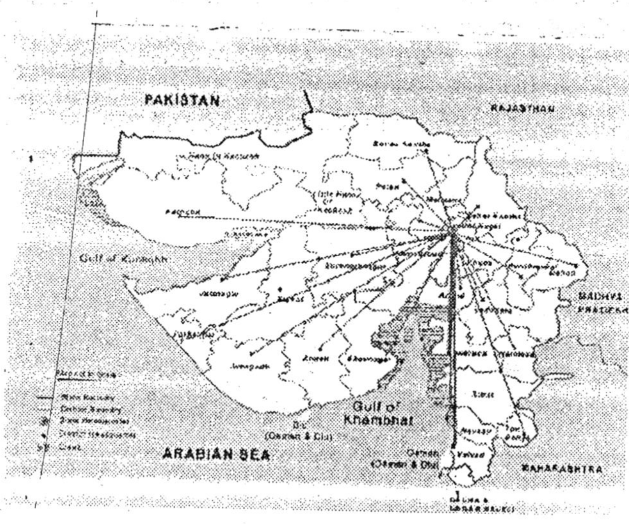

Fig. 1 : State of Gujarat — Capital at Gandhinagar

Bids were invited for qualifications and RFP (Request for proposal) were circulated to all qualified agencies. Work was awarded on lst march 2001 to the vendor for creation of GSWAN on BOOT (Built Operate Own and Transfer) basis. The BOOT period was fixed up for 8 years, after which project assets shall be transferred to Gujarat Government by the BOOT service provider at a nominal charge of Rs 1.

GSWAN was commissioned and accepted by Government of Gujarat on 26.12.2001. Gujarat Government has created a history in the area of state owned wide area networks in the country by having commissioned a total IP based, converged wide area network interconnecting even last and smallest administrative units in administrative hierarchy, *i.e.* Taluka, into the network.

GSWAN Network Architecture and Topology:

The network topology as conceived and designed for GSWAN was based on a **hub-and-spoke** design philosophy, with three tiers.

First tier - Secretariat Center (SC) at state capital, Gandhinagar, where from the highest office of Government functions in the state. Various departments and hundreds of subordinate offices located at the state capital are connected to SC horizontally through SCAN (Secretariat Campus Area Network). All districts and Taluka offices are vertically connected with SC (the hub of wide area network).

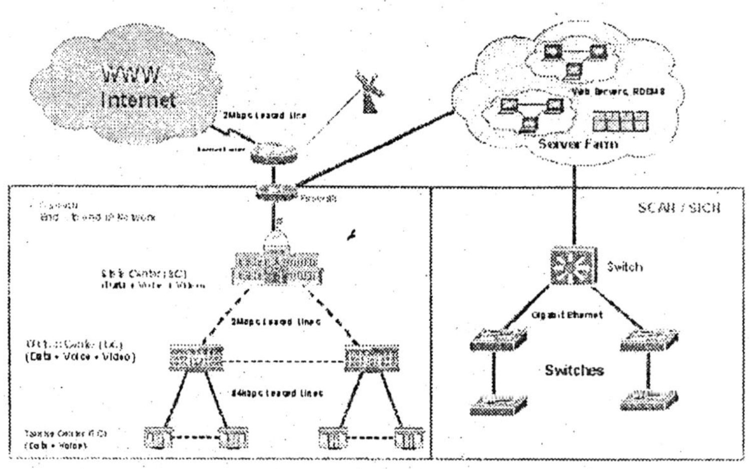

FIGURE-2: GUJARAT STATE WIDE AREA NETWORK ARCHITECTURE.

Second Tier- constitutes District Centers, or "**DC**"s, located at district collector's office, and multiple district level offices connected with DC horizontally.

Third Tier - constitutes Talukas Centers, or "**TC's**, located at Taluka Mamlatdar's office, and couple of Taluka level offices horizontally connected with TC.

Secretariat Center (SC) at capital is marked as tier -1. This is the network hub. Secretariat Campus Area Network (SCAN) integrates with GSWAN at SC (shown in figure above). SCAN has about 7000 Ethernet I/Os at capital city, Gandhinagar and all these I/Os are interconnected with GSWAN for information exchange. 300 Telephone connection given to various offices at Secretariat for direct voice communication to any GSWAN node in the state. Table given below summarises service (data, voice and video) to be commissioned in the beginning and after three years of commencement of the project.

Voice/ Data! Video service provisions for present and after 3 years

Place	Local Office Requirement		Other Office Requirement	
	Initial	After 3 Year	Initial	After 3 Year
VOICE Ports, LAN Ports, Video Port (VC), (Number of locations)				
TC	1,1 ,0,(I)	3,1,0,(6)	1,Dialup,0,(0)	I ,Dialup,0,(0)
DC	10,1,1 ,(25)	20,2,1 ,(25)	1,1 ,0,(33)	3,1 ,0,(60)
Super DC	10,1,1 ,(I)	20,2,1 ,(1)	1, 1,0,(50)	3,1 ,0,(100)
SC	100,2,25	200,4 ,25	200,1,0,(20)	800.1,0.(50)
	connectivity to existing Secretariat Network (SCAN)	+- connectivity to existing Secretariat Network (SCAN)	+ connectivity to existing Secretariat Network (SCAN) (This is an aggregate requirement for all other offices' requirement in SC)	+ Connectivity to existing Secretariat Network (SCAN) (This is an aggregate requirement for all other offices requirement in SC)

Tier-2 is the District Center (DC) and there are *25* such DCs in the network connected on 2 Mbps (El) leased lines with SC. Project design kept provision for connecting 20 number of other district level offices, which was subsequently enhanced to 33 due to demand received. All other offices located within 600 meter radius from their respective DCs are connected with OFC (MM) and copper cable and are capable of serving voice, video and data to the users. The offices beyond 600 meters of distance from the DC node of GSWAN are connected on 64 Kb leased lines capable of serving voice and data services to these locations.

There are 10 dialup PSTN lines terminating on remote access server (RAS) at DC. The dialup access is given to all those Government offices in that district, which are not considered for direct integration. Dial up access is designed to cater to Public Information Offices (PIO) or kiosks to be opened up at later date. GSWAN is ready to serve village level kiosks from the date of commissioning for internet (World Wide Web) and intract services.

Tier-3 represents Talukas Center (TC). Out of 225 Talukas in the state, 210 Talukas are connected with the GSWAN network on 64 Kb leased lines, and rest of 15 Talukas are connected directly Ethernet backbone because of the proximity of later with DC location. All Talukas are having internet/ intranet and voice services operational from the date of commissioning. Taluka node design has provision for interfacing Taluka LAN.

In each of the stations, there is a state-of-the-art Cisco router, which terminates the Leased Line. These routers route IP packets intelligently throughout the network, and provide the Quality of Service (or QoS) features necessary to enable convergence of voice, video and data on a single network infrastructure.

At the first and second tier, channalised interfaces are used to aggregate the links from the lower tier. The Cisco 7513 router at the SC uses Channalised E3 interfaces to aggregate the El links form the DCs, while the Cisco 3662s at the DCs use a Channalised E1 interface to aggregate the 64 kbps links from the TCs.

TECHNOLOGY AND DATA FLOW IN GSWAN:

GSWAN is a total IP network. Data, Voice and video travels as IP packets in the network, with a total convergence. An attempt is made to explain the data flow taking place in the network for Data, voice and video services, as given below:—

Data Flow from PC to PC in GSWAN:

- Application on computer encapsulates the data in Layer 7-Layer 5 headers.
- Network driver on PC then includes Layer 4 and Layer 3 information, packetization, and encapsulation in IP. This includes source and destination IP address, TCP port, etc.
- NIC encapsulates IP data within Layer 2 MAC header and sends it out over the LAN.
- If the destination IP address is not on the LAN, the frame reaches the router. Router strips off layer 2 MAC header and looks at the destination IP address.
- Router does a lookup in the routing table, finds appropriate interface to send the packet out of. If this is a WAN interface, then a Layer 2 PPP header is appended to the packet, and it is queued on the interface. At this time, appropriate QoS/Queuing mechanisms are applied to the packet, based on the configuration done on the router, and the information available in the IP header.
- Once the packet reaches the remote router, the remote router strips off the Layer 2 PPP header and looks at the destination IP address. This destination IP address will typically be on the local LAN.
- Then, the router encapsulates the IP packet into a MAC header and puts it on to the LAN interface. The packet now has the destination MAC address of the PC that the data is destined to.
- The destination PC receives the data, strips off the L2-L7 information, processes it and presents the data to the application after gathering all IP packets in that flow.

Voice calls flow from GSWAN phone to GSWAN phone:

- User picks up GS-WAN phone, dials access code for trunk line ("0" or "9").
- The PBX understands that this call is destined to another location, and therefore passes on the call to the router over the TDM link (El). Here, all digits are passed on to the router, one 64-kbps timeslot on the El is allocated to that call.

- The router receives the call on its voice interface. It understands the TDM signaling (El CAS), and converts it into H.323 standard for IP calls. It does a lookup and converts the destination phone number into the IP address of the remote router to which the destination user is connected.
- The remote router receives the H.323 call from the source router. It places that call on to the TDM link to the destination PBX. It also converts the H.323 signaling back to EI-CAS, which the PBX can understand. A 64-kbps slot on the El is allotted for this call.
- The remote phone starts ringing. Once the phone is answered, an RTP (real-time protocol) stream is set up between the two routers for transport of VoIP packets.
- At the source router, the digitized voice call travels from the PBX to the router. The router packetsize and compresses the voice from 64kbps to 8kbps (G.729a standard) using on-board DSP resources.
- IP and RTP headers are added to the compressed and packetized voice. The destination IP address in the IP header is of the remote router. This brings up the bandwidth per call to approximately 12kbps.
- The router identifies the voice traffic as high priority and puts it before the data traffic on the interface. If there are some large packets in the queue, they are broken up into smaller packets, and voice packets are then queued in between these. This ensures that voice does not face undue latency because of large data packets. This technique is known as Link Fragmentation and Interleaving.
- IP routing ensures that the VoIP packets traverse the WAN to the remote router.
- Once the voice packets reach the remote router, the reverse process is done — strip IP and RTP headers, decompress the voice, and put it on the designated 64kbps El link to the PBX.
- The PBX then switches the voice to the destination phone using TDM switching technology.

Video Call Flow

- User at Polycom end station dials the H.323 prefix (phone number of remote device). This may be for another end station in a point-to-point scenario, or may be an MCU.
- Polycom talks to the Gatekeeper in the network, and gets the IP address corresponding to that specific prefix. Once found, a call setup message is initiated over H.323 to the remote device.
- Once call setup is complete, a call is established. The Polycom digitizes and packetises voice and video from the camera and microphone and puts it onto the LAN port.
- While doing this, it classifies the traffic as high-priority, so that the router can identify it and give it the requisite treatment for QoS.
- Once the IP Packets are on the LAN, they are then routed to the destination device using normal IP routing, just like VoIP or data traffic.

TECHNOLOGY AND LA OUT OF DIFFERENT TIERS IN GSWAN:

Tier-I. SECRETARIATE CENTER (SC) Network

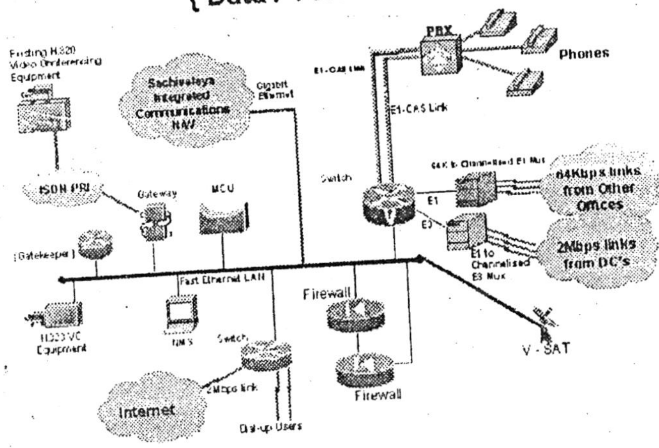

FIGURE-3: SECRETARIAT CENTER NODE -GANDHINAGAR

As shown in the above diagram, the network in the SC comprises all the components of a central hub site. There are 300 GSWAN telephones commissioned directly to GSWAN EPABX. Secretariat at Gandhinagar has one of the best internal voice, and video communication system using lucent technology. The integrated communication system at Secretariat caters telephone service to about 6000 subscribers. Current regulations forbids interconnection between secretariat internal communication network with the GSWAN, and that is why separate lines were laid for GSWAN telephones in the secretariat.

All existing data connections (7000) on the SCAN were interconnected to GSWAN, as regulators do not forbid the data interconnection between two closed user's groups. All Government offices and each of the 7000 users at Secretariat, in the capital city, are capable of doing VC to any one or all (MCU) in the network any where in the state.

The **Cisco 7500 series** is Cisco's premier high-end platform of multi-protocol routers. The series includes the Cisco 7505, the Cisco 7507, and the Cisco 7513. For the GSWAN, the 7513 was the platform of choice, which fit with the scalability, reliability and performance requirements of the network. CISCO Pix-520 provides necessary network security at SC.

Mobility feature introduced into GSWAN:

An extended c-band VSAT station is interfaced on to the LAN at SC, Gandhinagar to enable GSWAN connection with the portable VSAT mobile working at a distant remote location. This is first time in the contrary that wide area network services are made available to locations where there is a total telecom black out.

The events taking place at remote locations are covered and connected to GSWAN through portable VSAT terminal. This has given tremendous flexibility to the state administration in reaching to the public in remote areas during any emergency.

WLAN for important other offices beyond reach of cat-5 cable:

GoG has commissioned Wireless LAN, which is connected to the SCAN at Gandhinagar. Few important Government offices, which are not on the Ethernet backbone are connected using WLAN technology. There are six of such offices connected with the campus area network.

Server farm:

Multiple Servers are commissioned in server farm at Secretariat, Gandhinagar. All common IT services , *viz.* internet, web hosting and maintenance, data base storage and maintain, mail services, etc.. , are being managed from the server farm facility center, interfaced with GSWAN and SCAN.

Tier-II. DISTRICT CENTER (DC) Network

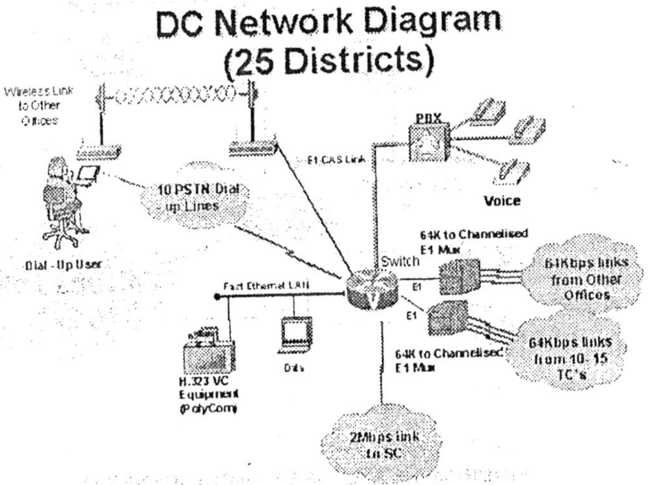

FIGURE-4: DISTRICT GSWAN NODE - GENERIC

The DC GSWAN node has all — voice, video and data communication faculties available. There are 33 other offices connected horizontally at DC in addition to all Talukas stations falling under its jurisdiction. 100s of offices authorized by Government enters into the network through dialup access. Remote Access Server (RAS) at each DC has 10 dialup PSTN lines enabling access to those who are not directly connected with GSWAN.

Cisco 3662 routers are installed. The Cisco 3660 series platform provides improvised density, performance, robustness and serviceability for use in larger branch-office applications or for Telco-managed services as Customer Premise Equipment (CPE).

Tier-III. TALUKA CENTER (TC) Network

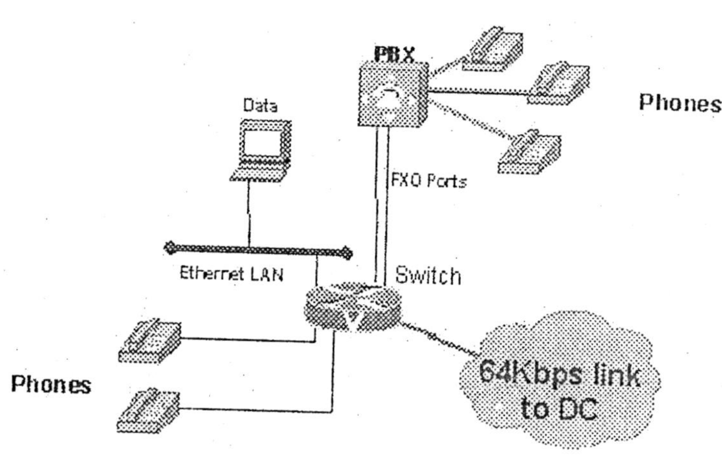

FIGURE-5: TALUKA GSWAN NODE -GENERIC

Talukas is the last and smallest unit of the administration in the state connected to GSWAN. Each Talukas has a LAN port, FXS/FXO port and capacity to expand. All offices located at Talukas level are authorized to access GSWAN on dialup lines in addition to direct LAN access. Cisco 1751 and 1750-4V routers have been installed in the talukas. The 1750 provides flexibility to adapt to changing requirements of growth at the TC's.

Conclusion

GSWAN is a state owned, IP based, converged wide area network connecting administration upto Taluka. The network was commissioned in Dec. 2001 and working satisfactorily. Integration of VSAT station at the hub of the network enabled GSWAN services omni present any where in the state /country. This is first, multi services (voice, video and data), wide area network owned by any state on IP technology. Network availability and quality of services are monitored and managed using powerful SLA monitoring engines. Long term objectives, technology obsolescence considerations, level of service (LoS) requirements in Government networks, were the key components of the project design. Use of IP technology has imparted immense flexibility to the expansion plan of Government.

(Source: WWW. gujaratindia.com)

Warana Wired Village Project

The Warana Project was jointly executed by NIC, Maharashtra State Government, and the Warana Vibhag Shikshan Mandal at a cost of Rs. 25 million (US $ 600,000) that was borne jointly by the three agencies in a ratio of 50.40.10. The services that include automation of the working of the cooperative societies, and provision of agricultural, medical and educational information to villagers are provided free. The kiosk manager is appointed by the village *panchayats* as a part-time activity. The panchayats acts as an interface between villagers and administration.

The system includes both web-based and Intranet-based applications. The web-based applications are the agriculture produce market information system, agricultural schemes and crop technology information system, computer learning aids, village information systems, educational and vocational guidance systems, government documents and procedures systems and computerization of the local cooperative market.

The Intranet-based systems are the wired management of sugarcane cultivation, land records computerization, the computerization of the Warana Milk Dairy, and a Grievance Registration and Redressal System. The content was created in the local Marathi language by the NIC office in Pune, Maharashtra State, through extensive interactions with the cooperatives. The content is regularly maintained and enhanced at the location of the central system within the local university.

Among the web-based applications, the most extensively used are the procedural information system and the computerization of the Warana bazaar. This has relieved the villagers of cumbersome processes and long waits at government offices for certificates and licenses such as ration cards and kerosene/gas licenses.

The bazaar has an inventory of more than 40000 items sold through twenty-nine outlets. Bar code technology has modernized management of the market and keeping track of the goods sold. NIC Pune was responsible for the design, development and implementation of the Warana Wired Village Project.

A team of thirty technicians and engineers were accountable for the implementation of the project in six months. The project design was implemented in collaboration with the already existing NICNET. The new system incorporated specific aspects of NICNET such as Very Small Aperture Terminals (VSAT). VSATs are small satellite terminals that can transmit and receive interactive communications *via* satellite.

Both the University and Business Centers of Warana were chosen to house the VSATs. The Institute of Engineering Technology houses the Central Hub.

The Central Hub facilitates all web, database, Intranet, Internet, and email applications. The Central Hub's servers store updated market information along with information pertaining to the many Information System (IS) databases, which includes dairy, educational, geographical and agricultural information. High-speed VSATs (very small aperture terminals) connected to the National Informatics Centre (NIC) in Pune and an electronic telephone exchange form the basic technology frame of the wired village project.

The VSATs provide Internet access and the electronic telephone exchange provides dial-up facilities to the central hub located at the office of the Warana sugar cooperative. For the network the NIC has developed a software package based on an accounting programme. The programme supports the local language. Communication is sustained between the IT centers, business centers and Village booths using dial-up connections over the local area network (LAN).

Application content is administered from the Central Hub.

Maintenance of the system is done in association with NIC, Pune. All IT Centers are equipped with UPS; however, power is not guaranteed over a substantial period of time. Some other observations made were in association with connectivity. Connections to the various nodes are maintained by a high-speed wireless LAN. The connections to the Internet however, were not very "high-speed". This may be attributed to weather conditions on the day of our visit or channel payload.

The applications related to agriculture produce, schemes and crop technology as well as for education are not being used to the fullest extent. One reason is the slow access to the Internet, insufficient awareness creation among the villagers, and the low levels of literacy in the area in spite of the high levels of income.

Similarly, the Intranet-based applications that are extensively used are the wired management of the sugarcane cultivation and the computerization of the milk dairy as these relate directly to the economic lives of the villagers. While sugarcane cultivation is the main occupation of the farmers, milk production forms their secondary source of income. The impacts of both web-based and Intranet-based systems on the villagers' lives are significant in their enhancement of the efficiency of the local economy and governance.

Computerized Interstate Check Posts in Gujarat

Gujarat has an extensive road network, which carries a large volume of commercial traffic. Major highway systems link Dehli to Mumbai and provide the principal link to the Kandla sea port on Gujarat's west coast. Gujarat's 10 check posts are positioned at the border with three neighbouring Indian states. Nearly 25,000 transport vehicles enter daily through these check posts.

Trucking companies want to maximize their earnings from each vehicle. Often this has prompted transporters to load their trucks beyond permissible axle load creating a serious safety hazard. The central excise and state sales tax is levied on the basis of a record of the weight/count of manufactured goods that are shipped out from the factory or shipped to a trader. Yet, the number of trucks dispatched in a day is the primary basis of this assessment. Thus, by overloading trucks manufacturers have evaded excise duty. (Some estimates are that 80-90% of vehicles are overloaded.)

The Gujarat Motor Vehicles Department (GMVD) controls the road transport activity in Gujarat. While the broad policies are laid down by India's central government in the Motor Vehicles Act, state governments are empowered to determine the penalties for infractions and procedures for enforcement. Nevertheless, state governments typically have been ineffective at reducing the number of overloaded vehicles. Inspection of 100% of commercial vehicles has been impossible; and check post inspectors have been notoriously corrupt. The GMVD department has 137 inspectors, of whom 27 were on suspension (under scrutiny for corrupt practices). It is common knowledge that inspectors' posts at lucrative check posts can be bought for as much as Rs. 10 million.

In Gujarat's traditional check post system, a suspect vehicle is flagged to a stop, and then weighed on a weigh bridge located away from traffic. The legal penalty for overload is Rs. 2,000 per ton. However, any fine often has been (illegally) negotiated. Inspectors are also expected to check for the driver's interstate transit permit, and vehicles registered in Gujarat have paid that the state's annual road tax. Corruption by departmental inspectors at these check posts has led to harassment of truck drivers and loss of revenue to the state.

The problem of corruption was particularly difficult to attack as politicians backed the corrupt. In the absence of any systematic inspection of vehicles, the transport companies also adopted various illegal practices. Duplicate copies of a single registration book from the Regional Transport Office (RTO) have been used for many different vehicles, using fake license plates.

Approach

In the computerized process, all the check posts are monitored at a central location using video cameras installed at every check post cabin. The video camera captures the registration number of all trucks approaching the check post. (There are flood-lights and traffic lights which make the check posts appear like a runway at night.) Software converts the video image of the registration number to a digital form and the details of the truck are accessed from a central data base. An electronic weighbridge captures the weight and the computer issues a demand note for fine, automatically. Drivers can use a stored value card for payment.

With the each revamped check post:

— A 10 lane approach road of 1.3 kms length has been built to receive the vehicles.

— Each lane has a video camera positioned high, on a pole, with a proper protective casing.

— There is a control room with 2 computer servers—the Data Base server that transmits the vehicle data through a 64 KBPS leased line, and a video server that captures & relays the video images, frame by frame, to a central server at the RTO. Power to the system is assured by dedicated lines from the State Electricity Board, backed up by a high capacity generator and 72 hour backup UPS.

— The video capture and transmit process (known as SIPCA— Satellite Image Processing and Capturing unit) has been supplied by a subsidiary of Phillips. The software for License tracking and the weigh-bridge equipment is also by Phillips. RTO has an IBM Server with DB2 RDBMS.

— Operators who man the cabins are from the private sector. Although GMVD employees have been trained to operate the new equipment, they are not operating the key nodes at the check posts.

— A database of all the 0.5 million commercial vehicles registered in Gujarat will be created at the HO in RTO premises. A powerful IBM server (AS 400) is installed there with DB2 as the RDBMS.

— With the vehicle's registration number the data base can retrieve information on the make of vehicle, whether or not the National Permit exists and is valid, insurance, whether the vehicle tax has been paid, etc.

— Once the vehicle arrives at the weighbridge, the un-laden weight, the actual weight, the amount of overload and the fine that must be paid is displayed on an electronic (plasma) boards. In this way, the process is made wholly transparent to the driver.

— Drivers hold a pre-paid card (in denominations of Rs.

2000 or Rs 5000) which are used for paying any penalty. This card costs Rs. 50.

— Operators also are expected to check head lights, tax payment, etc. Any shortfall is recorded in the computer. Only if corrective measure is taken and recorded in the system will the sensor-controlled barrier allow the truck to proceed.

— If the driver cannot pay the penalty, the vehicle must be parked in a designated parking lot. The RTO Inspector confiscates the vehicle's registration documents until the payment is made.

— Future plans include integrating payment of sales tax on the goods carried by the vehicles.

Implementation Challenges

The new system has teething problems. The central data base is being built, and for many vehicles it still does not hold the requisite details. Hence, the operator uses his judgement and, depending on the make of the vehicle, selects the permissible weight from a drop-down selection box.

The leased line (64 KBPS) connectivity is currently available at only 2 check posts (Shamlaji & Bhilad, the two largest). The centralized video monitoring is therefore not working properly. In some check posts inspectors may still harass the drivers to extort bribes.

The writing and pattern of license plates is often non-standard and not in compliance with the law. Hence, the license tracking software has not worked properly (only about 35 out of 5,000 numbers were read accurately). Now trucks with non standard number plates are required to replace them at the check post. A vendor is available to make the change, for a fee.

Initially the system issued manual receipts with limited information, since the automatic receipt generated by the computer, without a signature of the officer, was not legally valid. With passage of the central IT Act, the RTO's signature has been digitally incorporated on the receipt.

Data on the number of vehicles crossing the check post suggests that some vehicles have begun to divert through longer routes in adjoining states to avoid the penalty. Implementing similar systems in other states could plug the loop hole.

Benefits and Costs

Notwithstanding the implementation difficulties with the new system, the inspection of all vehicles has produced three-fold increase in tax collection over 2 years. Revenue increased from $12 million to $35 million, paying back the total project cost of $4 million in just 6 months.

On average, vehicles are cleared in 2 minutes instead of 30 in the manual system. Harassment of truckers continues, abetted by the problems with the video monitoring system.

The large and medium transport owners are happy with the system because they can come to know the exact date and time their driver passed the check post. The pre-paid card means that the driver does not have to carry much money.

Ur :ttp / /*www1* .worldbank.org/publicsector/egov/gujarats. htm, *http:/ /www.* incg.org. in

CARD

Registration to document changes in ownership and transactions involving immovable property is governed by the Indian Stamp Act of 1899. Deeds of various kinds are required by law to be written on stamp paper of prescribed value. Certain transactions require a fixed duty. For others the *ad valorem* method is used, whereby the stamp duty is a percentage of the property value or loan that is the subject of the instrument. The *ad valorem* method ensures that inflation will not erode the value of stamp revenues. This method accounts for over 90% of the total revenue from stamp duty.

Registration is carried out at the office of the Sub-Registrar of Assurances. In Andhra Pradesh (AP) there are 387 Sub-Registrar offices that register approximately 1.2 million documents per year. The work of the Sub-Registrar is supervised by a hierarchy of District Registrars (28), Deputy Inspectors (6), and the Inspector General (1). The traditional 11-step registration procedure is complex and time consuming, beyond the comprehension of most citizens. The age-old manual system of registering legal deeds like sale deeds, mortgage deeds, gift deeds and 44 other instruments—has been replaced by a simple, transparent and convenient system.

CARD Stands for Computer Aided Administration of Registration Department.

Implemented from 4 November 1998 at 239 offices of the sub-registrars in the State, over 3 million documents have been digitally registered till June 2002 under the CARD system.

Almost 60% of the documents, Encumbrance Certificates (ECs) and certified copies relate to agricultural properties, the success of the CARD project would greatly benefit the rural farming community. Agriculturists would also benefit from a possible link-up of the CARD network with the rural bank network, which would enhance the efficiencies of the rural credit services by eliminating the need for paper-based procedures.

OVERVIEW:*

The system has over 300 features providing an end-to-end solution to the automation of registration process—notable being valuation of immovable properties and conducting title search over the last 20 years in less than 15 minutes.

The various function of the Department are as follows:—

- Registration of Documents.
- Valuation of immovable Properties.
- Collection of Revenue Stamp Duty.
- Transfer Duty and Registration Fee.
- Preservation of Copies of Documents.
- Issue of Certified copies of Documents.
- Issue of Encumbrance certificates.

Registration Societies, Firms, Chit Funds, Non-Trading Companies, Marriages.

SERVICE LEVELS OF CARD ARE AS FOLLOWS*

S.No.	Service Provided	CARD Office	Non-Card Offices
1.	Sale of stamp paper	15 min.	30-60 min.
2.	Documents writing	30 min.	NA.
3.	Market Value Checkslip	10 min.	60 min.
4.	Cash receipt	10 min	30 min.
5.	Registration of documents	60 min.	3 days.
6.	Certifies copies	15 min.	3 days.
7.	Encumbrance Certificates	10 min.	1-5 days.

LIST OF COMPUTERISED SUB-REGISTRARS OFFICES IN THE STATE.

District	Category-A	Category-B	Category-C	Category-D
Srikakulam	Nil	1 Srikakulam R.O.	1 Palakonda 2 Kasibugga	1.Rajam
Vizianagaram	1 Vizianagaram R.O.	Nil	1 Bobbili 2 Parvathipuram	1. Kothavalasa
Visakhapatnam	1 R.O.	1 Sabbavaram 2 Gopalapatnam 3 Bhimunipatnam 4 Gajuwaka 5 Dwarakanagar 6 Anakapalli 7 Madhurawada	1 Narsipatnam	1. Nakkapally
Zone-i	2	8	5	3
East godavari	1 Kakinada R.O.	1 Mandapeta 2 Peddapuram 3 R.C. Puram 4 Thallarevu 5 Draksharamam 6 Samalkot 7 Pithapuram 8 Tuni	1 Alamuru 2 Biccavolu 3 Jaggampeta 4 Prathipadu	Nil
Rajahmundry	1 Rajahmundry R.O.	1 Rajanagaram 2 Kadiyam 3 Amalapuram	1 Malkipuram 2 Korukonda 3 Razole 4 Mamidikuduru 5 Ravulapalem 6 Anaparthy 7 Kothapeta 8 Mummidivaram	1. Ambajipet
West godavari	1 Eluru R.O.	1 Nidadavole 2 Kovvur 3 T.P.gudem 4 Chintaliapudi 5 Bhimadole	1 Ananthapalli 2 J.R.Gudem	1.Vegeswa-rapuram
Bhimavaram	1 Bhimavaram R.O.	1 Narsapur 2 Palakol 3 Akividu 4 Tanuku	1 Pentapadu 2 Ganapavaram 3 Penugonda 4 Veeravasaram 5 Attili	1. Achanta
Krishna	1 Machilipatnam R.O.	1 Movva 2 Kaikaluru 3 Gudivada 4 Avanigadda	1 Kanumole 2 Bantumilly 3 Pammarru	1. Pedana

District	Category-A	Category-B	Category-C	Category-D
Vijayawada	1 Vijayawada R.O.	1 Ibrahimpatnam	1 Kanchikacherla	Nil
	2 Patamata	2 Vuyyuru	2 Thiruvuru	
	3 Gunadala	3 Kankipadu	3 Nandigama	
		4 Mylavaram	4 Vissannapet	
		5 Nuzvidu		
		6 Gannavaram		
		7 Jaggaiahpet		
Zone-ii	8	31	26	4
Guntur	1 Guntur R.O.	1 Tenali	1 Tenali (west	1. Tadikonda
		2 Mangalagiri	2 Chebrole	
		3 Repalle	3 Prathipadu	
		4 Nallapadu	4 Duggirala	
		5 Ponnur		
		6 Peddakakani		
Narasaraopet	1 Narasaraopet R.O.	1 Chilakaluripet	1 Gurajala	1.Phirangi-puram
		2 Vinukonda		
		3 Sattenapalli		
		4 Bapatla		
		5 Piduguralla		
Prakasam	1 Ongole R.O.	1 Chirala	1 Markapuram	1. Kani ir
		2 Darsi	2 Addanki	
		3 Kandukur	3 Singarayakonda	
			4 Martoor	
Nellore	1 Nellore R.O.	1 Kavali	1 Venkatagiri	1. Kovur
		2 Gudur	2 Sullurpet	
			3 Naidupet	
Zone-iii	4	16	12	4
District	Category-a	Category-b	Category-c	
Kurnool	1 Kurnool R.O.	1 Nandyal	1 Dhone	1. Atmakur
		2 Adoni	2 Yemmiganur	
Cuddapah	1 Cuddapah R.O.	1 Proddatur	1 Rajampet	1. Mydukur
		2 Rayachoti	2 Pullampet	
			3 Jammalamadugu	
			4 Pulivendula	
Anantapur	1 Anantapur R.O.	1 Tadipathri	1 Dharmavaram	I.Uravakonda
		2 Hindupur	2 Rayadurg	
		3 Kadiri	3 Guntakal	
		4 Bukkapatnam	4 Kalyandurg	
			5 Penukonda	
Chittoor	1 Chittoor R.O.	1 Madanapalle	1 Kuppam	1. Vayalapadu
		2 Palamaneru	2 Punganur	
			3 Piler	
Sribalaji	1 Tirupati R.O.	1 Renigunta	1 Srikalahasti	1. Pakala
			2 Chandragiri	
Zone-iv	5	11	16	5
Warangal	1 Warangal R.O.	Nil	1 Janagaon	1.Ghanapur
			2 Mahabub bad	
			3 Warangal (rural)	

District	Category-A	Category-B	Category-C	Category-D
Khammam	1 Khammam R.O.	Nil	1 Kothagudem	1. Sattupalli
Karimnagar	1 Karimnagar R.O.	1 Jagitial	1 Metpalli	1. Mallial
		2 Sircilla	2 Husnabad	
		3 Peddapalli	3 Huzurabad	
			4 Vemulawada	
			5 Sultanabad	
Adilabad	Nil	1 Adilabad R.O.	Nil	1. Bhainsa
		2 Nirmal		
		3 Mancherial		
Zone-v	3	6	9	4
Nalgonda	1 Nalgonda R.O.	1 Kodad	1 Devarakonda	1. Huzurnagar
		2 Miryalaguda		
		3 Choutuppal		
		4 Suryapet		
		5 Bhongir		
Mahabub nagar	Nil	1 M.B. Nagar R.O.	1 Gadwal	1.Nagarku-rnool
		2 Shadnagar	2 Jadcherla	
			3 Wanaparthy	
			4 Kalwakurthy	
Nizamabad	1 Nizamabad R.O.	1 Bodhan	1 Kamareddy	1. Bhamswada
Medak	1 Sangareddy R.O.	1 Siddipet	1 Sadasivapet	1. Jogipet
		2 Gajwel		
		3 Zaheerabad		
		4 Narsapur		
Ranga reddy	1 Rangareddy R.O.	1 Rajendra nagar	1 Vikarabad	1. Parigi
	2 Medchal	2 Ghatkesar	2 Tandur	
	3 Uppal	3 Shamshabad	3 Maheswaram	
	4 Malkajgiri	4 Champapet		
	5 Kukatpalli	5 Hyderabad (east)		
	6 Saroornagar	6 Shamirpet		
	7 Vallabhnagar	7 Pedda amberpet		
		8 Chevella		
		9 Ibrahim patnam		
Hyderabad	1 SR.nagar	1 Doodbowli	Nil	Nil
	2 Golconda	2 Charminar		
	3 Chikkadpally			
	4 Secunderabad			
	5 Marredpally			
	6 Azampura			
	7 Bowenpally			
	8 Hyderabad			
	9 Banjara Hills			
Zone-VI	19	23	10	5
Grand total	39	95	78	

Note:

Category A - 39 offices with more than 5000 documents registered per annum.
Category B-95 offices with 2500-5000 documents registered per annum.
Category C - 78 offices with 1500 -2500 documents registered per annum.

CURRENT STATUS:*

DETAILS OF WORK TURNED OUT ON CARD IS AS FOLLOWS:

Statistics

	Feb 99 to May-01	June , 01	Total
No. Doct. Registered.	1950456	97353	2047809
No. of MV Checkslips issued	709986	31382	741368
No. of Registration Checkslips issued	1725531	90431	1815962
No. of documents scanned	1713721	89119	1802840
No. of Encumbrance Certificates issued	787365	45256	832621
Value of Stamps sold (in Lakhs)	75120.38	2851.14	77971.52

Department has computerised 214 Offices so far. Department is about to extend the same to another 25 Sub-Registrars offices in the immediate future.

MV assistant is being given in the web for Hyderabad Municipal Corporation. The same is being extended to 6 other corporations in the State *viz.*, Viskhapatanam, Rajahmundry, Guntur, Vijayawada, Kurnool, Warangal.

To give online Encumbrance information (Title Search) all Sub-Registrars Offices of Hyderabad City and Ranga Reddy District numbering 20 are being interconnected. The central Web Server will be updated immediately after a transaction is committed in the Sub-Registrar Office concern.

Web Services: *

Land rates of agriculture and non-agriculture properties of all computerised offices of the state are available on the web. They are available at igrs.ap.gov. in/Encumbrance information of all sub-registrar office of Hyderabad City is centralised at Inspector General of Registration. This is online updation the information is available over Internet at { HYPERLINK "http://igrs.ap.gov.in" }

LOCATIONS: LIST OF OFFICES*

	HYDERABAD
1	OFFICE
2	S.R.NAGAR
3	GOLCONDA
4	CHIKKADPALLY
5	SECUNDERABAD
6	MAR REDPALLY
7	AZAMPURA
8	BOWENPALLY
9	BANJARA HILLS
10	DOODBOWLI
11	CHARMINAR
	RANGAREDDY
1	RANGAREDDY R.O.
2	HYDERABAD (EAST)
3	UPPAL
4	MALKAJGIRI
5	KUKATPALLI
6	SAROOR NAGAR
7	VALLABH NAGAR
8	RAJENDRA NAGAR
9	CHAMPAPET
20	TOTAL

The cost of the CARD project was funded entirely by the AP government. The 1996 pilot project to computerise two Sub-Registrar Offices cost about $55,000. The original outlay for the full CARD project was about US$3 million; and this figure is likely to grow to $4.3 million. (This cost includes hardware, software, training, site preparation, data entry, air-conditioners, furniture, stationery and storage media, and other miscellaneous expenses.)

* **Source: HYPERLINK "http ://www. ap-it. com/cards.html**

"BHOOMI" - ONLINE DELIVERY OF LAND RECORDS IN KARNATAKA

Background

Sixty six percent of the population of the Karnataka State resides in rural areas and agriculture is the main occupation.

About 6.7 million farmers own 20 million land holdings. The crucial document which records various parameters and information pertaining to the land holding is the Record of Right Tenancy and Cultivation (RTC). In the earlier manual system, these records were maintained by 9000 Village Accountants (Vas) who serviced farmers in about 27,000 villages. The RTC is required for land transactions, for obtaining crop loans, other loans and concessions linked to the size of the land holding. The manual system of maintaining RTCs was exploitative. The VAs were not easily available. Bribes were extracted and since the records were not open for public scrutiny, there was scope for manipulations. Instances of even Government land being mutated in the name of individuals had come to notice.

The Central and State Governments have been acutely aware of the need to reform the land record system with the following objectives.

- Facilitating easy maintenance and prompt updation of land records.
- Making land records tamper proof.
- Allowing farmers easy access to their records.
- Collating the information to construct database regarding land revenue, cropping pattern, land use etc.
- Utilising the data for planning and for formulating development programmes.
- Enabling usage of this database by courts, banks, private organisations and ISPs.

Computerisation of land records in Karnataka was started in 1991 when a pilot was initiated by the Government of India. By 1996, projects for computerisation of land records were sanctioned for all districts in the State aimed at creating computer records from manual data. However, since no provision was made to install computers at sub-district level, where online updating was to be done, these projected failed without achieving the above objectives.

NEW BEGINNING

Bhoomi is a computerized system of land records maintenance. It permits online updating of land records making it radically different from land records systems attempted elsewhere in India, which update databases in offline model making it less current and therefore of not much use. The required software has been designed and developed in-house by the National Information Centre, and organisation of Government of India.

Under the scheme computerized land record kiosks have been set up in 140 sub-district offices from where farmers can obtain RTC copies on-line. At these kiosks a second computer screen connected to the kiosk computer faces the clients so that they can see the transaction being performed. Any number of copies can be collected for any land parcel belonging to anybody by providing the name of the owner or the plot number.

When a change of ownership takes place through sale or inheritance, farmers can file online requests at these kiosks for initiating the mandatory process known as mutation for effecting necessary changes in the RTC. Each request is assigned a number by the computer. Notices are then generated from Bhoomi, which are served by Village Accountant on interested parties. After waiting for a statutory period of 30 days from the day of serving of notices, the Revenue inspector (RI) passes the mutation order in a register maintained for this purpose. The mutation order passed by the RI is processed on Bhoomi and a new RTC is generated duly incorporating the details of the new owner. As a part of the process, the mutation order is also scanned to take care of non-repudiation. While the mutation records are pending for orders of the RI, farmers can trace the status of the application, using the computer number provided to them, on the Touch Screen Kiosks provided on a pilot basis in three of the computerised kiosks.

IMPLEMENTATION CHALLENGES:

Rolling out the application to 177 locations was a real challenge. In the first phase, the project was implemented on a pilot basis in a controlled environment in four sub-districts. After gaining experience in data entry operations and implementation of the software, the scheme was extended to one pilot sub district in each of the 27 districts. In the third phase, the project was rolled out to all the 177 sub districts simultaneously.

The whole exercise called for imparting intensive training and for bringing about an attitudinal change amongst departmental staff. Twelve State level seminars were organised for 1200 senior and middle-level officers. Four divisional level workshops were organised to train 800 officials. More intensive training was imparted to the officials who handle the computers at the kiosks. To clarify various technical and administrative issues more than 150 circulars were issued and compiled into compendia. A "Bhoomi-Help Manual" was printed and distributed at the sub-district level. A computer-lab for training was set up.

The political executive was completed involved. The State's Chief Minister and Revenue Minister highlighted the importance of the project in many public fora. The Chief Minister himself inaugurated many such kiosks and took several meetings to impress upon the team the need to commission this project in a time bound manner.

A participatory software development strategy was followed. Selected field level personnel were involved in the development of various modules of Bhoomi through a formal State Level Committee. Suggestions for improvement were elicited and where valid were incorporated in the software.

The data entry work was done in an offline mode through private data entry agents. Comprehensive software, which accommodated variations in manual records across districts, was developed. After the initial data entry, print outs were taken and validated by the VAs with reference to their original records. The entire software was developed in Kannada, the official language of Karnataka.

What is Unique to Bhoomi

Authentication with a difference — Bio metrics does the trick

The software incorporates the bio-logon metrics system, which authenticates all users of the Bhoomi software on the basis of their fingerprint and therefore makes offices accountable for their decisions and actions. This is not prone to hacking as is the case with traditional password based authentication. A log is maintained of all transactions carried out by officers.

No more Hand Written records

As an implementation strategy, manually written RTCs

were declared invalid from the day on which the computerized system became operational in a sub-district. This has forced the department to completely rely on the new system. This strategy worked because the application design was robust and did not falter. By simultaneous dismantling of the old system through this innovative and bold decision, success and self-sustenance of the new system was ensured.

User charges

An unique aspect of the project has been the imposition of user charges for all transactions. Rs. *15*/- per copy is charged for land records and mutation extracts. By November 2001. Rs. 5 million has been collected as user fee from the distribution of 3 million RTCs from kiosks, which have been operational for periods varying from 3 — 12 months. It is estimated that every year Rs. 30 — *35* million would be collected as user charge, which would be ploughed back to maintain and improve the Bhoomi programme.

BENEFITS ACCRUING OUT OF BHOOMI:

- Farmers can now get a copy of the RTC from the information kiosk at the sub-district headquarters without harassment.
- The farmer can file an application for effecting a mutation in the RTC and trace the status of the mutation application.
- A comprehensive database is now available which can be used for planning for agriculture and development programmes. For example — it is now possible to identify what percentage of the land holdings are held in the name of women.
- Land records are now in the public domain and in the true spirit of the right to information, it is possible to get information about the land holdings of any person.

What is planned for coming months

Banks, cooperative societies and other lending institutions would be provided electronic access to the database for processing requests for crop loans. Similarly the High Court, district and taluk courts will be able to access the database for resolving land-related disputes.

The Govemment has plans to web enable the database so that rural information kiosks can provide a copy of the land record at the doorstep of the farmer.

The Bhoomi programme would become the backbone for disseminating other relevant information, which will empower the citizens in the rural areas. This includes prevailing rates of agricultural commodities in rural markets, list of people getting social assistance from govemment like old age, widow and physically handicapped pensions and information on agricultural inputs for crops.

It is planned to extend these kiosks to the village level by involving private sector entrepreneurs and *gram panchayats* (local governance units), on revenue sharing basis.

The successful implementation of the programme has attracted the attention of many State Governments, the Government of India, the UNDP and the World Bank. The States of Tamil Nadu, Madhya Pradesh and Maharastra have started evolving models based n Bhoomi for implementation in their jurisdiction.

(Source : World Bank)

GYANDOOT

A COMMUNITY-OWNED, SELF SUSTAINABLE AND LOW COST RURAL INTRANET PROJECT

INTRODUCTION

On January 1, 2000, Dhar district began the new millennium with installation of low cost, self-sustainable and community owned rural Intranet project. Dhar district is located on the south western corner of the central India and has a population of 1.7 million, with 54% population being tribal (*Bhils, Bhilalas, patleiyas*) and 60% population living below poverty line. Computers in 20 village centres in five Blocks of the district were wired through an Intranet network (presently there are 31 such wired village centres).

Local rural youth act as entrepreneurs for running cybercafes-cum-cyberoffices on commercial lines without salary or stipend. The computers in the network have been established in *Gram Panchayats* (Village Committee). They have been called *Soochanalayas* (Information Kiosks). The *Soochanalayas* provide user-charge-based services to the rural people. This Intranet system has been named Gyandoot (Messenger of Information).

SOOCHAK (Manager/owner of the kiosk)

The person operating the *Soochanalaya* is a local matriculate operator and is called *Soochak*. A *soochak* is not an employee but an entrepreneur. *Soochak* only needs maintenance and numeric data entry skills. He needs very limited typing skills since most of the Intranet software is menu-driven.

The *Soochaks* for originally started 20 centres were selected interactively by village committees and the local community. Three member panels were selected by the community who received training at their own cost at the District Council. At the end of the training, the best trainees were selected out of a panel of three as *Soochaks*.

He/she runs the *Soochanalaya* on commercial lines. He has an initial one year agreement with the village committee. He does not receive any salary. He bears the cost of stationery, maintenance and electric and telephone bills. He pays 10% of income as commission to the *Zila Panchayat* (District Council) for maintaining the net.

The 11 centres started as private enterprise, the *Soochak* is the owner of the establishment who pays Rs. 5,000 as a license fee for one year to district council. Each *Soochak* is expected to earn a net income of at least Rs. 36,000 per annum at conservative projections.

SERVICES AND FACILITIES

During the formation of the project proposal a detailed RRA/PRA exercise was taken up involving the villagers and the community. The selection of the services was a result of this interactive exercise and was based upon the advice and the felt needs of the villagers.

In these meetings, it was learnt that due to lack of information regarding the current and prevailing *mandi* (agriculture produce auction centres) rates, the farmers were unable to get the best price for their agricultural produce. Villagers also informed that copies of land records were difficult to obtain. The villager who requires a copy of the land record had to go out in search of the *patwari* (village functionary who maintains all land records) who may or may not be available on that particular day at his headquarters.

For small complaints or for giving applications, people had to go to district headquarter which resulted in waste of time, money and potential livelihood earnings. The services offered on the Gyandoot network are:

Agriculture Produce Auction Centres Rates

The variety-wise current and prevailing rates of prominent cereal crops of the district like wheat, gram, soybean, etc. at local and other prominent auction centres of the country are available on-line.

Other statistics of the auction centres *e.g.* the volume of incoming agricultural produce, previous rates etc. are also provided on demand. The facility is available at a nominal charge of Rs. 5. Horticulture crops like tomato, potato, peas, green chillies, guava etc. are also produced in substantial quantity in the district. The rates of these commodities are also available.

On-line Registration of Applications

So far, the villagers had to go to the local revenue court to file applications for obtaining income/caste/domicile certificates or for getting demarcation done or for obtaining landholder's loan passbook *(rin pustika)* etc.

For this, they would again made repeated visits to the court to enquire about the progress of the application as well as to finally collect the prepared document. Now, through *Soochanalayas* they may send the application at a cost of only Rs. 10 and thereafter, in a maximum period of 10 days, preferably less, an intimation of the readiness of the certificate is sent back to them through e-mail at the concerned *Soochanalaya.* Thereafter, they may go to the concerned court to collect the certificate.

On-line Public Grievance Redressal

Wherever there is some problem in the delivory of services, the villagers travel at the cost of time, money and livelihood to Block, *tahsil* or district headquarters without any certainty that they would even be able to meet the officer concerned. Now through the *Soochanalaya,* a villager may send his/her complaint with assurance of reply within a maximum period of seven days, preferably lesser, at a charge of Rs. 10.

The reply to his complaint after redressal is sent back at the *Soochanalaya* through e-mail. Complaints available on the intranet include complaints regarding drinking water, scholarship sanction/disbursement, quality of seed/fertiliser, employee establishment matters (like leave or provident fund sanction) queries, functioning of school, public distribution system, beneficiary oriented schemes, functioning of village committee etc.

Rural e-mail facility

A fee based e-mailing facility, which is provided in the intranet, and it has all the features and facilities of a state-of-the-art web based e-mail.

Village auction site

This facility is started since July 2000 where auction facilities are available to farmers and villagers for land, agricultural machinery, bullocks or equipment or other durable commodities.

It opens a new horizon of e-transactions in the rural areas. The middlemen involved in the rural commodity transaction market are sought to be eliminated through this facility. One can put one's commodity on sale for charges of Rs. 25/- for three months. One can browse the list of salable commodities for Rs. 10.

On line matrimonial site

A fee based on-line matrimonial service for the villagers to choose the right match for a prospective bride/groom. Every entry from a *Soochana laya* by a villager gets added on to a centralized database with search facility on various criteria. The user charges for service rendered are Rs. 25/- for three months. The programme has been designed to suit the requirements of the v.

Information regarding government programmes

Detailed Information regarding over a hundred government programmes is now available on the Gyandoot Intranet.

The villagers have an access to the information regarding all government programmes related to rural development.

Sawaliram se puchiye

This site provides opportunity to school children to ask inquisitive questions regarding career counselling or any other field from *Sawaliram* at no cost. A team of experts at the district headquarter provide the answers within three days. The facility is created to promote inquisitiveness, ability to inquire and scrutinize among the school children.

Ask the expert

This facility is aimed at farmers and villagers who can inquire about latest techniques, advice for their problems, new technologies etc. from a group of experts pertaining to fields of agriculture, animal husbandry, health, or related to legal opinion. The service is provided at Rs. 5/- user charge.

Free E-mail facility on social issues

Free of cost option are available to the villagers to inform regarding child labour, child marriage, illegal possession of land belonging to Scheduled Tribes etc. Besides they can send e-mails to others connected through the net with the help of this facility in Hindi.

Avedan Patra

This facility provides on-line application formats required by local administration and departments of the state government. Thus, application forms are available at the doorsteps of the villagers and avoid their running from pillar to post for these application forms.

Transparency in government working

Updated and latest information regarding public distribution system, list of below poverty line families, beneficiaries of social security pension, beneficiaries of rural development schemes, information regarding government grants given to village committees, etc. are available on the intranet which makes the government functioning transparent.

Gaon ka *Akhabar (Village Newspaper)*

A local web-based newspaper is available to cater to the rural people. The newspaper delivers micro-news about the happening around the villages where Soochaks act as correspondents.

E-education (shiksha gyandoot)

This site contains reading material to supplement and help the students in understanding and learning their subjects in a better way. It contains things like syllabuses of various subjects taught in class X and XII, question banks developed by a team of experts to help in preparation of exams, chithi to help them keep in touch with other schools connected to the intranet etc.

Employment News

This site contains employment news for semi skilled employees.

Below Poverty line list

The site contains the whole list of below the poverty line families and anyone can check his/her name in the list.

STRENGTHENING OF PROJECT

In order to make *Soochanalayas* economically viable entities and to improve the functioning of the project following steps are being taken:

Additional facilities at Soochanalayas:

To make *Soochanalayas* economically viable *soochaks* are given licenses to vendor government judicial stamps and powers of petition writer are also delegated to them. Due to the delegation of above mentioned powers additional incomes are possible and the *Soochanalayas* are becoming virtual cyber offices.

On-line linking of all departments with gyandoot server

A local Area Network (LAN) linking all the major district offices has been installed. As a result, the district heads of various government departments like health, education, tribal development, revenue, food, agriculture, public health engineering, District Council and District Magistrate etc. are connected directly to gyandoot network. This provides backup support and logistics to gyandoot network.

Wireless in Local Loop

The Gyandoot Samiti is introducing low cost TDMA based Wireless in Local Loop (WILL) technology in collaboration with Indian Institute of Technology, Chennai.

This technology will facilitate large scale multiplication of *Soochanlayas* in the hinterland where traditional plain old telephone system has not reached. The technology has power to increase access speed and provide reliable connectivity. The technology will also help the kiosk operator to run two connections at a time, *e.g.* STD/PCO (voice connectivity) and Internet/Intranet (data communication).

E-education initiatives

The Gyandoot Samiti, with the help from Member of Parliament, has established 34 kiosks at the high schools and higher secondary schools. We are providing them local educational contents through the server. They are also accessing internet for other educational contents. Each school is having Computer Club to promote activities related to IT among rural students.

EXPANSION OF THE PROJECT

Some fundamental guidelines were framed for future expansion. They were:

(1) Centers to be opened only in the villages where local telephone exchange is having OFC and fair connectivity.
(2) New centers to be created through private investment.
(3) New services and facilities to be introduced in phased manner.

THE NEW FACILITIES PLANNED OVER NEXT TWO YEARS

1. E-News for the district
2. Distance education
3. Registration of property transaction
4. Feedback system on the development programmes
5. "Bare foot doctor"

ACTION PLAN FOR INCREASING USAGE OF THE NETWORK

A comprehensive and integrated multi-media mass campaign concentrating on IEC activities has been launched in the district. The campaign focuses on penetration and propagation of the project in the hinterland of the district. Indian Institute of Management, Indore is collaborating to provide structured inputs for the IEC activities. The steps taken include:

Gyandoot medhavi chhatra (talented students) scholarship:

From the funds available with gyandoot, two scholarships each of Rs. 1,000/- per month for 5 years have been announced. For the scholarship, only those students of the district would be eligible who motivate 10 or more villagers to use gyandoot facilities between the period 1st September to 31st December 2000.

The scholarships will be finalised through an on-line test of the eligible students and the result of the test would be declared on 26th January 2001. This scheme uses the services of the students to propagate new technology and its power among the rural masses.

Visit of school children to nearest Soochnalaya

Students of class IX, X, XI, XII are taken to the nearest *Soochanalaya* on study tour. These students are given elaborate demonstration on the gyandoot Intranet system and the facilities available at the centre.

Gramsabha in the villages in the project area

Special *gramsabhas* (Meeting of all villagers) in each village in the project area have been started which will be completed by January, 2001. These specially convened village meetings will deliberate on gyandoot and its services, which are available there at nominal cost.

Audio-Visual campaign

Posters and pamphlets have been distributed to all the concerned village committees. TV cable network and cinema halls are being used to popularise gyandoot services.

Audiocassettes carrying gyandoot messages are being used in weekly *haat* bazaars (market places).

Use of ISRO-DECU communication project

A communication project has been established by ISRO (Indian Space Research Organisation) which is already functional in 200 villages of the district. The said project carries message on the gyandoot project.

Gyandoot Computer Clubs

Gyandoot Computer Clubs are being established in major high schools and higher secondary schools of the district.

Incentives

Incentive in the form of cash awards (Rs.5,000, Rs.3,000, Rs. 2,000) along with certificate of excellence were given to three best performing *Soochaks* and certificate of appreciation were given to the village head of the concerned village committee on 15th August 2000. These incentives are being offered twice a year.

Sir Ratan Tata Trust Healthy Child Competition

Sir Ratan Tata Trust has granted Rs. three lakhs to organise healthy child competition based on *Soochnalayas*. The scheme has dual objective of promoting good practices of child rearing among rural masses and at the same time let them know about IT and its usages.

The competition is organised with *Soochanalayas* as nodal points. It will motivate villagers to come to the kiosks. This competition was recently organised (between 9th to 19th April 2001) and was a huge success with 29140 children (12113 boys and 16027 girls) participating in it. All the people coming to the *soochanalaya* for this purpose were explained the utility of the Gyandoot network. It is expected that this will popularise the use of the network for various purposes.

Source: Madhya Pradesh Government.

Bibliography

ASTEC (1994) The networked nation. Canberra : Australian Science and Technology Council.

Abramson. J.B. Arterton, F.C. and Orren, G.R.(1988) The electronic commonwealth. The impact of new media technologies on democratic politics. New York: Basic Books.

Adonis, A. and Mulgan, G.(1994) Connecting each to all. Washington, DC : A-P-T.

Angell, I .(1995) Goodbye to nation. Hello the world', Parliamentary Brief, 3(7):39-40.

Artherton, F.C.(1987) Can technology protect democracy? Washington, DC: Roosevelt Centre for American Policy Studies and Sage.

Arthur Anderson (1994) Predictable patterns. Navigating the continuum from protected monopoly to market competition. Los Angeles, CA: Arthur Anderson & Co.

Audit Commission (1986) Computing in local government. Bristol : Audit Commission

Audit Commission (1992) Citizen's Charter performance indicators. London: Audit Commission.

Audit Commission (1995) Talk Back. Local authority communications with citizens. National report. Bristol : Audit Commission.

Bangemann, M.(1995) Europe and the global information society. Recommendations to the European Council Brussels: European Commission.

Bangbemann, M (1995) Policies for a European information society. Charles Read Lecture, 1995, given under the auspices of ESCR/PICT.

Barber B.R. (1984) Strong democracy. Participatory politics for a new age. Berkeley, CA: University of California. Press.

Barker J. and Downing H.(1985) 'Word Processing and transformation of patriarchal relations of control in the office', in D. Mackenzie and J. Wajcman (eds). The social shaping of technology. Milton Keynes: Open University Press.

Barlett, W.(1991) 'Quasi-markets and contracts: a markets and hierarchies perspective on NHS reforms', Public Money and Management 11:52-61.

Beamish, A (1995) 'Communities on-line: community based community networks', unpublished MA Thesis, Massachusetts Institute of Technology.

Becker T. (1981) 'Teledemocracy, Bringing power back to the people', The Futurist, December 6-9.

Becker T. (1993) 'Teledemocracy: gathering momentum in state and local governance', Spectrum : the journal of State Government, 66,14-20.

Bell, D (1973) The coming of post-industrial society. A venture in social forecasting. New York: Basic Books.

Bellamy, C. (1994) 'Managing strategic resources in a Next Steps department: information agendas and information systems in DSS', in B.J. O'Toole and G. Jordan (eds) Next steps: improving management in government? Aldershot: Dartmouth Publishing Co.

Bellamy C. (1996) 'Transforming and social security benefits administration for the twenty-first century: towards one-stop services and the client group principle', Public Administration 74:159-79.

Bellamy, C. Horrocks, I. and Hambley, N.(1996) Community governance in the information society. Unpublished report prepared for the Foundation for Information Technology in Local Government, Nothingham Trent University.

Bellamy C. Horocks. I. and Webb.J. (1995a) 'Exchanging information with the public, From one stop shops to community information systems', Local Government Studies, 21(1):11-30.

Bellamy C. Horrocks, I. and Webb.J (1995b) 'Community information systems: strengthening local democracy?' in W.B.H. Van de Donk, I.Th.M.. Snehallan and P.W. Tops(eds) Orwell in Athens. A perspective on informatization and democracy. Amsterdam:IOS Press.

Bellamy C. and Taylor JA. (1992) 'Informatisation and new public management. An alternative agenda for public administration', Public Policy and Administration, 7: 29-41.

Bellamy C. and Taylor, JA. (1994a) 'New public management and the information polity. Towards theoretical development', Paper given to European Consortium of Political Research Joint Sessions, Madrid.

Bellamy C. and Taylor, JA. (1994b) 'Introduction, Exploiting it in public administration: towards the information polity', Public Administration, 72 :1-12.

Bellamy C. and Taylor J.A. (1998) 'Governing in the Information Age'. Open University Press, Buckingham, Philadelphia.

Bellamy C. and Taylor J.A. (1994 c) 'Reinventing government in the information age. Proceedings of a workshop organized for OPSS. London: ESRC/Programme on Information and Communication Technology and CCTA.

Benjamin R. Rockart, J. Scott Moarton, M. and Wyman, J.(1984), 'Information technology, A strategic opportunity', Sloan Management review Spring: 3-10.

Bhatnagar Subhash, Schware Robert (2000), 'Information and Communication Technology in Development - Cases from India'. Sage Publications, New Delhi/Thousand Oaks/ London.

Blackburn, P. Coombs, R and Green, K(1985) Technology, economic growth and the labour process, Basingstoke: Macmillan.

Braverman, H. (1974) Labour and monoply capital : the degradation of work in the twentieth century, New York: Monthly Review Press.

Bridgeman Report (1932) Report of the Commission of Inquiry on the Post Office, Cmnd 4149, London: HMSO.

CCTA (1990) Information technology in central government. Changes and trends. London: HMSO.

CCTA: The Government centre for Information Systems (1) 995b) BPR in the public sector. An overview of business process re-engineering. London: HMSO.

CCTA: The Government Centre for Information Systems (1995a) Report on information superhighways, Norwich: CCTA.

CCTA: The Government Centre for Information Systems (1 995b) Information superhighways. An update on opportunities for public sector applications Norwich: CCTA.

CCTA: The Government centre for Information Systems (1995c) Making the best use of the Internet, Norwich: CCTA.

Cabinet Office (1982) Efficiency and effectiveness in the Civil Service, Cmnd 8616, London: HMSO.

Callon M. (1987) 'Society in the making. The study of technology as a tool for sociological analysis', in W.Bijker (ed) The social construction of technological systems. Boston: MIT Press.

Carter Report (1977) Report of the Post Office Review Committee, Cmnd 6850. London: HMSO.

Carter D.(n.d) "' Digital democracy" or "information aristocracy": economy regeneration and the information economy', Discussion Paper, Department of Economic Development, Manchester City Council.

Castells M. (1989) The informational city. Oxford: Basil Blackwell.

Castells M.(1996) The rise of the network society: Economy, society and culture I. Oxford : Blackwell.

Cawson, A. Morgan, K. Webber, D. Holmes P. and Stevens, V (1990) Hostile brothers, Competition and closure in the European electronics industry. Oxford: Clarendon Press.

Child J. (1987)" Information Technology, organization and the response to strategic challenges", California Management Review, 30 (Fall): 33-50.

Colllingridge, D and Margetts. H(1994) 'Can government information systems be inflexible technology? The Operational Strategy re-visited', Public Administration, 72: 55-72.

Coombs, R. (1992) Organizational politics and the strategic use of information technology. PICT Pclicy Research Paper No. 20 Newscastle: ESRC, Programme on Information and Communication Technology.

Corrigan, P. (1996) No more big brother, Fabian Pamphlet 578. London: Fabian Society.

Crick B. (1964) In defence of politics. Harmondsworth : Pelican Books.

Danzigar, J. Dutton, W. Kling R. and Kraemer, K.(1982) Computers and politics. New York: Columbia University Press.

Davenport, T.H. (1993) Process innovation. Re-engineering work through information technology, Boston, MA: Harvard Business School Press.

Davies A.(1994) Telecommunications and politics. The decentralised alternative. London: Pinter.

Dawson P. Buckland. S and Gilbert N. (1990) 'Expert systems and the public provision off welfare benefit advice', Policy and Politics, 18(1): 43:54

Department for Education and Employment (1995) Education superhighways for education. The way forward. London: HMSO.

Department of Trade and Industry (1996) Development of the information society. An international analysis. London: HMSO.

Depla P. (1995) 'Technology and the renewal of local democracy: Dutch experiences after 1990', paper given to the UK Study Group on Information, Communication and New Technology in Public Administration, De Montfort University, June.

Dizard W. (1989) The coming information age. (3rd edn) London: Longman.

Doctor R.D. (1994) 'Seeking equity in the National Information Infrastructure', Internet Research, 4(3): 9-22

Donk, W.B.H.J. Van de and Tops P.W.(1992) 'Informatization and democracy: Orwell or Athens, A review of the literature', Informatization and the Public Sector. 2:169-96.

Donk, W.B.H.J. Van de Snellen, I.Th.M. and Tops, P.W.(1995) Orwell in Athens. A perspective on informatization and democracy, Amsterdam:IOS Press.

Dosi F. Freeman, c. Nelson, R, Silverberg, G and Soete, L. (1988) Technical change and economic theory, London: Pinter.

Doulton, A. (1993) Exchanging information with the public. EIP Report 10992 and case studies. Oxford: Dragonflair and CDW& Associates.

Dutton W.H.(1994) 'Lessons from public and nonprofit services' in F. Williams and J. Pavlik (eds.) The people's right to know: media, democracy and the information highway, Hillsdale, NJ: Lawrence Erlbaum Associates.

DuttonW.H. (ed.) (1996a) Information and communications technologies:visions and realities Oxford: Oxford University Press.

Dustton W.H. Guthrie, K.K. O'Connell. J. and Wyer J. (1991) State and local Governemnt innovations in electronic services: the case in the western and northeastern United States, a report to the Office of Technology, US Congress, Los Angeles : Annenberg School of Communications.

Dutton, W.H. Blumler, J. Garnham N. Mansell, R. Cornford, J. and Poltu, M.(1994) The information superhighway. Britain's response PICT Policy Research Paper 29, Uxbridge: ESRC/P ICT.

The Economist (1995) 'The future of democracy, and democracy and technology', the Economist, 17 June:15-16 and 21-3.

Edwards A. (1995) 'Informatization and views of democracy' in W.B.H.J. Van de Donk I.Th.M. Snellen and P.W. Tops (eds) Orwell in Athens. A perspective on informatization and democracy. Amsterdam:IOS Press.

Efficiency Unit (1995) Resource Management Systems: London: HMSO

Etzioni, A. (1972) Minerva. An electronic town hall', Policy Sciences, 3:457-74

Eulau H. (1977) Technology and civility: the skill revolution in politics, publication no.167. Stanford, CA: Hoover Institution, Stanford University.

Europeon Commission (1993) Growth, competitiveness and employment. The challenges and ways forward into the twenty-first century. White Paper. Brussels: European Commission.

European Commission (1994a) Europe's way to the information society. An action plan Brussels: European Commission.

European Commission (1995 c) G-7 Ministerial Conference on the Information Society. Summaries. Brussels: European Commission

Fallon I(1993) The paper chase: ten years of change at DSS. London: Harper Collins.

Fenchurch, R.A. (1994) 'Network wonderland', Demos 4:11

Fishkin J. (1991) Democracy and deliberation: new directions for democratic reform. New Haven, CT: Yale University Press.

Fishkin J.S. (1992) ' Talk of the tube. How to get teledemocracy right', American prospect. qq (Fall): 46-52.

G-7 Government On-line Project (1995) Publicity document available at http://www.open.gov. uk.

Gans. H.J. (1994) 'The electronic shut-ins. Some social flaws of the information superhighway', Media Studies Journal, 8:123-7.

Garrett, J.(1980) Managing the Civil Service, London: Heinemann.

Gibbs, D. and Leach, B(1992) 'Telematics and local economic development: the Manchester Host computer network', paper presented to the PICT National Conference, Newpaort, Wales, March.

Goldman, H (1986) Co-ordination of computerization of the criminal justice system. London: Home Office, unpublished

Gore A. (1991) 'Infrastructure for the global village', Scientific American, 265 (September): 108-11

Gore A (1993) Creating a government that works better and costs less. New York and Harmondsworth: Plume Books and Penguin.

Greer P. (1994) Transforming central government: the Next Steps initiative. Buckingham: Open University Press.

Grint K. and Willcocks, L (1995)' Business process re-engineering in theory and kpractice. Business paradise regained?' New Technology, Work and Employment, 1 0(2):99-1 09

Gulick L (1937) Notes on a theory of organization ', in L. Gulick and L. Urwick (eds) Papers on the Science of Administration. New York: Institute of Public Administration.

Gutherie K.K. and Dutton. W.H. (1992) 'The politics of citizen access technology. The development of public information utilities in four cities,' Policy Studies Journal, 20(4): 574-97.

Gyford J —(1985) The politics of local socialism. London: George Allen and Unwin.

Hambleton R, Hoggett 0. and Tolan. F (1989)' The decentralization of public services. A research agenda,' Local Government Studies, 15(January-February) 39-56.

Hammer M. (1990) 'Reengineering work. Don't automate, obliterate,' Harvard Business Review, July-August:104-12.

Hammer M. and Champy, J(1993) Re-engineering the corporation, New York:Harper Collins

Hawker, I. Tandon V. Cotter D. and Hill A (1994) 'New network infrastructures for the 21st century', British Telecommunciations Engineering, July;103-1 10

Heeks Richard (1999), 'Reinventing Government in the Information Age -International Practice in IT-enabled Public Sector Reform'. Routledge, London and New York.

Henderson, A.M.C. (1993) 'Informatization of the delivery and administration of social security. Developments And issues in the Australian DSS', paper given to ESRC Study group on Information, Communication and New Technologies, London.

Hepworth, M. (1989) The geography of the information economy. London Belhaven.

Hoggett P. and Hambleton, R (1988) Decentralization and democracy. Localising public service. Bristol: School for Advanced Urban Studies. University of Bristol.

Holman K. (1994) Plan large, deliver small. Balanced decentralisation in the country councils. London : Association of County Councils

Home Office (1993) Police reform: a police service for the twenty-first century, Cm 2281. London: HMSO.

Home Office Science and Technology Group (1994) The national strategy for police information systems. London: Home Office.

Home Office (1995a) Annual Report 1995. The government's expenditure plans 1995-96 to 1997-98 for the Home Office and Charity Commission Cm 2808, London: HMSO

Home Office (1995b) Identity cards. A consultation document Cm 2879 London: HMSO

Home Office (1996) Annual replort 1996. The government's expenditurue plans 1996-97 to 1998-99, Cm 3208, London: HMSO

Humbert M. Meijer J. Niewwehuis, M. and Schouten, R. (1992) Government service centres : final report. The Hague: B and A Policy Group on behalf of the Ministry of Home Affairs

Information Society Forum (1995) theme paper, Brussels: European Commission.

Information Society Forum (1996) Networks for people and their communities. Making the most of the information society in the European society in the European Union, first annual report to the European Commission from the

Information Society Forum, Brussels: European Commission.

Information Technology Advisory Panel (1983) Making a business of information London ;HMSO.

Information Technology Review Group (1995) Clients first. The challenge for government from Information Technology. Canberra :Ministry of Finance. The references in this book are to the on-line versions downloaded from the Ministry's web site.

Inland Revenue (1994) Electronic lodgement. Consultative document. London Inland Revenue Change Management Division.

Jarillo, J.C. (1993) Strategic networks. Creating the borderless organization. Oxford: Butterworth-Heinemann.

Jones M. (1994) Don't emancipate, exaggerate:rhetoric, reality and reengineering in R. Baskerville et al.(eds.) Transforming organizations with information technology Amsterdam: North Holland.

Jones, S.G.(ed), (1995) Cybersociety. Computer mediated communication and community. Thousand Oaks, CA: Sage

Josevold, R. (1994)'Improving public services through inter-governmental cross-level and cross-professional organization, paper given to the Nordic Network on One-Stop Shops, University of Bristol.

Kable (1995) Civil Service IT market profile 1995-6, London: Kable Keane J. (1988) Democracy and civil liberty. London: Verso

Keen J. (1994a) Information management in health services. Milton Keynes: Open University Press.

LGUA (1996) Your local authority in the information society. London: Local Government. Users Association. The Labour Party (1995) Communicating Britains's future London : The Labour Party.

Laudon K. (1977) Communications technology and democratic participation. New York. Praeger.

Leach S. Steward Jand Walsh K. (1994) The changing organisation and management of local government, Basinggstoke: Macmillan

Lipietz A. (1987) Mirages and miracles London : Verso

Lythinen K. and Hircheim, R (1987), Information systems failures. A survey and classification of the empirical literature" Oxford Surveys in Information Technology. 14: 257-309

Mackenzie, D (1996) Knowing machines: essays on technical change. London Mit Press.

Mackenzie D. and Wajcman.J(eds) (1985) The social shaping of technology. How the refrigerator got its hum. Milton Keynes: Open University Press.

Mclean, I (1989) Democracy and new technology, Cambridge: Polity Press.

Macpherson, C.B. (1973) Democratic theory. Essays in retrieval. Oxford: Clarendon Press.

Margetts, H (1991)' The computerization of social security. The way forward or a step backward'? Public Administration, 69:325-34

Margetts H. (1995) ' The automated state', Public Policy and Administration, 10(2): 88-1 03.

Martin J.(1978) The wired society. Englewood Cliffs. NJ: Prentice Hall.

Marvin 5. (1994) 'Accessibility to utility networks. Local policy issues'. Local Government Studies.

Masuda Y. (1990) Managing in the information society. Releasing synergy Japanese style. Oxford: Basil Blackwell.

Mathews, R.S. (1979) 'Accountable management in the Department of Health and Social Security,' Management in Government 34: 125-32

Metcalfe, L. and Richards, 5 (1987) Improving public management. London: Sage and European Institute of Public Administration.

Miles, I.(1996) 'The information society: competing perspectives on the social and economic implications of ICT's in W.H. Dutton (ed.) Information and communication technologies, : visions and realities. Oxford: Oxford University Press.

Miller D. (1995) 'Citizenship and Pluralism', Political Studies, 43: 432-50

Mills M. (1996)' Changing the project culture for procurement,' Information Technology and Public Policy, 14(3):167-9

NCC (1996) The information society. Getting it right for consumers. London:

National Consumer Council.

NHS Management Executive (1992) IM&T strategy overview. London: Information Management Group, NHSME.

National Audit Office (1986) The Financial management initiative, London: HMSO.

National Audit Office (1991) Office automation in government departments. London: HMSO.

National Computer Board of Singapore(1995) IT 2000. Visions of an intelligent island, Singapore: National Computer Board.

OECD (1992) Information technology in Government, Management challenges. Paris: Organization for Economic Co-operation and Development.

OFTEL (1994a) Households without a telephone London: OFTEL

OFTEL (1 994b) A framework for effective competition. A consultative document on inter connection and related issues. London: HMSO.

Palfreman, J. and Swade, D(1991) The dream machine. Exploring the computer age. London: BBC Publications.

Peltu, M. Mackenzie, D. Shapiro, S and Dustton, W.H. (1996) ' Computer power and human limits,' in W.H. Dutton (ed.) Information and communication technologies: visions and realities. Oxford : Oxford University Press.

Percy-Smith, J. (1995) Digital democracy, Information and communication technologies: in local politics. London : Commission for Local Democracy.

Ponting C. (1989) Secrecy in Britain. Oxford: basil Blackwell.

Quinn, J.B. (1992) Intelligent enterprise. A new paradigm for a new era. Berkeley: University of California Press.

Raab C. Bellamy, C. Staylor, J. Dutton, W.H. and Peltu, M (1996) 'The information polity: electronic democracy, privacy and surveillance', in W.H. Dutton (ed.) Information and communication technologies; visions and realities. Oxford: Oxford University Press.

Ranson S. and Stewart J. (1989)' Citizenship and government:

the challenge for management in the public domain', Political Studies, 37:5-24

Ranson S. and Stewart J. (1994) Management for the public domain:

enabling the learning society. Basingstoke: St. Martin's Press.

Rawlings C. Temple, M. and Thrasher M. (1994) Community identity and participation in local democracy. London: Commission for Local Democracy.

Rhleingold, H (1993) The virtual community in a computerized world. London Secker and Warburg.

Rhodes, R. (1981) Control and power in central-local relations. Alder shot: Gower.

Richardon J. and Cram L. (1992) Citizenship and local democracy. A European perspective, Luton: Local Government Management Board.

Index

A

B

C

D

●●●